I Brake for Meltdowns

I Brake for Meltdowns

How to Handle the Most Exasperating Behavior of Your 2- to 5-Year-Old

MICHELLE NICHOLASEN
and
BARBARA O'NEAL

Da Capo
LIFE
LONG

A Member of the Perseus Books Group

Designed by Brent Wilcox
Set in 11.25 point Adobe Garamond by the Perseus Books Group

Library of Congress Cataloging-in-Publication Data
Nicholasen, Michelle.
    I brake for meltdowns : how to handle the most annoying behaviors of your 2-to-5-year-old / Michelle Nicholasen with Barbara O'Neal.
    p.   cm.
Includes bibliographical references and index.
ISBN 978-0-7382-1167-1 (alk. paper)
    1. Preschool children.   2. Discipline of children.   3. Parenting.   I. O'Neal, Barbara.
II. Title.
HQ774.5.N53 2008
649'.64—dc22

                                                                          2008006497

Published by Da Capo Press
A Member of the Perseus Books Group
www.dacapopress.com

Da Capo Press books are available at special discounts for bulk purchases in the U.S. by corporations, institutions, and other organizations. For more information, please contact the Special Markets Department at the Perseus Books Group, 2300 Chestnut Street, Suite 200, Philadelphia, PA, 19103, or call (800) 810-4145, ext. 5000, or e-mail special.markets@perseusbooks.com.

10 9 8

To my husband, Jim, who recruited me for
the toughest job I ever loved.
–M.N.

To my husband, Frank, and my family
for their support and belief in my life's work.
–B.O.

CONTENTS

Introduction

Why are they screaming at me?

Young children seem programmed to drive us precariously close to the cliff. Impulsive, stubborn, and a tad psychotic, these little people have the ability to transform us into tricksters, fast-food waiters, goofballs, and pushovers. Our passion for them is matched by the level of exasperation they induce. We parents carry the universal balance scales on our shoulders: equal parts love and *Ugh!*

I think it's accurate to say that small children sometimes behave as if they are, in fact, crazy. If adults ever acted like a two-and-a-half-year-old, they would be arrested. (Some adults do, and they are.) As parents, we often feel our toddlers' insanity rubbing off on us. On the other hand, children are the only members of our society who can undress in public, pee on a tree at the park, and mutter to themselves feverishly without attracting much attention. And let's admit it; deep down we really envy their lack of inhibition. When we embrace the loveable wackiness of our little psychiatric patients, then we start to have fun—and forbearance.

It seems that cracking the nut of parenting young children involves two elusive skills: knowing when to be control freaks—or

1

not—and being able to see the humor (or absurdity) in the situations that are momentarily out of our control. Understanding the differences among these subtleties is a process a parent never stops learning.

Today's parents have benefited enormously from the child development research of the past four decades. Our generation understands so much more about children's emotional lives than past generations. Gone are the days when a child was forced to stay at the table until he finished eating. No longer do we see a child getting spanked over his mother's thighs. By now, you probably have internalized all the "corrections" that need to be made from your own childhood. Never spank. Don't dismiss your child. Acknowledge and talk about feelings. Don't break a child's spirit. Talk to children. Respect them. Be affectionate! We know that children need love, guidance, boundaries, autonomy, and strong bonds with their parents to form healthy selves. That's light years away from what my mother's generation knew about children.

But here's the rub: psychologists and educators report that many parents today are so afraid of damaging their kids' delicate psyches that they sometimes forget what they are supposed to be doing as parents. They get confused about what boundaries to set, and worry about harming their child's self-esteem when in fact they need to be firm. Who can blame them? Parenting is a confounding job. But somehow, we parents have to find a way to nurture our kids, let them explore, take risks, and "be themselves," while at the same time consistently upholding healthy, reasonable boundaries.

This book will help you figure out when and how to draw those boundaries. It will help you scrutinize which battles are worth fighting and identify the many things you can just let go of. Use the Contents or Index to look up the behaviors that really get your goat. (You know what they are.) We give suggestions for what to say to your child, interventions you may or may not have considered, and ways to think about the situation if nothing seems to work. Because children have different temperaments, our suggestions will work for some and not others. We give you a variety of ideas for managing each tricky behavior so you can try out what feels right for you and your child. For example, one child who stubbornly refuses to put on her shoes might respond to silliness or a game to get her started. Another child might get motivated by a ticking timer. Each parent has his own strengths and vulnerabilities, too, when it comes to dealing with young behaviors. Then again, one child's struggle may not even be an issue for another. And so it goes.

We don't propose a new way of parenting or a novel "method" that you can apply to all your perplexing issues. Rather, what we do is share all the tricks we know about managing two- to five-year-old children in an effective, respectful way based on the behavior that is driving you bonkers!

The language we suggest you use with your little one is just that—a suggestion. You should freely adapt it to your own style or diction. We sometimes offer two different versions of a response, one example for younger and one for slightly older children, but youngsters can vary greatly in their level of comprehension. You should use whichever example feels right. Some phrases you won't see are: "good job," "big girl/boy," and "use your words." We find these to be devoid of meaning and more trouble than they're worth. ("But you said I was a big boy, so why can't I have gum?") Instead you'll see: "Thank you for helping me." "You finished that puzzle by yourself!" "You are really growing up." "Whoa, hold on. What do you want to tell me?"

This guide was inspired by my children's preschool, Arlington Children's Center in Arlington, Massachusetts, where Educational Director Barbara O'Neal takes phone calls every day from parents who are stuck. They have tried everything and need some quick advice. One child has come home from school with a stolen item, and her mom is not sure how to handle the situation. Another dad wonders why his son is having meltdowns right after school and what he can do about it. Still another is worried that her daughter is not making friends. Barbara sees her job as not only directing the school's curriculum and training teachers, but also being a family partner. She gives advice. That's her job. And she always knows what to say to kids. She's been doing this for thirty years.

I, on the other hand, have learned about kids in a trial-by-fire kind of way. Our children came to us fast and furious: five children in four years, with triplets in the middle. On the domestic front, my life can best be described as a military operation (and with luck, it will bring lifelong rewards). Five children with very different temperaments propelled my husband and me to try different approaches constantly, to weed out strategies that weren't working only to introduce them again at later stages in development. While our son is so easygoing he can be talked into just about anything, one of our daughters is so intense that when she was small, we often watched helplessly as she kicked and scratched out her anger on the floor. Talking with Barbara, I saw that the approaches we use with our children at home are well aligned with the methods and spirit she brings to preschool.

Together we have put our strategies into this book as a tool for others who are managing the challenging toddler-and-beyond years. While we don't espouse a particular philosophy, our suggestions are in tune with the theory that children learn from the logical and natural consequences of their actions. Psychologist Rudolph Dreikurs first popularized this theory in the 1960s. The best way to understand how this learning works is to take the example of a child who refuses to put on his coat to go outside in the middle of winter. A parent can prod, coerce, and cajole, or offer logical explanations for why he ought to put on his coat. She can also threaten or bribe him. But the most effective way of handling the conflict is not to have an argument at all, but to let him go outside without a coat. He will soon learn that it's cold outside and ask for a coat, which the parent has brought along. Obviously, this approach is not practical in all circumstances—like when your daughter insists on driving the car—but it can be applied to a lot of mini-battles that spring up during the day.

Talking to other parents of young children, I discovered that they generally do not turn to parenting books for help. They do, however, turn to other parents. We see this book as a place to turn, to commiserate with two moms who have been in the trenches, and still are. We also see this book as an opportunity to remind parents that they have rights too, and that setting healthy limits is essential for the growth and security of the whole family.

As a conscientious parent, you've learned how to appreciate the joys of childhood, celebrate the highs, and comfort the woes. The suggestions on the following pages are designed to help get you through the other, teeth-clenching moments of parenting. Good luck!

—*M.N.*

CHAPTER 1

Meltdowns, Tantrums, and Screaming Fits

Every child has them. Every parent dreads them. Small children get frustrated because they can't easily solve their own problems. Many can't even articulate them. So they collapse into anger and tears. Sometimes there's not much we can do but wait it out, since hollering at them to stop hollering will only make them more angry and inexpressive.

One key strategy that parents often don't consider is to talk in advance with their kids about what it means to "calm down." It's useful to show your child some specific ways to calm down. Try taking three deep breaths, or stretching and taking breaths. You can be creative. Perhaps hugging herself will be calming for one child, and humming to herself works for another. Practice these calming techniques with your child when he is in a good mood. Then later, when he's coming down from a tantrum, you can coach him to use these methods. Teaching him calming techniques in advance is like an insurance policy that works over time. You can't stop tantrums, but you can sometimes help your child come out of them.

Public Meltdowns

The fear of your child losing control in public is enough to make you want to stay home, order takeout, and shop online. When my child is in the middle of a loud, thrashing tantrum, and folks nearby are starting to stare, I imagine there are two groups of people watching: those with children, and those without. Parents, I imagine, are looking at me with sympathetic smiles and sending me positive thoughts: "I've been there and I feel your pain." The other group contains nonparents who have absolutely no idea how baffling it can be to raise a small child. This is the kind of person who would leer at you accusingly even if you tried to explain how it's not *your* fault this time, because you did everything in your power to prepare your child for this trip, and so on. Any self-respecting parent should ignore these onlookers because they are manifestly clueless in the child-raising department. So now that you have summed up all the people around you—those on your side and those who don't matter at all—you should feel safe to let the tantrum happen, and get ready to take action.

There's another important thing to keep in mind when your child is losing it in public. Most people are staring at you, the parent, not the child. They are watching to see if you will keep your cool. Think about the last time you saw a child freaking out in a store; weren't you secretly hoping the parent didn't lose control too? It must be a subconscious record we replay from childhood, when we wanted our parents to love us even when we were horrid. This is the time to put on a knowing grin, and adopt a mellow "children will be children" attitude. Even if you have to fake it.

Shopping

By now, you are likely aware of the two critical rules of shopping with a child: he must be well rested and fairly well fed. Success is mostly about timing. Don't take your child to the store if it's too close to naptime or lunchtime. (You might get away with it if you stave off his hunger with a snack, but you'll have to shop fast.) Bring your arsenal to the store:

- A drink and snack
- A book or toy
- Review the rules with your child before you go inside, for example:

We're going shopping today, and you're going to have a big job: you get to pick out one cereal and one fruit (or two cereals, etc.). But that's all. Mommy will pick out all the other foods. Are you ready?

What if he picks out an unacceptable cereal? Redirect:

We don't eat this kind of cereal because it has a lot of sugar, and that can hurt your teeth. You can pick a cereal from this side over here.

Or offer two or three cereals and let your child choose one.

It's hard for a child not to want everything when he goes inside a store. If a meltdown happens in the grocery store, park your cart out of the way, and try taking your tot outside to your car or to a bench to see if you can calm her down, or until she calms herself. Inside a mall, you can retreat to a bench.

After the shrieking stops, you can say:

We can't go shopping together until you calm down.
Do you think you're ready to go back inside?

Review your plan again for who chooses which items.

But how can you leave the store when the ice cream is melting in your carriage? And what if you have another child with you? If your youngster takes a long time to calm down, you can ask a clerk to restock the cold items in your cart, or even make a list of them so you can re-shop. But the multiple-child scenario is more challenging.

- If grocery shopping with two children, take them both outside to a bench or to the car, and give the non-crier a pad of paper and a pen or crayon (or another diversionary toy stashed in your car or bag).
- Let the non-crier pretend to drive the car while you sit with the crier in the backseat. Make sure the emergency brake is on!
- When the crier has calmed down, and you've offered a drink or snack, return to the store and try playing a game if you have the energy. For example, search for the letters of the alphabet on products or signs. The children can take turns calling out the ones they find. Do the same with numbers, colors, or animals. This is commonly known as the "I Spy" game.
- If your child wants to hold something unbreakable from the shelf, like a box of cake mix or pasta, but you don't want to buy it, you can say:

We don't need that food at home, but you can hold it while we are shopping, and I'll put it back when we're done.

Depending on the child, you might ask her to give the borrowed item to the cashier when you are about to leave. But don't give merchandise to your two- or three-year-old if you think it will end up in her mouth.

- If the source of conflict is that your child wants candy or some other forbidden object, stick to your policy of no candy, but tell her she can have a snack when you are back in the car. This might result in a big protest, but don't give in. Distract your child by asking her to help place some of your groceries on the belt at checkout. Or start a "Where's the Rice Chex?" hunt as you check out. (Also see "How Much Should You Negotiate?" on page 269 in the Ongoing Adventures section.)

If your child will not calm down outside the store, or if the meltdown reoccurs, it's time to shelve the whole shopping plan and go home. Some children are high-strung by nature and have a hard time controlling their impulses, especially in a stimulating store environment. If you can, avoid taking a high-energy child shopping. Try again in a few months, and be sure to review the rules in advance.

What about those pesky onlookers who try to intervene? If you're the kind of person who just cannot ignore them, you can say:

We're fine, thanks.

Or you can put on the smile of an experienced parent and say:

Benny is very frustrated because he wants a bag of sweets, but Mommy said we are having a snack in the car instead.

This should reassure the concerned bystanders that you are torturing your kids for a very good reason. (Hey, weren't they three years old once?)

Restaurants

You might ask yourself, "When will I be able to have a civil meal with my whole family?" Little diners are tricky customers to please, but, mercifully, the whole restaurant experience gets better as they approach age five and exhibit more self-control. Meltdowns in restaurants are especially frustrating for parents, who are hungry and really deserve the chance to let someone else cook for a change. When ordering for children at a restaurant, remember a few things:

- Give your child a choice of two items you think he might like from the menu.
- Children have no concept of seasonings or sauces. As a rule, order all toppings on the side. Even foods that you think are served plain sometimes arrive with parsley, basil, pepper, or butter on them. If you know this is a showstopper for your child, tell the waiter you don't want any condiments sprinkled on top.
- Bring sippy cups for younger children.
- Bring special small toys that you reserve just for restaurants.
- Bring emergency snacks, like cheese and crackers, and serve them as an appetizer if your food is taking too long to arrive. If it ruins your children's appetite, don't sweat it. They will have eaten a fairly nutritious snack in place of a big meal. Not a bad trade. Try to enjoy your own meal, because you deserve this break from making dinner!

> ### Been there. . .
>
> Your child's pasta arrives with red sauce. It doesn't matter that she ordered it that way, because now it seems offensive to her. She starts whining and bucking in her chair. What do you do? Do you order something new? Do you ask the waiter to wash off the pasta? Do you go into the bathroom and try to do it yourself?

Although you're feeling keenly exasperated in the situation above, try to act indifferent. Don't scold your child. Just tell yourself that small kids act like this about 50 percent of the time, so you are just playing the odds when you go out to eat anyway. You might say:

Oh, gee, that's what we ordered tonight.

Start eating your own meal and don't fuss over the pouting diner. If your child strongly insists she does not want it, you might ask:

Does anyone else want to eat this pasta?

Don't try talking her into eating over and over again. This is too much work for you, and it will just stress everybody out. Don't reorder at your child's whim either, or you'll be going down the slippery slope of having to accommodate more mind-changing in the future. There are practical reasons for establishing such boundaries at mealtime, like wanting to avoid waste and added expense. And it's a good chance for your child to see the consequences of what happens when he rejects the food that he chooses. Never scold in this situation, because your child is still learning. Shrug your shoulders and stay coolheaded.

If your youngster suddenly wants someone else's food, you can try to arrange some food sharing, with permission from the other person. Or ask the waiter for some bread for your toddler to nibble on.

What if. . .

After rejecting his order, your child sits civilly in his chair but eats only bread and juice?

Call it a meal (or at least sustenance). That's what he ate, and there's nothing you can do about it. He'll get his nutrients from all the other things he eats that day. Next time, you can order something you know he will enjoy.

What if. . .

Your little one's behavior in a restaurant is getting out of control?

You or your spouse should pick her up and take her outside or to another part of the room until she calms down. Be prepared to spend a few minutes with a thrashing child. You can say:

I'm going to wait with you until you calm down. When you are feeling calm, you can join us at the dinner table.

If she will not calm down within, say, ten to fifteen minutes, pack up the food and go home, even if you have more than one child with you.

Next time try to start your dinner before your child gets out of her mind with hunger or fatigue. If the source of conflict is a meal that is unappealing, next time order food that is more pleasing to her taste or with more eye appeal, such as squiggles, shapes, or colors. You can also try cutting a sandwich, for example, into triangles, squares, or sticks.

Role-Play

If eating at restaurants is a particularly difficult time, try role-playing at home. Pretend you're at a restaurant with the table already set. One parent can be the child, and the other parent can be the waiter. Go through all the potential issues with the child (getting out of her chair, trying to stand up on her chair, playing with her drink, rejecting food). Do it the wrong way, and then model the correct behavior. Then it's your child's turn to show good manners at the table. Children will be fascinated by this playacting and will even remember some of it. Note that role-play is not as effective for kids under three, but there are always exceptions.

If nothing seems to improve your restaurant experience, then take a break from eating out for a while, and try it again in a month or so. A restaurant hiatus falls in the category of "Things we have to give up for our kids." You won't have to say good-bye to dining out forever. As your child matures, you'll have better experiences eating out.

Visiting Others

What are the odds that when you take your child to visit a friend you see only once or twice a year, the snapshot that you leave behind is that of a petulant little tiger in the throes of a tantrum? You can bet the odds are fairly high. Here are some ways to make your visit successful:

- You wouldn't leave the house without activities for the kids, right? Keep markers or crayons and paper in your car so you can grab them in a pinch. Buy some new stickers or tiny notebooks to use during your visit. Interactive gadgets like containers with lids that come off will hold the interest of two- and three-year-olds longer than static toys.

- Never schedule a visit during naptime. Unless your child easily falls asleep anywhere, there's no way to salvage a visit with a cranky, exhausted child.
- Anticipate your visit by describing what your child can expect to see and do. Will there be other children there for her to play with? Or particular activities or people to look forward to seeing?
- Luckily, houses have rooms you can visit with your child to calm down and talk. If she throws a tantrum, chances are she just wants you to hold her until she feels comfortable. Is there anything you can do to remedy her distress? Does she have to go to the bathroom but is afraid to go in a new place? Is she freaked out by the dog?
- Get the stroller, if needed, and go for a walk in the neighborhood to reboot your toddler.
- Give your child some activities to do in a place removed from all the strangers; you'll have to participate for a while until he is comfortable. Then, if needed, move somewhere you can talk to your friend while he plays on your lap.
- If you are visiting with two or more children and a meltdown occurs, depending on the ages of your children, they might all follow you into a separate room because they don't want to be left behind. If the non-criers start getting bored, ask your spouse or a friend to set up crayons, cars, or books to lure them out of the room.
- If your friends are easygoing, another good distraction is putting on music and having a ten-minute dance party. Anything with a good beat will do. Wooden spoons and bowls make decent drums.

- Guaranteed to work is water play outside or on the kitchen floor. Use plastic cups, bowls, measuring spoons, and a tub or pitcher of water. Line the floor with towels. Water is your friend and better than any toy. It entertains young children for minutes on end, and virtually cleans itself up. (Water play also gives you a good excuse to use the bag of extra clothes you stashed in your trunk. Or, if you're like me, just smile at your child's blotchy shirt and say, "Hey, that will dry by itself, no problem.")
- Remember, if things are not working out, you can always pack up and graciously offer to reschedule the visit. A true friend will understand.
- If your child is shy and demands a lot of your attention in a new social situation, see "Clingy Behavior" on page 57.

Private Meltdowns

Inside a Car

If you have one child in the car who is coming unraveled, pull over and listen to him. See if you can fix the problem quickly. When you have covered all the bases, drive on and you probably won't have to stop again. If your child simply wants out because she hasn't had enough time running around outside, try to work a pit stop into your schedule if you have the time. She'll be a much more contented traveler when she's expended a little energy. A park, a store, or even walking down a sidewalk can be helpful. But sometimes we don't have the option to stop, and our child might pitch a fit in his car seat. Turn on your music, sing, and accept that the little screaming banshee whom you love will calm down in her own time.

The checklist for car trouble:

- Try to solve a problem (snacks, drink, diaper, temperature, toy, music).
- Distract by starting a search out the window for dogs, bikes, or diggers, for example, or playing a version of "I Spy." If that works, keep asking questions. "What color was that dog?" "Was that lady wearing a helmet?" "Was that digger working or parked?" And so on.
- Start singing a song your child knows.
- Go for a walk or take a pit stop if you have time.
- If you can't stop, and you've tried everything else, turn on relaxing music and have faith that your child will calm down in her own time. Occasionally reassure her that you'll soon be at your destination.

Been there. . .

It happens nearly every day on the way home from day care. Your two children get into a screaming fight over . . . who knows? Does it matter? It does not. Do you urge them to work it out? Do you interrogate them about who said what? Can't you just ignore them? Unfortunately, none of these gentle approaches is working, and you feel like climbing out of your skin.

If one or more of your children are having a scream fest in the car, just pull over to the side of the road. When the yelling subsides, calmly explain that you cannot concentrate on driving when it's so loud in the car. Explain that when everyone calms down and keeps their hands in their laps, you can continue home. When they urge you to drive again, tell them that you can only continue when they have stopped yelling—because the yelling makes it hard to drive. Be prepared to wait calmly without talking to them; read a magazine; take several deep breaths. Thank them when they quiet down, and drive on.

What if . . .

Only one of your children is the instigator and won't stop provoking the others? In fact, she is acting in an unrelentingly horrid way. You are finding it hard to ignore her continuous loud ranting, and it's starting to distract you from driving.

Try this: the Sidewalk Time-Out. Pull over to the curb and park (preferably in a residential area). Explain to your passengers that Betty needs a time-away on the sidewalk. You are going to sit with her on the sidewalk until she calms down. The other children will be able to look out the windows and see that you are still close by. Put on some nice music for the ones who are waiting inside the car, or get out your stash of books or toys. Put on the emergency brake.

You'll have to sit on the sidewalk, or on a nearby step, and wait with the howling one. And you'll have to act as if you don't mind waiting, which you could do for an hour if you had to. Take a deep lungful of air, and wait. Remind yourself that what you are doing is a safety measure for everyone. You're not a distracted driver anymore, just a parent taking a much-needed break. I have used this tactic very effectively with my children, who each on average get one or two sidewalk time-outs per year. The beauty of this tactic is that your child will be so surprised to find herself sitting in the middle of nowhere that she will calm down fairly soon. When she begins to settle down, you can say:

It looks like you are trying hard to calm down. I can't drive the car when there is loud yelling, because I can't concentrate. Is the yelling out of your system? (Is your yelling all done now?) Do you think you're ready to go back inside?

What if. . .

You do exactly the wrong thing and *you* scream at your kids?

It's not so much wrong as it is useless. Everyone does it sometimes. In our constant effort to control our own tempers, we parents harbor a lot of tension. It feels good to yell in the moment, but it almost never solves the problem. In almost every case, yelling will make the situation worse by getting your child more entrenched in his behavior. There are a few exceptions when you might have to yell as a reflex, like when your child runs into the street. But other than emergencies, screaming back just makes everyone angrier. For strategies to stay in control, and suggestions on what to do when you don't, see "Losing Your Temper; Keeping Your Cool" on page 278 in the Ongoing Adventures section.

At Home

If only our children came with a reboot switch for those times when even our calmest, most compassionate language is swallowed up by rants and protests.

What can you do to help a child who's stuck in a frustrated tantrum?

A. Solve the problem or redirect.
B. Take your child to another room or time-away area if he is being disruptive.

C. When nothing else works, give your child a safe space to kick and scream it out.

A. Solve the problem or redirect.　It probably feels as if you're trying to solve your child's problems and complaints all day long. If the problem is solvable, you have already figured out what to do: help zip a coat, help point out what a child wants if he can't say it, and so forth.

But some problems cannot be "solved." Most tantrums erupt when a child is denied something she wants; for instance, when she wants to play with something really off-limits, like your car keys or wallet. Don't give in to these requests, but do explain why she cannot have it; then try to get her interested in something else and move to another room.

It sounds like you really want to hold my keys. I can't let you have them because I need them to drive the car, and I don't want them to get lost. Let's go play with the fish puzzle instead.

Try to counter negative language with positive:

I know you want to hold the whole bag of crackers, but we don't eat our snacks from the big bag.
Would you like a bowl or a snack bag? How many pieces, three or four?

Don't cave in because you can't bear the hounding and harping. This will erode your credibility with your child. If the whining gets really bad, then either try to ignore it, or explain that you will take her to the time-away area for a while until she calms down or stops asking for what she cannot have (see part B).

If you find yourself hopping around like a nutcase, filling all of your child's requests, however wacky or sensible, it may be time to ask if your child is starting to take advantage of your willingness to do everything for her. There are two things you can do to remedy this. The first is to foster independence by encouraging her to fill her own needs, suitable to the age of your child. It's OK if you need to give assistance, like holding the cereal box while she shakes some out. The second is to stop fulfilling every single request. Without yelling, tell her no, you have already gone upstairs twice and you are tired and don't want to do it again. She can go up and get her own shoes, or in five minutes, after you set a timer, you can do it together. If the tantrum escalates, see part B below.

B. Take your child to another room or time-away area. If the tantrum escalates to the point where your youngster is really disturbing others (e.g., provokes another sibling repeatedly, won't stop whining at the dinner table, keeps repeating her demand), then say you'll have to take her to a different room if she does not stop. If the behavior continues, count to five out loud. If nothing improves, take her to a designated time-away or quiet area in your house.

Once you are in the time-away place, here's some language you can use if your child is not screaming at the top of her lungs:

I'm here to help. I love you and can hold you until you are more comfortable or until you calm yourself down.

With children older than two, you can choose to give yourself a time-away during the tantrum. Briefly explain why you are taking a break; for example, you can't concentrate when there's so much noise and protesting.

THE TIME-AWAY PLACE

Think of a time-away as a last resort to check unacceptable behavior. A first-time offense should be an opportunity to teach and learn. (*We don't hit other people; hitting hurts.*) Your first choice is to check behavior include:

- Re-instruct and redirect. (*You cannot tear up Julia's painting. Let's go and find a game or toy.*)
- Keep your child by your side. (*It looks like you are having a hard time taking turns. I want you to stand by me/play next to me for five minutes.*)
- Take him away from the other person or activity, and talk to him briefly and simply about your expectations.

When your child knows the rules, but continues the unacceptable behavior, then a time-away is an appropriate consequence. Remember, you can always give him a final chance to check his behavior by counting to three or five before removing him to the time-away area. (You can choose to count to three each time, as the author Thomas Phelan instructs in his book *1–2–3 Magic,* or you can pick another number that feels right for the situation.)

A separate room or enclosed porch is ideal. Make sure there are no breakable, pointy, or sharp objects in the room—like scissors or pencils. For more easygoing children, a bottom stair or small chair in the hallway may be enough. Ideally, this room should not be the child's bedroom or playroom, but rather a boring place with no toys so the child doesn't look forward to being there. A guest room or other unstimulating room can work well, too.

I've never liked the phrase "time-out" because it's not very descriptive. You can make up your own name for the time-away place. Some examples include: The Quieting Down Room, The Calming Down Chair, The Quiet Space, and The Yelling Room (where a child can go to scream as loud as he wants without hurting other people's ears).

Your child runs out of the room? Of course your child will run out of the room. How do you keep the little buggers in the time-away spot?

- Pick him up or take his hand every time and return to the designated spot without talking or scolding.

If he keeps coming out, stay inside the room and be the human barrier in front of the door. Many times I have closed the door behind me and sat down in front of it. I sit there calmly, resting my arms on my bent knees, until my thrashing child calms down and I can talk to her. Don't argue; don't engage much; just wait calmly. It can take a while. It's understandable if *you* feel like screaming. But don't. Close your eyes for a few seconds and regroup.

Arriving at the time-away place, you might say:

You have to stay here until you calm down, and I can help you.
You must stay here until you calm yourself down. I will be back to
  check on you in two minutes. (You can try leaving for brief
  periods with a child older than three.)

When your child calms down a little:

I see you've stopped kicking and thrashing and you're ready to go
  back to play. That's great. Let's take a deep breath together.
  (Take a couple of deep breaths together before allowing
  him to leave.)
You calmed yourself down. I bet that feels better. (Give a brief
  hug of support.)

Acknowledge your child's feelings by empathizing with him:

It seems like you were really angry. . . It seems like you really wanted to scream out there. . . I noticed you got really angry and decided to hit your sister.

Show him what he can do the next time he gets angry, instead of hitting or biting. Stomp your feet and say *I am really angry!* Ask him to try it. If he doesn't want to engage, just end the time-away. Later down the road you can say:

You got angry and decided to hit your sister. But hitting really hurts her. What can you do the next time you get angry?

By the time a child is four or five, less explanation is needed. They already know that they shouldn't be hitting, and that hitting hurts. Nevertheless, they must have a consequence if the behavior continues, and a time-away serves that purpose well.

Keep in mind that when small children are lost in a tantrum, they usually don't recall why it escalated. It could be a combination of daylong issues, like lack of sleep or overstimulation. Back off on the "Why did you do that?" interrogations.

What if. . .

You can't stay in or near the time-away room?

Let's be honest: you can't always stay with your melting-down child because you might be the only one at home and have other children to monitor. You may have to leave your child alone in the time-away area for a few moments. Here are some ways to do this:

- For kids who can't climb out, put a locking gate inside the doorway of the room and keep the door open. It's best if a small child can see you from a distance. Tell her you will return in two minutes (or one minute for each year). Set a timer because you'll never remember when you started.
- A four- or five-year-old may order you out of the time-away room. That's OK. Just come back after the designated time, and hopefully your child will be calm enough to return to an activity.
- If your child readily climbs over the gate and gets out, you will have to keep returning her to the gated area until the timer rings. It might also be helpful to place the timer somewhere she can see but not touch it, to give an indication of an ending point. If she spends the whole time climbing out, then re-do the time-away with her (and reset the timer), as soon as you are free.

C. When nothing else works, give your child a safe space to kick and scream it out.   If your child is too wound up to hear you, talk, or be reasoned with, or if she screams when you come near, then let her have the tantrum she needs, in a safe place and with supervision if possible. Hold back; she's probably too tired for any interventions or discussions. It can take quite a while before she settles. When she finally calms a little, be available for a brief hug. Then say something along the lines of:

You calmed yourself down. I bet that feels better.

Another approach is to sit nearby as she is winding down and start to read one of her books to yourself. Don't urge her to join you. She may get interested and climb in your lap. If your child did not get her usual nap, give her one now if you can. (If your child gets very aggressive with you when you are setting limits, see Chapter 7: Getting Really, Really Angry, and see "Using Physical Force on Your Child" in Ongoing Adventures if you feel your youngster is a danger to herself or others during a tantrum.)

Reality Check

Tantrums are a part of life for two- to five-year-olds. The good news is that they become less frequent as your child gets close to age five. Most tantrums occur when a young one is tired or hungry and can't get what he wants. Painful as it is, think of a meltdown as a thunderstorm. Long or short, it will pass. And sometimes the most you can do is make sure your child doesn't hurt herself while it's rolling by. It's fine to give your child support at the end of a storm, so she knows she is not a bad person. (However, don't go overboard with the affection. It could have unintended consequences. You may think you are giving her positive reinforcement for calming down, but what you may be doing is teaching her that acting out is the way to get lots of your attention.) When your child has calmed, you can have a discussion about the different things she can do the next time she gets angry.

If your child is having frequent or prolonged outbursts in specific, recurring situations, it may be time to step back and look at what else is going on in her life. If you sense that your child is struggling for more attention or acting out because she feels bad about herself, then you may have to make some changes. You might need to give her one-on-one special time with a parent every day—even if that means spending just fifteen minutes doing what she chooses. You may need to make your schedules and routines more consistent, or break a negative feedback cycle that you may be in. (For example, do you get into the same battle with your child every day that ends

with both of you feeling horrible?) Your first step should be to discuss the tantrum problem with a valued preschool teacher, your pediatrician, or another experienced parent. If the situation is very
complex, the advice might be to see a child psychologist to talk over
some of the issues or routines in your family life that may play a role
in your child's difficulty. Even one or two meetings with a recommended child psychologist can be very illuminating.

CHAPTER 2

Social Graces,
or the Lack Thereof

Up until toddlerhood, we pretty much give our kids a free pass on using good manners. We've all been told that the best thing we can do to teach our children is to model good manners ourselves. (We've been doing this all along, right? Even when talking to our spouse?) Modeling is critical, but not necessarily enough. There comes a point, usually after age two, when a child is more aware of people and social interactions, when it's time to teach her directly about manners. As they begin to learn manners, kids can get some pretty confusing messages when it comes to interacting with "strangers." On the one hand, they're instructed not to talk to strangers, but on the other, they're nudged to say hello to the person you bump into at the store. The earlier you start modeling and practicing good manners, the better the results. For a two-year-old, simply saying "bye-bye," "please," and "thank you" is a wonderful start; you can add more as your child catches on.

Modeling, practicing, and praising good manners (even when you're not feeling particularly polite yourself) are all ways to help put your child on the path to civilized behavior.

Won't Say Hello to Greeters

Often toddlers need prompts to learn how to say hello politely. Don't assume that it comes naturally. When someone greets your child, you might say, for instance:

> *In our family when somebody says hello, we like to say "Hi" back. It's the polite thing to do.*
>
> *It's OK to have shy feelings. If you don't want to say "Hi," you can just give a little wave. Or a nod.*
>
> *It's always polite to say hi when you're with Mommy or Daddy (or whoever is taking care of you).*

Role-Play

At home, rehearse and practice introductions and greetings. Pretend you're somebody your child knows, like her grandfather, then somebody she doesn't know, like a former colleague. Your child can decide to say hi, nod, or wave. Always explain who a new person is by giving context, even to the youngest children.

> *Josie, this is Madge. She used to work with me a long time ago at my office. (Hi, Josie.) Can you say hi to Madge?*

Of course, the next time a real visitor appears, your child might turn away or ignore the greeting. You can say:

Tommy, here's Dana. Let's say hi to her.
I heard Dana say hi. Let's say hi to Dana together.

What if. . .

Your child turns away in shyness?

When starting out, go easy on your child and expect some non-compliance. Fill in the appropriate response for him:

Hi, Dana. How are you?

After a bit of practice, you can choose to:

Get down low and whisper: *Josie, in our family when a friend says hello, we look up.*
Say to the visitor: *Josie is having shy feelings right now.* (That's enough. Don't discipline.)

What if. . .

It still doesn't work?

When teaching manners, repetition is your tool. Practice a few times a day, but not so much that your child tunes you out. Give your child some slack to get it wrong, and lots of chances to get it right. Always praise or reinforce good manners.

That was so polite when you said, "Hello."
You seemed like such a growing-up boy when you said, "Thank you."
You really showed good manners when you said hi to my friend.
I can tell you are trying hard to use good manners.

You have spent a good amount of time on manners, perhaps months, and you think your child understands, but then suddenly he doesn't feel like cooperating anymore?

At two to three years old:

First, model the right thing to do by saying the greeting for him.

Hi, Margaret. How are you?

Then the consequence should be more practice and role-playing at home.

At four to five years old:

Get down and whisper, in a tone that is straightforward but not naggy:

Alan said, "Hello." I want you to look up and give a wave.

Things you can say later:

When we're out and someone says hello to you, I'm going to expect you to say hello or give a smile.

I was very uncomfortable because someone spoke to you and you ignored him.

The Stranger Conundrum

You can imagine a small child thinking, "Hey, this person is a stranger, so why should I talk to him?" Explain to your child that it's OK to talk to strangers when Mommy or Daddy is with her. If a grown-up is being friendly, it's OK to be friendly back when Mom or Dad (or other caregiver) is near.

What is the appropriate response to compliments from all those well-meaning people who want to be friendly?

I like your shoes! What a lovely skirt! You have beautiful curls!

For a two- or three-year-old, say "Thank you" for your child. Don't expect her to respond graciously to compliments; she still doesn't understand the social context.

For a four- or five-year-old, you can tell your child:

It's polite to say thank you when someone says something nice. It's OK to talk to strangers when Mommy is with you.

Don't push your child or be heavy-handed about it. Responding to compliments should be a low priority compared to all the other manners she is learning. If your child ignores the compliment, just say thank you for her.

Annoying Strangers.   Don't urge your child to say anything to people you don't know, or someone who makes you feel uncomfortable. If an overbearing person makes a comment about your child, just say:

Thank you so much; let's go find the strawberries.

You can tell your child:

When we are out and people come over and make you uncomfortable, you don't have to say anything. Mommy or Daddy will take care of it.

Been there. . .

One night I brought two of my daughters to get take-out food at the burrito shop. The friendly owner of the shop came around the counter to tell my daughter Josie that her coat was pretty. Josie was four, and she really did not like strangers talking to her. Her lips curled into a pout as she glowered at the man. Before I could whisk her away, she grumbled, "You're stupid!" Mortified, I left the store wondering, *Where did we go wrong?*

If your child says something unkind to a greeter, start by taking a deep breath to keep your anger and embarrassment under control. Addressing both the person and your child, you can say:

> *I'm very sorry; Josie is still learning good manners (or learning how to be polite, considerate, respectful, etc.).*

If this has been happening for a long period of time, choose an appropriate, immediate consequence, which can be challenging when you are running errands. Some examples might include leaving the store as soon as possible, taking your child to a bench where you can talk about her behavior, or banning shopping trips with your child for a few days.

Back at home, rehearse the scene again. And when you are both calm, talk to your child about other ways of handling the situation. Teach her phrases like "I don't want to talk right now," or "I don't feel like talking." Remind her that it's OK if she doesn't want to talk, but she may not say mean words. Like any unacceptable behavior, start out by explaining why the behavior is inappropriate or offensive, and give your child alternatives to use.

If your child's behavior doesn't improve, you'll need to be firmer:

If a person comes over and makes you feel uncomfortable, you don't have to say anything. Mommy or Daddy will take care of it. But I never want you to say anything impolite like "You're stupid."

Or

It's not OK to say mean things to people because it really hurts their feelings. You can say in your head, 'stupid head,' but you can't say it to the person. That's really inconsiderate. You can tell Mommy or Daddy how you feel, but you cannot be rude to another person.

Won't Give a Relative a Hug or Kiss

You can't expect your child to hug or kiss a person he doesn't know very well. Whenever your child refuses, you should respect this decision and defend it, in spite of outside expectations.

If your child shrinks away from Auntie Eleanor, here are some things you can try:

To Auntie: *Lucy hasn't seen you in such a long time.*
Lucy, can you shake Auntie's hand? Let's shake her hand together.
    (Try this only once. If your child pulls away, don't force her; because you certainly don't want a battle.)

If you have particularly old-fashioned relatives who expect children to act a certain way, you might try to head them off in advance,

THE FAMILY POLICY BOOK

It can be very handy to write down your important family policies in a notebook that you store in the kitchen or living room. You can refer to it when you are in the midst of a discussion with your children about why they have to do something like say hello. What's in your policy book will no doubt reflect the behaviors and routines needed to keep your family functioning and growing.

Below is a sample from our Family Policy Book. You will identify things that you disagree with because your values are, of course, different. But my hope is that it might serve as a working model for your family.

- Everyone must sleep in his own bed at night.
- We do not eat or bring food into the living room or upstairs.
- Everyone must brush his or her teeth twice a day (or let parents do it).
- Everyone must try to use good manners, such as saying please, hello, and thank you (a work in progress).
- No one may hit, bite, pinch, push, or scratch (also a work in progress).
- We never, ever say "Shut up" in our family. Whoever does so gets an automatic time-away.
- We all do age-appropriate chores on Saturdays.
  (For example, a two-year-old can help move toys from floor to bin or pick up books; a three- or four-year-old can help carry unbreakable dirty dishes from table to sink or re-cap markers; a four- or five-year-old can put away clean utensils but not knives, tidy up the shoe area, help take out the recycling, or set the table.)
- All safety rules must be followed. (You must sit in a car seat. No wearing flip-flops on climbing structures, etc.)
- Any important routine we are all trying to learn is non-negotiable until it is well established.
  (Examples include settling in to school drop-offs, learning to sleep in one's own bed, or going to bed at roughly the same time each night.)

or in the moment, by saying something like: *Just so you know, John is still learning manners and isn't big on hugs or kisses right now.*

Ignores You or Others

Being ignored can really make your blood boil. That feeling of being invisible is not something we adults take lightly. When our children ignore us, however, we must not take it personally. There's much more going on inside that little head than being rude to Mom and Dad.

Here are some reasons why your child might be ignoring you:

- She is truly focused on a task and doesn't want to be interrupted.

Concentration is a precious skill. If your little one is really focused on a project or task, don't interrupt her unless absolutely necessary. Don't feel compelled to chat about or direct her actions unless she asks for help. (It's OK to ask her once if she wants help.) The way to cultivate a long attention span is to do nothing. Try to keep other adults and happenings from interrupting her as well. Giving her brain the time and space it needs to explore and process sets a solid foundation for learning. It's also a critical antidote to our rushed modern lifestyle.

- She is completely distracted by the talking, noise, and activity around her.

Don't yell over the din of your environment. Wait until you can find a quiet spot to talk.

- She is overstimulated by the environment and needs to tune everything out.

Remove her from the busy environment to talk. If that's not possible, it's comforting just to hold her on your lap.

- She doesn't know how to answer or respond to your request.

Use simpler, shorter sentences that she can understand, or turn your request into two choices.

- You are talking too much and your story is too long. (You know who you are.)

Sometimes less is more. Remember, little children have very short attention spans. Change your approach. Be concise. Find a hook that will interest a small child.

When I was a little boy I used to wonder. . .
Do you know what I learned today?

- She doesn't want to do what you have asked her to do.

At this point ask yourself: Is what I am asking her to do reasonable? Is it really necessary or can I let it go until later? Make requests only when you really have to. Let your child make his own choices and decisions whenever possible. That said, when you set reasonable boundaries, like coming to the dinner table or getting into the tub when the timer rings, then you must follow through. There is a gray area you can operate in, however. It's OK for both of you to compromise. Here's a simple example: If you are in a battle over putting on shoes, you can offer to put on one, if she puts on the other. (Read more about creative compromising and giving choices on page 219 in Chapter 11: Particularly Annoying Refusals.)

- She doesn't believe you will enforce any of your mild threats.

When you calmly warn your child of a consequence (*Please sit down on your chair, or I will have to take you away from the table*), you must follow through with it. Of course it is easier to let the violation slide, but you will lose credibility and effectiveness—and ultimately you will lose control of your child.

When you really need to get your child's attention, try some of these approaches:

- Get down low and look her in the eye.
- Touch her shoulder, make eye contact, and say: *I need you to listen right now, not talk.*
- Come in gently from the side rather than making a frontal approach.
- If your child responds that she is busy doing something, tell her you can wait until she is done (if you can, come back in a minute or two), or use a timer if necessary.

Won't Play with Others or Make Friends

Somewhere between two and three years old, a child will start to acknowledge playmates, interact with them in a limited way, seek them out, and even refer to one or more of them as "my friend." Until your child reaches this developmental stage, you may be anxious that something is wrong or antisocial about him. To you, it may not seem like your child is showing an interest in other kids. But there's more to it. Even if a child is watching, eavesdropping, or within earshot of other children, he is learning a lot about social behavior and play without getting directly involved. Kids love to watch other kids. Even babies do it from their strollers. There is no need to rush or co-erce a child into social interactions. All you need to do is give your child regular exposure to other children, and his interest will slowly and naturally develop.

What if. . .

After weeks of going to the playground every afternoon, your three-year-old still plays by himself and shows no interest in other kids?

Some children have naturally reserved and introverted personalities. This is normal. Respect your child for who he is, but at the same time step back and ask yourself some questions about your own social style:

Does my child see me being friendly or talking to other people at the playground?
Do friends come over to my house to visit?
Do I sometimes bring my child to visit friends?
Do I feel awkward around new people?
Am I isolated from other people?

Even if you score low on the social scale, you can still do things to help your child have healthy social experiences. If you are shy and re-served by nature, remember that you don't have to change and sud-denly become a social butterfly, you don't have to become best friends with other parents or host potlucks every week. Here are some things you can do:

- Enroll your child part-time in a well-respected preschool. Ask your teachers about your child's social experiences during the day. Did he play in a small group? Did he join in the dancing? Over time, you and the teachers should see a gradual blossoming of interest in other children.

- If your child is not in toddler school or preschool, set up a recurring playdate with a neighborhood child, someone who your instincts tell you might be a good companion for her. During the playdate spend some time talking to the parent, and if you want, you can sit on the floor with the children as they play. The key here is to make the playdates recur—once or twice per week, for example. This allows time for your child to get used to a new friend within short, structured periods of time.

- Join a moms' or dads' group that meets regularly at a nearby park. Go every week, so your child gets used to seeing familiar faces. This is a great alternative to going into someone's home for a playdate because you don't even have to set it up. You just show up. The only thing to keep in mind is that some children can feel overwhelmed by a large group of children. Watch your child to see how she reacts.

- If at first your youngster shows no interest in playing with others, don't worry. Keep going. Feeling comfortable in social situations takes time and lots of exposure to others.

- After establishing a regular routine, you can try to facilitate play, very gently. For example, start playing ball or trucks with another child, and calmly invite yours to join in, or vice versa. As your child starts to play more comfortably with others, you can get more creative.

- If you have established relationships or friendships with some of the parents—and your little one feels comfortable too—you can try to take small trips away from the playground (or playgroup) while another parent looks after her. This is a great way to help her feel comfortable and secure away from you, and to learn that you will always come back. Start out by leaving for fifteen minutes at a time (for example, walk around the block), and take it from there. Explain to your daughter what you are doing and when you'll be back. Don't abandon your plan just because your child looks anxious and runs for you. Have the trusted parent pick her up and redirect her at the time you leave, and see how it goes. Cheerfully wave and walk away. This is great practice in separating and reuniting.

Reality Check

In the beginning, regular exposure to peers is the most you can and should do for your tot. It may be uncomfortable to see her acting indifferent in social settings. Don't force her to do or say things just to be polite. Be patient, and gradually you will see small changes in her interest in other kids. By age three, she'll have a natural interest in others. She needs some freedom and breathing space away from you to explore these relationships, if only at the other end of the playground. If by age four your child doesn't seem to relate to other children, then it's time to speak to a professional. Ask your pediatrician or preschool director for suggestions.

Difficulty Sharing or Taking Turns

To expect your two- or three-year-old to share her toy may be a well-intentioned idea, but it's also a myth. First of all, the word "sharing" is fraught with confusion. All too often, sharing becomes synonymous with capitulation in a child's eyes. A youngster might hear a parent say, "Share your wagon with John." But what she's really thinking is, "My mom wants me to give up this wagon. No way." Sharing is too vague a concept for young children to understand, and it is best used only when a child has lots of something to distribute, like popcorn. A better phrase to use is "taking turns." It can be suggested that a child give his friend a turn with a toy, after he himself has had a substantial amount of time to play with it first. It's not fair to immediately impose taking turns right after a child has picked up a toy. Don't pounce on him. He deserves a few minutes of uninterrupted time and space to play—it gives his brain a chance to process what he's doing.

What if. . .

Your little one is at a playdate and starts to play with her friend's ball ramp, and the friend comes along immediately asking for it back? His dad is not there at the moment to intervene, so how do you protect your child's space?

Ask your child (who has the toy): *Tommy, can Marcus play with you?* If the answer is no, don't force the issue.

Tell the other child: *Tommy is playing with that right now. Let's come back in five minutes to see if he's done.*

If that approach doesn't work: *Tommy, Marcus would like to take a turn when you are done. How many minutes do you need, three or five?* (Or hold up your fingers to ask a little or a lot.) Set a timer or use a watch. Give your child a one-minute reminder before his time is up.

Vice versa:

- When your child is angling or grabbing for a toy that a friend has, encourage him to do the asking, even at age two:

Why don't you ask Marcus if you can play with him?
Ask this boy if you can have a turn with the yo-yo when he's done.

- At home, review the rules of playdates or playing with friends:

In our family, when a friend comes to our house, we let them play
with our toys, and we take turns with each other.
Before our friend leaves today, she will help put the toys back and
won't take any home with her. (This last part assuages the
anxiety your child may have about losing his toys.)
When we visit a friend's house, we play with his toys and take
turns with him.
Before we leave, we always put the toys back and we don't take any
home with us.

- Review the policy again before a playdate starts.
- Before the playdate, give your child a chance to store the toys
that she doesn't feel like sharing with her friend. Be prepared for
the slippery slope. In the middle of a playdate, she can't suddenly
designate something off-limits just to get it away from her friend.
These decisions must be made before the friend comes over.

Aggressive or Disruptive Toward Playmates

If correcting and redirecting your child's disruptive behavior doesn't
do the trick, then remove him to a place where you can talk to him
alone. Don't scold him in front of his friends because that can make
him feel ashamed, and he may act out in anger.

If your child is disturbing the other playmates around him, you can
respond by giving him a time-away. Here are some ways to do it:

- Have him sit next to you until he calms down and listens.
- Take him to a different part of the playground to calm down and talk.
- Take him to a separate room at the playdate location.

Stay with him; don't isolate him. When he calms down and understands that hitting or (continually) wrecking sand castles, for instance, is not acceptable, then he can go back to play. Throughout this process, you do not have to raise your voice, although you may feel the urge to express your outrage at him. Usually separating him from the situation and telling him what's what will do the trick. Although outrageous, your child's behavior is pretty typical of small children who are experimenting with their own power.

What about Pushing or Kicking?

Little kids can go from being best friends to rivals and back very quickly. And a child can sometimes go through short phases of disruptive behaviors with playmates. For example, a toddler might take on a pattern of pushing or pulling hair for a few days in a row. In this case, first calmly and repeatedly try to hold or redirect her. You can simply say: *Oops. No pushing* and take her hand and offer a choice of something else to do. If the behavior escalates, you can try the following:

Take your tot to a place where he can push/pull/hit/kick something safely. For example, he can push a wall, kick a ball against a wall, or pull a toy. *Balls are for kicking; I like the way you are kicking the ball.* There is no need to be preachy to a very small child.

You can say to a child older than three: *I notice that you really want to kick a lot this week. So let's go someplace to get all your kicking out of your system. It's OK to kick a wall because walls don't have feelings. Friends do have feelings, and kicking really hurts them.*

What if. . .

Your child obviously needs a time-away at a playdate? Are all the rules and procedures the same at playdates?

All the rules of conduct are the same, but the time-away procedures should be a little different. The only case where a full-blown time-away makes sense is when both children are implicated, and both have a separate time-away. Otherwise, stay with your misbehaving child and do not leave him alone, as you might do for short periods at home. It's not a good idea to make a big scene in front of your child's friends: humiliation is a tough emotion to process at a young age. The best you can do is to take him by your side or into another room for a few minutes until he switches gears or calms down. If his behavior is uncontrollable, then pack up and go home.

I don't know why, but today it looks like you are feeling irritable.
Do you know what that means? It's when you go like this—
(demonstrate). *It looks like everything is bothering you.*
I can help you calm down. Let's go home now, and we'll try to play
on another day.

What Not to Do

Don't make excuses in front of your child, like the popular: *He got up so early today. I think he's just tired.* This does not excuse the behavior, or the reasonable consequence you have established. Your child can also use this excuse against you someday to justify his poor behavior.

If your child has a long-term problem with aggressiveness toward other children, then step back and evaluate the situation from a few different angles.

- Are there changes or disruptions in my child's life that he's struggling to cope with?
- Is he showing this behavior at school? If so, how is it handled by the teachers? Could the teachers' response be exacerbating the situation by isolating him? For example, by putting him at a separate table alone?
- Have I been giving him enough attention lately?
- Does he show his aggression toward adults? In what situations?

If it's hard to be sure what's going on, confide in a valued preschool teacher or experienced parent to get advice. You can also ask your pediatrician for the name of a professional who might be able to observe your child and offer help.

Doesn't Respect Personal Space

Does your child unabashedly walk over to a stranger's table and eavesdrop? Does she insert herself into a game that's already in progress? We adults don't even have to think about the borders of personal space, because it's so ingrained in our culture and behavior. Children start out oblivious to this hidden rule of human interaction. They learn by picking up social cues over time and, of course, guidance from their parents.

Anticipate your child's natural curiosity by intercepting him right before he acts. You can say:

Let's ask this man if we can watch his chess game.

Let's ask her if you can help with the puzzle.

Take one step back so the lady can have some space for her news-
  paper.

This is not our popcorn. It belongs to someone else.

Bosses or Bullies

We often think of bullying—harassment that aims to cause emotional distress—as something that rears up in the middle school
years. Unfortunately, preschool and kindergarten teachers are now
reporting more of it too. Don't confuse bullying with bossiness. The
bully has the intention of causing harm or distress. Bossiness, on the
other hand, is one way young children experiment with feelings of
power and control. However, if you notice your child being overly
controlling of another child, to the point where the other child
protests, it's a good idea to talk with your child about it. When necessary, find a gentle way of reminding her to check her behavior
when she's playing. Intercede but don't discipline. Feelings of self-
confidence and power are good things; you don't want to banish
them entirely.

Been there. . .

Your daughter and two friends are happily playing "school." As usual, your
daughter assigns herself the role of the teacher and proceeds to tell the
others who they are and where to sit. When one of the friends starts to
stand up, your daughter orders her to sit down. The other friend picks up
a book, but your daughter pulls it out of her hands, and tells her to sit
back down because she is a student. Is this bossiness a normal part of
imaginative play? When does a child cross the line?

It's a good idea to let the actions among children play themselves out (as long as no one gets hurt or breaks the obvious rules). Children learn a lot from negotiating with one another, even if it ultimately ends in frustration, at which time a parent can help them understand what happened. You certainly don't want to break the spirit of a child who loves to be a leader. The vast majority of bossy interactions will work themselves out on their own. On occasion, a line will get crossed. For example, one of my daughters is so controlling of her little brother that she will browbeat him until he gives up his toy, and she will even lead him around by the neck to get him to do what she wants. She doesn't intend to cause him distress; she's just a very persistent child. We are constantly giving her reminders to give her brother some space. If your child is acting overbearing to the point where her playmate is upset, then you should talk to your child about it:

> *Beverly, when you keep telling Tommy what to do, he can't make his own choices. You are not in charge of Tommy; Tommy is in charge of himself.*
> *Tommy needs to have some space, and make his own choices.*
> *Tommy needs a turn in the game.*
> *Your brother is younger and can't play as long. Now he's done with this game and wants to do something else.*

Whenever you can, point out the way the other child is responding; for example, he might move away, cry out, or wear a sad or confused expression. These cues will help your child learn about feelings and develop empathy.

> *When you keep giving Joey orders, his face goes like this—* (demonstrate). *He doesn't like it.*

When you pull him around, Joey goes like this, "Aaaaa!" He doesn't like it.

When he walks away like that, he's telling you he needs a break.

Another good idea is to invent a special signal that you can use with your child to remind him to back off a little. For example, tapping him on the shoulder and giving a hand signal or a word.

I have figured out that when you play with Tommy, you start to give him a lot of orders. I am going to help you stop doing that by tapping you on the shoulder. If I see you giving lots of orders to your friend, I'm going to do this (a tap or signal) *to remind you to stop (or give him some space).*

In older children, one natural consequence of bossiness is that friends will stop wanting to play with them. But a four- or five-year-old needs help from a parent or teacher to understand this dynamic. If your child is suddenly sad about a friend losing interest in her, you can ask why she thinks this is happening. You may never know the real reason, so it's important not to jump to conclusions. You can encourage your child to talk to her friend by suggesting some language she can use.

Sabrina, why don't you want to play with me today?

Whatever answer she gets, help your child understand it and put it into context. For example, your child's friend might tell her she is too bossy. You can talk to her about what this means, and how she might play differently. (Or perhaps friends just need to take a break for a while, as they get to know other friends, but that doesn't mean they stop being your friend.) You can ask teachers for their take on your child's bossiness. If you discover it's actually interfering with relationships, suggest some ways she can interact without giving orders. Say something in a bossy way, and then in a friendly way. Ask your child to pick which is which.

> *Give it to me, it's my turn!... May I have my turn now?*
> *I'm the princess and you're the baby ... I want to be the princess first. What do you want to be?*

What if . . .

Your child complains that you are bossing her: "You're not the boss of me!"

It's always helpful to spend a few seconds asking yourself if you have been too bossy or naggy today. Have you spent most of the day making requests and giving instructions? Chances are you have had a pretty normal day, and your child is digging in her heels in response to a reasonable request. You can say:

> *Actually we are the bosses about certain things. There are lots of things you are in charge of, but Mom and Dad are in charge of keeping our family healthy and safe.*

Or

> *You won't like all of our choices, but there are certain things you have to do because we know what's best for you. Brushing your teeth is one of them.*

When the nagging has reached a fever pitch, try to stay calm but firm:

We have decided our family is going to Grandpa's tonight. That's Mommy and Daddy's final decision.

Reality Check

It's perfectly normal for a small child to think the world is all about him, him, him. That's his job after all—to be self-centered—and one of the crazy, outrageous things we love about our kids. Most children will grow out of bossy stages as they get older and realize the rest of the world doesn't always bow to their demands. The appearance of bossiness in our children should remind us to do a little lifestyle check on ourselves. Too many demands, orders, interruptions, and transitions in a small child's life can make him feel powerless and cause him to respond by trying to exert control over his friends. Consider whether or not your child gets enough unstructured play time at home, and if you are communicating with your child about many different things—books, friends, nature, his own projects, you name it—and not just nagging him about what he should do next. And of course, if you see signs of real bullying in your child (intentionally causing distress in another child), it is not advisable to let it go. It's something that should be addressed and stopped right away.

One-upmanship

Age five is the golden year of bragging. "I have three Barbie dolls at home," "I'm going to the circus and getting cotton candy," "My shirt has more sparkles than yours," "Well, I have a whole giant box of stickers at my house." Just like bossiness, bragging is not a problem unless you know your youngster is deliberately making someone else feel bad. You have to use your judgment to determine when that line gets crossed.

Here are a few ways to reframe a competitive interaction that is heating up:

You are feeling really good about your new bike, and your friend is feeling happy about his new bike too. (This line is good to use in a "mine is better than yours" exchange.)

In our family, if we have something that our friend does not, we don't make her feel bad about it.

We don't tease someone for not going to the circus; that could make her feel sad. Would you like to tell Molly about your favorite part of the circus?

If you want to tell a friend about your truck in a friendly way, that's OK. You can say, "Ella, do you want to see my new truck?"

Separation Problems

Whether it's transitioning to a caregiver, or saying good-bye at preschool drop-off, there is only one way to remedy separation problems, and that is with consistency. That means you and your spouse should have a routine that you stick to nearly every day. A child is most secure when he has the same caregiver or group of caregivers, and knows when he can expect to see his parents again.

Here are some guidelines that many preschools give to parents who are trying to improve the morning separation scene:

- Decide on a short routine you will do with your child when she arrives at school. For example, read a book or work on a puzzle for a few minutes. Then give your child a kiss or a hug and leave. Stick to this routine as long as you need to, or until his drop-off anxiety decreases. Some children, however, do much better with a fast drop-off and no lingering. If your extended routine is only making your child more anxious, you might want to adopt the quick drop-off approach.

- When it's time to leave, give your tot a kiss and say, *I'll see you after naptime/after the playground,* using a more specific time frame than "the end of the day." Smile, wave, and leave. Do not look worried or stressed when you leave. Fake it if you have to. (Parenting is just like acting, but without the fancy clothes and awards ceremonies.) You can also ask her to make a choice: *Would you like one or two hugs/kisses?* Note: If kissing or hugging just makes her cling more, then use only a wave. If she is crying, clinging, and won't let you go, then place her in the arms of a teacher. A teacher should be prepared to comfort her like this every morning, if necessary. You may even find that the best system is to say good-bye right at the door to the classroom, as long as there is a teacher ready to bring her inside.

- Believe it or not, you can actually role-play the drop-off scene at home. Pick a doorway, and pretend it is the door to the classroom. Have one parent play the teacher and the other play the parent. Go through your miniroutine all the way through to saying good-bye. Knowing what to expect goes a long way.

- On the way to school, if your child is pleading with you to stay home, it can be helpful to list all the things you need to do that day. *No, sweetie, we can't stay home today because Mommy has to go to work/clean the house/work on my computer/go to meetings with grown-ups.* Or explain the benefits of staying at school: *Preschool has a lot more toys and friends than we have at home. I think you will have much more fun at school today, while I am running errands/working. If you stay home today, there will be no one there to take care of you and keep you safe.*

In our family, parents go to work and children go to school to have fun and learn.

- Remember, as pathetic as your child looks when you drop her off, most children snap back into a good mood just minutes or even seconds after you leave, with the help of a caring teacher. It's one of the hard-to-believe facts of preschool.
- If you're worried about your son or daughter to the point of distraction, leave a message for the teacher to call you later with an update on your child. We grown-ups sometimes need a little reassurance too.
- If you will be transitioning your child to a new school, ask for the names of one or two children in your child's class and set up some playdates with them before school starts. Familiarity with a few new friends prior to starting school will help your child feel more comfortable in the first days.

Playdates are another opportunity to practice separating and reuniting. Between the ages of four and five is a great time to start trying drop-off playdates. Talk to your youngster about what will happen. Decide together whether you should stay at the playdate for ten or fifteen minutes. If she vehemently resists the idea, wait a while and assume she is not yet ready. Present the idea again in a few weeks or months. Invite her friends over for a drop-off playdate so she can see peers who are comfortable in this situation. When she completes her first playdate without you, she will feel very proud of herself. Be sure to praise her for her independence and for being such a nice friend.

Adjusting to Babysitters

Here are some ways to smooth your child's adjustment from being with you or your spouse to being in the care of a babysitter.

- Familiarity breeds comfort. Try to set a time for your child or children to get to know the babysitter before you make a date to go out. Hire her for an hour to come over and play. If you can't prepare in advance, ask the babysitter to arrive at least an hour early to get to know everyone.
- If possible, get a photo of your babysitter and give it to your child.
- If you think your child will be anxious, don't tell him about the actual babysitting event until the day before, and mention it only once. On the morning of the event, remind him again; that's all. Too much discussion about it may make him more anxious.
- Decide on a special project or activity your children can do with the babysitter: make popcorn, watch a special approved video, go to the playground, bake cookies. Try to keep some special activities reserved for babysitting nights.
- When you leave, say supportive and encouraging things, such as:

Mommy and Daddy will come home tonight when you are sleeping, and we will check on you in your bed.
I know you will be a big helper tonight for Kim.

- Start a good-bye ritual. Sometimes kids like to do something special right before their parents leave (like pushing them out the door!). It might be waving from the window or starting a project they will make for you to see when you get back. What works really runs the gamut, and for some children, a quick good-bye works best because it doesn't stir up emotions.

You might feel horrible when you walk away from a screaming child at drop-off time, but if you maintain a consistent routine, your child will most likely recover immediately after you leave. It's hard to believe, but true. If separation continues to be a struggle, step back to see if there are other issues going on in your child's life that are making her insecure. Is your child anxious because she does not know when she will see you or your spouse again? Have there been some shifts in your schedule? Is there a big change going on in your family? Of course every child needs to spend quality time with a parent every day. When it comes to separation anxiety, though, it's not the amount of time you spend with your child that counts, but how consistent you are about when you leave and return. If he can depend on the same routine every day, he won't spend his time worrying about when you will come back.

Clingy Behavior

Some children are naturally shy, and they need support in social situations. Other kids are shy only when entering a new scene. In either case, it's usually not a problem for a parent to hold a child for a while after entering a new setting, and then let her get down when she gets bored. But what about the child who really doesn't let you go? We expect a two-year-old to be clingier than a five-year-old who has achieved more independence. If you have a problem with clinginess, you can gradually add boundaries to your child's behavior, in an effort to slowly, but gently, pry her away for a while.

- Take the example of visiting a friend. Before you go, explain to your child what's going to happen.

When we get there, we are going to say hello, and I am going to put you on my lap while I talk to Jane. After a little while, I will put you on the floor next to me where you can draw or play a game.

• If the clinginess happens in the middle of a visit, take a ten-minute break to play with your child if she really needs your undivided attention. But tell her that when you are finished playing, you are going to stay close by and talk to the grown-ups.

What if . . .

It doesn't work? Your child keeps interrupting you, even after you have spent time playing with her, making it impossible for you to talk to your friend.

It could be that your child just wants to be physically close to you while in a strange environment. You can try to sit at a table and hold her on your lap while she plays with something—cards, crayons, blocks. Explain to her that if she wants to stay on your lap, she'll have to play quietly and not interrupt. If she can't do that, you will have to put her down on the floor to play. (Also see "Interrupting" on page 60.)

What if . . .

The clingy behavior just gets worse?

The best response to a clinging, whining child in this situation is a real judgment call for you. On the one hand, if you keep letting her interrupt you to give her a time-away or to simply leave the scene, she has succeeded in getting what she wants: attention from you. (At a different time, you must assess whether or not your child is getting enough time overall with her parents. Do you have a consistent routine with your child, or does she always have to adapt to your absences?) If you feel your youngster is otherwise well-adjusted, and you see her at predictable times each day, you may conclude that episodes of very clingy behavior are a way for her to manipulate you. Instead of giving in, try to use constructive resistance as a way to help her learn to entertain herself nearby. Here are some suggestions:

- Ignore the whining. Shake your head once and say, *I can't help you right now because I'm busy talking to* ____. Don't react or give your child extra attention. More laid-back children will get bored waiting for you and will find something to engage their interest—or become more open to the toys you have offered.

- Set up intervals of time, say five minutes, where you won't talk, interact, or make eye contact with your child because you will be busy doing something else. Of course, you must explain this. *I need five minutes to talk to my friend. So for the next five minutes you need to sit right next to me and play quietly.* Your next step is to ignore her, within reason, for the designated time.

- Have your spouse take your child to another room, find an activity to do together for a few minutes, set her up with an activity she can do on her own, and then come back. When she comes back to get you, review the rules about sitting on your lap and not interrupting.

- If your child is being deliberately disruptive and annoying, you or your spouse can take her to another room for some quiet time-away. But make it a short time and come right back. If you feel you need to leave the visit, don't do so immediately. Wait a little while, or else your child will have won the battle.

Has your child not yet learned to feel safe when he's away from his parents? To begin the practice of separating, have your child spend time away from you with someone he sees a lot. For example, a grandparent, an aunt or uncle, or a close friend can take him shopping, out to lunch, or to the playground. It's important that you start with someone your child knows very well. After that, you can move on to babysitters or other adults you trust. You don't have to do this frequently, just often enough for your child to feel confident and safe outside of your care. In our family, we have the same babysitters (yes, we need two) who come one night a week, so my husband and I can go out. Our children have come to look forward to Thursday nights with the babysitters, because they get to bake, watch a movie, or put on kids' tattoos.

Interrupting

Sometimes I fantasize about a time in the future when my children will no longer whine, have tantrums, or interrupt me when I am so obviously and clearly talking to someone else. Of course by then they'll be brooding preteens, and I'll probably be desperate for them to talk to me at all. For now, with small children around, interrupting is a fact of life. Over time, they will get the hang of the etiquette for how to get your attention politely, but it will take a lot of patient teaching on your part.

There are two major strands to dealing with chronic interrupting: teaching your child to say, "Excuse me," when she needs to break in; and using a hand signal that tells your child, *I hear you, and I will talk to you in a minute.*

- For two- and three-year-olds who thrive on instant gratification, you can simply say, *One minute, honey, Mommy's talking,* while holding up your sign for "Please wait." This hand signal can be holding up one finger or two, as in a peace sign. You may have another idea for a hand signal. For the littlest kids, use words and the hand signal together. Eventually—perhaps a year from now?—you will be able to just hold up your signal and your child will get the message.

- For four- and five-year-olds who now have the skills to learn how to wait for short periods of time, take them aside and introduce them to the hand signal and what it means.

At the same time, you should also teach older children to say "Excuse me" when they need to get your attention while you are in a conversation. (You might prefer a tap on the shoulder instead.) Practice this with them in a role-play while you pretend to be on the telephone. Explain to them that saying "Excuse me" will get Mom or Dad to notice them, but they also might receive a hand signal if a parent needs to finish up a conversation with someone else. "Excuse me" should not be just a sugarcoated interruption. In other words, you shouldn't drop everything just because your child said, "Excuse me." Use your hand signal.

You're growing bigger now, and I know you will learn how to wait until I'm done talking. That's good manners when you wait for me.

(**What if. . .**

Your child keeps interrupting you anyway?

Try to ignore her as much as possible, while holding up your hand signal.

Hold up your hand signal as you walk into a different room.

Don't keep chatting on and on. That's not fair to your kids. Wrap up your conversation soon, and when you're done, don't forget to thank your child for waiting.

Thank you for waiting!
You are so patient. I know you wanted to tell me something and you waited for me.
Wow, you had a lot to tell me, and you waited so patiently. Thank you! You really are growing up.

While we're on the subject of good manners, here are some phrases we parents should try to use more often. It's really easy to let formalities slide with our family, but it's a great chance to model the behavior you want your children to learn:

To your spouse:

Excuse me, honey. I'm sorry for interrupting, but I wanted you to know that I already gave Sophie her vitamin.

To your children:

Excuse me. I'm sorry for interrupting, but I wanted to tell you that your juice is on the table now.
Excuse me for a minute, guys. I have something I need to tell Grandma.

Do you feel like Mister Rogers when you talk like this? Well, that's understandable, since being the perfect parent is not second nature to you, or to me, or to most of the parents I know. Practice this way of speaking nonetheless, and it will come to feel more natural.

Let's go one step further with the good manners idea. What about the person on the other end of your conversation? Is it fair to turn away from him because your child is whining for you? Suddenly ignoring the person you were talking to is kind of rude. Here's a more polite way to handle an interruption:

> *Excuse me; I am just going to talk to Jenny for a second.*
> *Can you excuse me for one moment? Jacob seems to need me right now.*

After you help your child, you can tell her:

> *I can help you this time, but please don't interrupt me again—I'll be finished soon.*

Afterwards, if needed:

> *I know you really, really wanted to tell me something, but I was talking to my friend on the phone, and I did not want to be interrupted. I did this—*(hand signal). *Do you remember what that means?* (Let her answer.) *That's right; it means I will talk to you as soon as I am done. Next time I do that, will you please wait for me to finish?*

Reality Check

Teaching our children to be civilized, social beings can feel like a long, fruitless effort. It's often easier to look the other way or make excuses for our child's failure to be polite. They are so young, after all, and oblivious to the everyday expectations of society. It's easy to understand why parents get frustrated. Children don't seem to absorb what we teach them for the second or third time. That's the remarkable thing about little kids—they are like a slow train arriving at the station. But rest assured, they do learn and grow, as long as we parents deliver calm and compassionate guidance over and over again.

CHAPTER 3

In Search of Sleep

His smiles reassure you; his hugs lift you on your worst days. You would overcome anything that stands in the way of your child's happiness. But . . . does that mean you have to let him sleep in your bed?

Many families struggle with the issue of nightly sleeping arrangements, because parents are conflicted about whose needs should come first: their children's or their own. Sleep is so critical to our functioning as parents—not to mention it makes you feel and look younger!—that it's worth rearranging our lives for. Does that mean we all should train our children to sleep in their own beds? Not necessarily. The bottom line is that whatever arrangement makes both parents happy and gives everyone enough sleep is the one that works. Some parents who work long hours feel that the closeness of a family bed makes up for some of the time they are not with their children. But if you are like many parents who need some separation from your children in order to achieve peace of mind and a good night's sleep—not to mention a little time with your long neglected spouse—you should establish healthy bedtime rituals and boundaries.

The Case of the Family Bed or Co-Sleeping

Here are a few questions you should ask yourself to see if your co-sleeping arrangement is working.

- Are you doing it for you or for your child?

Most healthy, secure children don't need to sleep with their parents. If you have a strong bond with your child, and she sees you at consistent times during the day, then you can help her transition to her own room with minimal pain. On the other hand, if you work ten-hour days, for example, and get very little time to spend with your child, how could you pass up the chance to be close at night? If you want to separate at night, but find it hard to begin, try to incorporate more fun and closeness with your child at other times of day, so that bedtime is not the only time for cuddles.

- Are you sleeping together in order to avoid conflict?

Big transitions almost never occur without tears. It's not your job to make sure your child never cries. It is your job to be consistent and calm, and follow through with the new routines once they are established. If you are consistent, your child will learn faster. You might have two or three nights of conflict—and yes, even ear-splitting protest screaming—followed by literally months or years of happy sleeping. (See page 307 for a list of recommended sleep-training books.)

- Do you stay with your child until she falls asleep, even in a family bed?

Falling asleep on one's own, when tired, is one of the best early skills your child can learn. Why? If a child can recognize and feel the signs of being tired, he can learn to take care of himself—or soothe himself—by falling asleep. If his routine is consistent, your child will come to enjoy sleep and do it more quickly and more deeply. And a good night's sleep is critical to a child's learning process. You work hard getting all the bedtime rituals in place, and when you leave the room, your tired child should eventually fall asleep.

• When do you expect your child to leave your bed?

Most families that have a communal bed—where a child or children sleep in a parent's bed most nights—report that sometime between the ages two and five, a child will spontaneously choose her own bed over her parents'. The right response is to let your child do it; don't make him stay with you. This transition into a bed of his own will be important to your child's sense of independence and autonomy. If the transition out of your bed doesn't happen spontaneously, you might want to think about a cutoff age. Will it be OK for a ten- or thirteen-year-old to sleep with you every night? If you opt for the family bed, ask yourself if you are encouraging and nurturing autonomy in your child in other ways, such as age-appropriate self-dressing (around age four), decent hair brushing (by age five or six), drop-off playdates (by age five), going out with a trusted relative (any age), serving herself "easy food" (by age four), or doing or helping with simple chores (as soon as possible).

• Are you, the parent, getting enough sleep?

Moms are notoriously light sleepers. If a lack of sleep is making you miserable and short-tempered, it's time to make some serious

BEDTIME ROUTINE CHECKLIST

Start bedtime rituals at the same time each night. Keep the last half hour before bedtime very mellow, with no roughhousing, tickle attacks, or races.

Get all of these things in place before you settle down with your child in her bed:

- Sippy or other cup of water (optional)
- Special cuddly animal or blanket (or both)
- Night-light installed
- Teeth brushed
- Use or attempt to use potty; or put on diaper
- Specific number of books picked out

This is a lot to remember, so make a checklist and stick it on the wall. It doesn't mean you are losing brain cells! It's very comforting to have this list, because it makes you so efficient.

changes to the bedtime situation. It doesn't matter that your spouse sleeps through everything and doesn't mind tiny feet climbing up his back or the thwack of a restless arm. If it's not working for one of you, it's not working.

Finally, if you think it's time to kick a well-entrenched co-sleeping habit, get advice from your pediatrician or the several helpful books listed on page 302 in the Ongoing Adventures section. It won't be easy at first, but the rewards will far outweigh the challenge.

Throws Tantrum at Bedtime

Your child has her own bed and bedtime routine, but she loudly and stubbornly resists going to bed. Here's what you can do:

After a five- or ten-minute before-bedtime reminder, take your child's hand and lead her to the bathroom/bedroom. If she physically resists, tell her that if she doesn't come along, you will have to pick her up and carry her to bed. If she still resists, announce calmly that you are going to count to five, and then start. If there's no cooperation, pick her up right away and carry her. Whenever you set a strict boundary like this, you have to follow through immediately. Don't get talked into another minute or another book. You already gave a five-minute warning. Keep doing this night after night and the resistance will fade. The key is to stay calm and not vacillate; otherwise your child might perceive your actions as a battle and keep on fighting.

Won't Let You Leave the Bedroom

What happens after you turn off the light? Whatever you choose to do, make it a consistent length of time every night. Sing a song, cuddle for two minutes, ask your child to close her eyes and think about what color balloon she would pick for her birthday party, etc. Say goodnight and leave. Here are some handy responses to the pleadings that may follow:

"I'm scared of the dark."

You really want to tell me that you're afraid of the dark. This is a safe, cozy house. Let's open the door a little so you can see the light in the hallway. You can look at your night-light, too. What color is it? Can you see it when you lie down?

"I'm afraid of bad dreams."

I know you don't like bad dreams. But remember, bad dreams are not real. We can turn them into happy thoughts. Let's go over what you are going to think about tonight in bed. (Do you know what we're doing tomorrow? What kind of card will you make for Dad's birthday? What kind of flowers will we plant in the yard?)

Naturally, you are on the hook for delivering anything you propose, so it's best not to make things up.

"I don't want to be alone."

You're telling me you really don't want to be alone. We never leave children alone. We're all sleeping together in the same cozy house. Mommy and Daddy are at home all night long; we're not going anywhere.
Mommy and Daddy will be sleeping all night long in their bed just like you.

"I need more cuddles."

How many cuddles, two or three? (Deliver on your offer. Tuck in.) *Do you want your covers on or off? Good night; see you in the morning.*

"One more minute."

You really want Mommy to cuddle more, but in the morning when you wake up, we'll have lots more time to cuddle.

"My belly hurts."

Going to sleep is the best way to make your tummy feel better. (Only if your instincts tell you she is not sick.)

I'LL CHECK ON YOU LATER

Here's another idea that can work well for children starting around the age of three. Tell your little one that if she stays in her bed, you will come back and check on her in ten minutes, or after you finish cleaning the kitchen, for example. If you return and she is still awake, cuddle very briefly before quietly announcing that you will return after another (longer) interval. She will likely be asleep on one of your return visits. This exercise is especially helpful in teaching children to fall asleep without a parent being present. After you fall into a good routine, you might tuck in your sleepyhead one night and be asked, "Will you check on me later?" And you will only have to do it once.

"I'm not tired."

I understand you may not feel sleepy right now. But little by little sleep will come. (You might offer a cup of milk.)

"I want my duck" (or my doll . . . or my bear . . . the horse I left in my backpack, etc.)

You already picked out your cuddle toys for tonight. On a list for tomorrow night, I can write down "Don't forget the bear at bedtime." (Write it down on one of the sticky pads you have stashed all around your house, and hopefully nearby.)

If your child is consistently wide-awake at bedtime, then either cut down or eliminate naps. Most naps disappear between the ages of three to four, some earlier, some later.

For now, you can offer the following to help her pass the time:

- Give her a child's tape recorder with calm music she can play while she tries to fall asleep. The key is that she must be able to operate it independently.
- Give permission for her to stay awake in her bed and listen to the grown-ups making noise. It can be comforting to listen to dishes clanking and being loaded in the dishwasher, or to the hum of her parents' conversation. Contrary to our instincts, we should talk in a regular voice and make noise downstairs. It may actually be soothing to our children.
- Give her a light wand or flashlight she can turn off by herself.

Then, you must be consistent and leave the room, even if your child protests.

What if. . .

After your meticulous bedtime routine, your child needs to pop out of bed to go to the bathroom just before you leave the room?

Of course you are going to let a child go to the bathroom if he asks to go. In fact, you might spend two nights responding to all the requests to go to the potty.

- If this is a recurring request, anticipate it the next night by having her stay on the potty a little longer just before bed.
- If you think she is just making excuses to get out of bed to get your help and attention, as younger children will try to do at some point, let her know you are on to her.

I have just figured out that you are saying you have to go to the potty because you want to get out of bed all the time. You already went two times, so now you can get into bed. (Lead her to her bed.)

After your child is potty trained (usually by age four at the latest), you must give her the freedom to get out of bed (or a crib) multiple times to go to the potty. You must tolerate the footfalls that you hear after the lights go out. There's no need to stop her, unless you find her playing with her toys in the bathroom instead of getting back in bed!

Tips for Transitioning from Crib to Bed

Don't move a child out of his crib until he climbs out (or has physically outgrown the crib). The longer your child uses a crib, the less trouble for you. Enjoy the final months of self-containment! There is no deadline for phasing out the crib and no harm to your child's growth if he stays in—get rid of it when there's a logical reason to do so. When he climbs out regularly—or has completed potty training—it is time to transition.

> *You are getting bigger and bigger, so the crib is not comfortable for you anymore.*
> *You can stretch your legs out in a special bed of your own.*

Involve your little one in the process of setting up his growing-up room. He can help you decorate the walls, set up a toy basket, put books on shelves, and witness the next step:

Place the crib mattress on the floor and add blankets and a pillow. This is your child's temporary new bed. You can remove the crib in a few days, or earlier if it's becoming a distraction.

Been there. . .

When two of our triplet daughters started climbing out of their cribs, around age three, we put the sides of their cribs down, so they could get in and out of bed on their own. We removed almost everything else from the room. After the bedtime rituals, we closed the bedroom door upon leaving and listened to them on the monitor. Whoever came out of the room got ushered back inside with minimal fanfare. All of these steps were explained to them ahead of time. They adapted within a week.

Like any two- or three-year-old confronted with new freedom, she will come out of her room repeatedly at night. At this point, it's important to establish a new bedtime routine or ritual, including book reading or perhaps a tape player for soothing music.

Be supportive on the first few nights, giving your little one lots of chances to return to her new bed. If she comes into your room at night, calmly bring her back, tuck her in, blow a kiss, and be relaxed in posture and demeanor, but don't hesitate or linger.

Whisper: *You are learning to sleep in your own bed. I will tuck you in.*

When you have had enough of the pop-goes-the-weasel scenario, it's time to buy the tallest gate you can find and put it in the bedroom doorway. Remove any hard objects, toys, or lamps from the bedroom. Follow the guidelines above (see page 68) for setting up a consistent bedtime routine and sleep training.

Keeps Getting Out of Bed or Calling You Back

Unless there is a specific problem, you don't need to respond each time your child calls you back. If you have to go back in, make your interactions as minimal and boring as possible. If your child is crying in bed, out of anger or protest, that's OK, as long as she stays in her room. She'll eventually get tired and fall asleep.

Been there. . .

You and your spouse have finished cleaning the kitchen. Now you are enjoying a glass of wine in the living room, congratulating each other for having left the kids' rooms by 8:00 p.m., your bedtime goal. Just as you start to think about curling up on the couch to watch a grown-up movie, you hear the telltale squeak of floorboards. The unmistakable padding of sneaky feet. You feel a primal scream rising in your throat. . .

Calmly and quietly, you must take your child's hand and lead him back to bed. Don't talk or scold or grumble. Be businesslike. You don't have to make your child stay in the bed; he just needs to stay in the room. Some brief things you may choose to say:

It's bedtime, time to stay in your room.
Bedtime is not negotiable.

Two- to three-year-olds who first transition out of their crib to a new bed will most likely go through a pop-goes-the-weasel phase, where they repeatedly try to get out of the room. And even after transitioning successfully, children might also go through isolated periods of trying to leave the room. As mentioned above, you must be calm and not too chatty when ushering them back to bed.

Here's the frustrating part: you may have to do it fifty times for very willful children. (Don't expect to get too much done for yourself on those nights you are sleep training.)

After this point, you are really out of options, so you may choose to escalate. This is a last resort, and it often involves a lot of hollering on your child's part, but it works. For children ages two to four, you can put a gate in the doorway (as mentioned above) that will keep them from leaving the room every two minutes. It's not a foolproof barrier, as a child might climb over it, but it still acts as a deterrent while allowing them to feel connected to the world outside the door. It should buy you some time in between your visits.

Remember that you are not a cruel-hearted despot. Millions of parents have done this, and more, but they won't necessarily talk about it unless asked. Just be sure to take the gate down once they are asleep (kids need a safe passage to the bathroom), and, as always, remove any dangerous objects from the room ahead of time.

On your last return trip before escalation, tell your child:

If you don't stay in your room, I will put the gate up to help you.

The next time he comes out, calmly lead him back to his room or bed, and say:

I'm going to put the gate up to help you stay in your room and fall asleep. Goodnight. I'll see you in the morning.

The hardest part is what follows; most likely there will be angry protest screaming. Your child may even throw things around or pull clothes out of her drawers. Eventually, she will get tired enough to fall asleep. If you get through the first night without caving in, you have shown your child that what you say (or the consequence you propose) really has teeth. On subsequent nights, your child will probably agree to stay in his bed in exchange for leaving the gate down.

What if. . .

The gate is useless?

If your child can easily step over it, then there's no point to using a gate. After all the rituals have been done and all the needs met, sit in a chair in the hallway outside your child's room. Read a newspaper. Every time your child tries to come out of the room or engage you, lead her back to bed. Say practically nothing. Don't make deals. Don't raise your voice. Keep at it until your child gets bored or frustrated enough that she goes back to bed.

What if. . .

Your hard-won routine gets derailed?

Once you have established a pattern with your child, you can occasionally deviate from it without too much trouble. You might take a child into your bed when she is very sick, or when something unusual or scary is happening; for example, sleeping in a new house or in a hotel. Better yet, you might even sleep with a child in his room during these times. When things return to normal, you should have minimal trouble reacquainting your child with his familiar routine. In other words, the retraining process should go much faster than the initial one.

Comes into Parents' Bed in the Middle of the Night

The parent who doesn't struggle with this problem is probably a very deep sleeper. Interrupted sleep can be a real drag on an adult's well-being. There are two things you can do to protect your sleep. Get up each time and bring your child back to his bed, and teach your child the importance of sleeping all night long without waking you up (easier said than done, we know).

Being awakened from a delicious slumber feels so miserable that it's no wonder many parents cave in and let a child get in their bed at any hour. If this routine works—that is, everyone gets enough sleep in spite of the late night visits—then there may be no need to change anything. If you decide that boundaries are necessary to ensure adequate sleep, you should bite the bullet and usher your child back to his bed. But first, find out the reason for the visit. If your child isn't feeling well, had a bad dream, or needs a drink of water, you can try to address those needs first. If it's just a middle-of-the-night "I can't sleep" visit, you can say that you'll cuddle with him for one minute in his bed.

The other part of your response involves a lot of explaining, even to younger children. At bedtime, talk to your child about how important it is that she stay in her bed because Mommy and Daddy really need their sleep so they can have energy in the morning to make breakfast and read books. Tell her that children also need sleep so they can grow up healthy and stay healthy and strong. Tell her what you will do if she comes into your bed at night—you will take her back to her room. You can even tell her that in the morning when the sun comes up she can climb into your bed for cuddles. Be aware of the slippery-slope effect: she may appear at your bedside earlier and earlier. Set the routine straight by calmly bringing her back to her own bed if it's too early.

You can come into Daddy's bed when the sun comes up.
I'll see you tomorrow when the sun comes up.
We can have lots of cuddles tomorrow morning when the sun comes up.
Peggy is such a growing girl; she is going to sleep all night in her bed.

One useful idea starting around age three and a half is to set an alarm clock (with a soft ring) that will indicate when they can come into your room in the morning to wake you up.

Always use positive reinforcement in the mornings when your child has made it the whole night through in her own bed. You may even try putting a sticker on a chart for every night she slept in her own bed.

> *What a great sleeper you are. You stayed in your bed all night. I bet you feel so good.*
>
> *Peggy, you have really learned how to sleep in your bed all night. Let's celebrate.* (Choose your own method for celebrating: a sticker or balloon, baking cookies, putting on dress-up clothes and dancing to music, etc. Whatever appeals to your child.)

Bad Dreams

Bad dreams are understandably scary for a small child. Take your child back to her own bed for a cuddle and be reassuring.

> *You had a bad dream. I bet you thought that was real. But it's just make-believe (or pretend), and it's all gone now.*

Whisper some happy things she can think about while she's falling back asleep, like her favorite part of the playground or what color balloon is her favorite. She can make "new dreams" out of those happy things. Stay with her until she relaxes, then kiss her goodnight and tell her you'll see her in the morning.

Some parents even try things like spraying the room for bad dreams (using water in a spray bottle) before their child goes to sleep.

In fact, your pediatrician might be able to prescribe the same thing and call it "monster spray." Another fun idea that can help to ease a child's fears is to hang a Native American dream catcher in her bedroom. Legend describes it as a beautiful spider web that catches all the bad dreams at night but lets the happy dreams sift through.

You may not be able to prevent bad dreams, but keep in mind that an overtired child is more likely to have difficulty falling asleep, and disordered sleepers tend to have more nightmares. Also, children who watch violent or frightening TV shows, movies, or videos are more likely to have bad dreams. It's important to consider the age appropriateness of what your child is watching, particularly if you have an older and a younger child in the same household.

Naptime Trouble—Won't Nap on Weekends

If you are certain your child still needs naps, and is taking naps at school, then you should try to maintain that pattern on the weekends. Nap success depends on your being consistent. In short, be a Nap Sergeant. Arrange your schedule so you can put him down around the same time on weekend days. Do your errands and activities in the morning or late afternoon, or arrange for another adult to be home during naps so you can go out.

If your child is still giving you a rough time even after several well-timed attempts, and even after you have applied the basic principles of getting a child to stay asleep (see page 74), perhaps your child is growing out of naps. (Most naps go away between the ages of three and four. If your unnapped child is fairly civil, composed, and not too cranky at bedtime, he probably doesn't need naps anymore.) In that case, turn naptime into quiet time. At his regular nap hour, your child can play quietly in his room, doing calm things, for an hour or half an hour depending on his age and temperament. An older child will probably agree to the quiet time scenario with little resistance. A two- or three-year-old might put up a fight. In this case, you can stay inside the room with him for a little while, or even lie down on the floor if you want. Just don't get to the point where he depends on you to stay with him, because then you are locked in for the duration of quiet time. Your child may or may not decide to sleep. She can play quietly with trains or look at books. Another great idea is to listen to soothing music or a story from a recorded book on tape.

How long should you keep up quiet time? Until your child leaves for college. OK, that's wishful thinking. Rather, try to do it each day that you are home. Kids and parents of all ages can benefit from a peaceful, low-key break after lunch or in the afternoon. Resist the urge to tackle your to-do list, and give yourself a meditative half hour or more with your child. Good things happen when you slow down!

What if you fall asleep in your child's room? I can only admire a parent who finds sleep in the midst of it all. Unexpected, unplanned, spontaneous sleep is one of the best grown-up treats. But if you turn your child's quiet time into your own nap, then you must consider that your child may expect you to stay for the duration every time. If your child has already gotten into the routine of playing quietly in his room without you, then your occasional snooze probably won't set him back. But every child is different, so be warned.

Reality Check

If it seems like your whole life revolves around sleep, you are not alone. The good news is that whether you sleep train or co-sleep, kids turn out just fine as long as they have consistent routines. That means bedtime rituals start at the same time each night, and your child sleeps in the same spot nearly every single night. So far no study has proven a correlation between either co-sleeping or sleeping in one's own bed and later behavioral problems. Ultimately this means that when it comes to a sleeping plan, you can focus on the needs of you and your spouse—imagine that! Many experienced parents believe that when you have a healthy, loving relationship and feel in tune with your child, she can quickly learn to sleep in her own bed and feel secure.

Sleep is an indispensable need, like food and water. It helps big and little brains process and learn, and keeps the immune system strong. Sleep researchers know that a typical two-year-old needs around thirteen hours of sleep per day (including nap), and by the time he is five, he needs about eleven hours per day. Young children are often unaware of how much rest they need, and that's why it's up to parents to establish a good, solid routine to ensure they get what they need. If your child has ongoing problems with interrupted sleep or night wakings, I suggest reading some of the step-by-step strategies found in the sleep-related books listed as resources on page 307. Remember that if everyone is getting enough rest—parents included—then your sleep arrangement is probably working.

CHAPTER 4

Eating Your Heart Out

Just like potty training, eating is an area where all the control belongs to your child. Mealtime can be stressful when you are counting the uneaten morsels on a plate. You have so many good reasons for wanting your child to eat: she might get cranky later if she doesn't eat; she might wake up hungry in the night; she might feel weak on the playground. If your child is not underweight, chances are these worries are overthought, and if any of the above scenarios happened, none would be a tragedy. Your job as a parent is not to pressure your child to eat—a very difficult rule to follow.

Won't Sit at the Dinner Table

At our house, when we see a little person leaving the dinner table, we announce:

Bevin, I see you left the table, so you must be all done. I am going to take your plate away to clean it up.

OR

It looks like you are finished eating. I'm going to clean up your plate.

If the child is hungry, he will come back to the table. But first he may have to learn the consequence of leaving; that is, having his plate cleaned up or taken away. What if he doesn't return? Older children who do not return should be considered finished with dinner. Two-year-olds will take a little longer to understand the consequences, so you can give them a few opportunities to come back to the table. Another useful tactic is to set a timer for fifteen or twenty minutes, telling your children that when it rings, it will be time to clean up all the dishes.

Also keep in mind that kids are more likely to stay seated if at least one parent sits down at the table to eat (or nibble) with them. It sounds obvious, but at some point the cook has to stop filling orders and sit down with the rest of the family.

Won't Eat Any/Much Food or
Eats the Same Things Over and Over

Picky eaters can drive you mad. If your child is picky, you probably long ago abandoned the idea that everyone eats the same food for dinner. This is OK, and not a moral failing. You just have to guard against becoming a short-order cook.

The best you can do is to serve your child something that you know she likes, or has eaten before. If she stubbornly eats only chicken nuggets or peanut butter and jelly, fine. You may need to buy crates of this stuff, but so what? Don't sweat it. You can buy healthy nuggets and peanut butter in the natural foods section of your store. Children get what they need, believe it or not, if given plenty of stress-free opportunities to eat three meals and two to three snacks per day, plus drinks. If you are worried about a lack of variety in what your child eats, give her a kids' chewable vitamin every day. (Check the label for dosage.) As she gets older, her curiosity about food will increase, but it may take many years before she is an adventurous eater.

Remember to serve small portions to your child, whether it's on a plate or in a lunch box. Too much of a serving or too many choices can overwhelm your child, and she may choose to pass on the meal altogether.

It will be hard, but you have to let your child walk away from a full plate. Just tell yourself that she will make up the calories and nutrients later, because it's true. That said, at the end of dinner, the kitchen is closed. If your child gets hungry just before bed, explain to her that dinner is over, but you can offer her water or milk.

We already ate dinner, when all the food was on the table. That was the time to eat.

Yes, there will be moaning and whining to raise the roof. If you want this tactic to work, though, stick to the plan without getting angry. You may feel like a tyrant, but in a couple of days, your children will understand the dinnertime protocol. Rest assured that by the age of two, your child will most likely not wake up in the middle of the night due to hunger. Like adults, their digestive systems slow down during sleep.

Tosses Food

Make it a family policy that whoever throws his food or tosses it on the floor must pick it up—either right away or by the end of the meal. You can get down on your knees with your two-year-old and participate; less of your modeling is needed for a four- or five-year-old. As long as he is doing some of the work, the point—or the consequence—has been established.

If throwing food continues, calmly explain that if the behavior doesn't stop, he will have to be removed from the table and taken to a time-away or quiet room. If he continues, calmly pick him up and carry him toward the time-away area. Eventually, your child will learn the consequences of throwing food and will decide to correct his behavior more quickly the next time (if there is a next time).

Children usually throw or play with food when they are no longer interested in eating or when they've gotten a lot of negative attention for doing it. In the latter case, you should try to ignore the food throwing, not give it any attention, as impossible as that may seem, and then at the end of the meal or before going to the next activity, have your child pick up the bits (or at least some of them). If your child is playing with food out of idleness, you can say this before allowing her to leave the table:

> *You're telling us that you're all done with dinner. Let's wipe your hands before you get down. . .*

Refuses to Eat Vegetables

Some kids love to eat the same veggies over and over. Some just won't touch them. If your child spurns veggies entirely, then make sure he gets plenty of fresh fruit at meals and as snacks—they contain many of the same benefits as veggies. If you want to introduce a new vegetable, let your children see you eat and enjoy it at dinner. Ask your daughter if she would like to try some, but if she says no, let it go. If a child refuses to eat any veggies or fruit, make sure she gets a children's vitamin each day. (Be sure to check the label to determine the proper dosage.)

Some mild tricks that can help:

- Serve cucumber rounds and show them how to make a moon by taking a bite out of yours and holding it up; they might want to try it.
- Broccoli can be pitched as tiny little trees that are yummy to eat, and carrots can be sliced thin and served with ranch salad dressing or dip. Some kids never seem to tire of anything they can dip!
- You can use colored peppers to make hearts (by slicing a heart-shaped ring off the side), or arrange them to make a face with ears on your child's plate.
- Have an occasional "toothpick dinner." I use this when we've had a wacky day of eating and I'd like to get some protein into my kids. I roll up slices of ham, warm up some frozen peas or other foods, and spear them all with a few toothpicks.
- Serve the vegetables as appetizers before the main course comes. A child can sit at the table nibbling on them before you bring out the rest of the meal.
- To break up the monotony of dinnertime, have a picnic on top of a big sheet spread out on the floor. Use foods that everyone can eat with their hands, like burritos or hot dogs.

Beyond these fun diversions, there's not much you should do to coerce kids to eat. Eating, like pooping, is out of our control. Best to just let your children see you enjoying your own food, don't be overly attentive to what they're doing on their plate, and soak in the relative calmness you have just added to mealtime, simply by respecting their choice not to eat.

Your child will readily eat vegetables when you bribe her with dessert? Is it OK to hold dessert hostage until your child eats her broccoli?

Psychologists who study eating disorders insist you should never bribe your child to eat. They say if you are having fights with your child about food, you are being overly controlling and should stop. It makes sense that micromanaging what your child eats (for example, never letting them have junk food) can make your child feel guilty or ashamed about his choices—not to mention powerless. There are so many good reasons to be lenient about eating. Here are just a few:

- Your child will learn his body's natural cues for hunger and fullness if his eating is not coerced. (The importance of this concept is described in the book *Let Them Eat Cake!*, a great resource for parents who wonder how much to intervene in their child's eating habits.)
- He will enjoy mealtime and special events more if he can eat what he wants and not feel guilty.
- You can avoid getting locked into food-related battles with your child that can, unfortunately, transform into other kinds of struggles. (In one drastic example I know, a pair of strict parents insist that their son stay at the table as long as it takes to finish his meal. Now, at age seven, he has regressed to wearing diapers in a desperate attempt to gain control of something.)
- You can foster feelings of independence and self-sufficiency in your child if she can take care of her eating needs by herself— that is, to eat or not.

It all sounds sensible, but I can never seem to follow this advice 100 percent. After all, I want my children to eat fiber to avoid constipation. Lots of parents I know won't let their children have dessert until they eat their vegetables. Yes, we parents, especially moms, care far too much about eating. Maybe it's because feeding our children is synonymous with nurturing, and we can't just turn off this instinct. (Remember the Italian grandmother who orders her middle-aged children to mangia, mangia?) Because I know I'll never be able to completely detach myself from what my kids eat, I try a compromise. At home, I tell my children they have to eat something on their plates before I bring out dessert. I don't browbeat them (at least I try hard not to), and if a child refuses, I don't push it. Also, dessert doesn't happen every night, just a few times a week.

Rejects What You Make for Dinner

Cooking a meal that you and your spouse love to eat and serving it to your children is an impressive feat. And if you have the time to cook, why not keep doing it? If you don't, you are not a bad parent for making frozen food. But whatever you serve your children, the key is to offer one standard alternative that your children can choose if they turn up their noses at your offering. Too many choices can overwhelm a child, resulting in indecision or lots of mind changing. Make option B a peanut-butter-and-jelly sandwich, a cheese sandwich, or another very simple alternative that doesn't require cooking. Even better, get your four- and five-year-olds to make it themselves (with some help). Be sure it is something they like to eat, of course. The first time you introduce this policy, you may encounter lots of hounding and wailing from little people who suddenly want to create a new plan-B menu every night. Don't give in to such demands; not only is it too much work for you, but it will also make rejecting the main meal too much fun. Stay your ground and the bellyaching will go away in a day or two.

Spills and More Spills with an Open Cup

Are spills accidental or sometimes intentional? The truth can be fuzzy. Sure, it's a good idea to give your child practice with an open cup starting around age two. But do it only as long as you can stand wiping up the spills, and then switch to an open cup that is one-quarter filled with water. Or go back to a sippy cup with the beverage of your choice. All parents love water for obvious reasons—it doesn't stain or need to be cleaned up. Don't reprimand your child too harshly for their spills; their coordination is not yet fully developed. You should see improvement between the ages of three and four.

If you think your child is intentionally spilling his drink to get attention, switch to a sippy cup.

I'm going to give you a sippy cup until you are ready to drink from an open cup.

And when you go back to open cups a few days later, enlist your child's help in cleaning up any spills. Make it a policy that whoever makes a spill has to help clean it up. But be careful to remain positive, or at least neutral about this step. If you express your dismay at the accidents, not only could it cause your child to feel ashamed but it could also encourage him to keep spilling to get a rise out of you. When facing spills, be a robot. Don't react much.

Poor Table Manners

Before you launch a major campaign to upgrade your child's table manners, introduce them in a role-play with a a tea party. Use play dishes and cups, or buy a toy tea service. Demonstrate good manners, and then deliberately make mistakes and see if your children can catch you.

This is how I put my napkin on my lap.
Can you please pass the milk?
May I have more cupcakes?
Oh, what good manners I see.
Give me that bread!
This macaroni is yucky!

Here are some ways to explain manners:

We use good manners at the table. Good manners mean that we chew our food calmly, and we take turns talking and listening. It makes dinnertime pleasant for everyone.

When we use good manners, we have less mess on our face and hands and lap. Cleaning up is a lot quicker, so we can go back and play sooner.

When we practice our good manners at home, then we can use them in a restaurant (or at our friends' houses for dinner).

Small children need to be told (calmly) a million times not to do something before they really internalize it, and progress is a function of getting older. You may feel like a broken record, but it does eventually pay off. First, make sure that the required table manners in your home are reasonable for little kids. Here's a short practical list:

- No climbing on top of the table. (*We do not climb on the table. Please sit in your chair.*)

- No standing in a chair. (*Please sit down, or the chair could fall backwards.*)
- No throwing food. (*Food is for eating. If you don't stop throwing it, you'll have to leave the table.*)
- Wipe your hands on your napkin, not your clothes. (This will take some time.)

If your entreaties don't work for the first three rules, tell your child you will count to five, and if he doesn't stop, you will take him away from the table. If he persists, follow through by having him sit at a small table next to yours or, if he is getting disruptive, take him to the time-away area. (See "Private Meltdowns at Home" on page 17.)

As your children get closer to age five, you can get a little more sophisticated about table manners by adding:

- Food is chewed with your mouth closed.
- Napkins belong on laps.
- Elbows belong off the table.
- Take turns talking.
- Carry dirty dishes to the sink or counter.

Don't forget to check your own grown-up manners at the table and model good language, too. *Can you pass the ketchup, please?* (See page 301 for recommended books on teaching children good table manners.)

Eats Constantly

A child who seems to graze all day long could just have a fast metabolism, or it could be that you are trying too hard to prevent him from feeling hungry. Giving little snacks throughout the day is easier than setting up a structure for meals or sticking to the routines outlined above. If you are feeding your child constantly because you are concerned he is not gaining enough weight, ask your pediatrician for advice on your feeding routines. If he is growing fine, then stick to three nutritious meals a day plus two to three snacks. If your nibbler wants to eat in between meals or snack times, and you sense it is more of a bad habit than a true need, engage him in an activity, read him a book, or offer a drink of water.

(**What if. . .**

Your child always wants a snack right before dinner?

When your child asks you for a particular snack, and it's very close to dinner, consider doing one of the following:

- Serve that snack with his meal, instead of handing it out immediately.
- Make a plan for one piece now, and the rest after dinner.
- Better yet, anticipate the pre-dinner munchies by putting a few nutritious appetizers on the table, like veggies or fruit.

Eats with Hands; Won't Use Utensils

If this is a problem you face, try providing your child with smaller utensils like baby spoons and forks until fine motor skills appear more coordinated, usually by the age of three or four. Provide small portions, finger foods, or sandwiches at most meals. If your child sees people around her eating with utensils, she will eventually want to copy them. Be sure to provide toddler-sized cutlery. These utensils are not always easy to find, but they should include forks with effective tines (not the baby forks with blunted tines) and a small safe knife.

It's so easy to obsess about our kids' eating patterns. When your child turns up his nose at something new, it gives you a sinking feeling (especially when someone has invited you over for dinner!). You worry: Will he ever get enough of the good stuff in his diet? Will he ever eat like a normal person? The bottom line is that if your doctor tells you that your child is growing and gaining weight just fine, then all of your worrying is just extra work. A lot of kids are picky eaters. Don't give up on introducing new foods, but don't expect major changes in your child's preferences until he's well past the age of five. You might be tempted by the new cookbooks that suggest ways to hide veggies in your child's food. If you have the time, go for it. But you are making a trade-off between spending time in the kitchen working on a recipe, and doing something meaningful with your child like playing a game or reading a book. And there's always the chance that he'll turn up his nose at the new dish anyway. Most likely, you'll come back to what is practical. Provide a child-sized multivitamin. Provide the nutritious things your child likes to eat over and over, if that's what he wants. Try to add small new items. Let him see his parents enjoying more adventurous foods that are accessible to him if he wants to try them. Sit back (if you can), enjoy your mealtime as a family, and assume that your child's palette will evolve on its own.

CHAPTER 5

The Trials of Potty Training

Because the successes are so exciting, and the lows are *really* low, potty training can be a roller coaster for parents. The job of potty training your child—an inconvenient, frustrating, tedious job that can stretch on for months—can feel counterintuitive. We spend so much time cajoling our children to do things we want them to do, why shouldn't the same apply to the potty? But parental pressure can backfire during potty training, and it often does. Why? Because children are, in the end, the ones who control the process, not us. Pressuring a child can make her feel that her self-control is being taken away, and thus can trigger her to dig in her heels and refuse to go. Children may also have anxiety about "losing" part of their bodies when the toilet is flushed.

Potty training is a time when we have to stop being control freaks and pretend we are mellow, laissez-faire parents. (*You had an accident? It's cool, buddy.*) Get your child interested and excited about the potty, and give him plenty of opportunities to go, but don't browbeat him. Your little one is in control of his poop and pee—that's it. We must bite our tongue. In the beginning, when he is willing to sit down on the potty, that's cause for praise. Later, the chance to model other children on the potty, as in a toddler or preschool class, will accelerate your child's motivation.

No matter how long your child takes, be respectful, positive, calm, and consistent. How do you do that over months? A year? Expect disappointments and setbacks at every turn. In fact, embrace them. You are the parent, and you know how to be helpful to your child during this long process. Not freaking out over an accident is the way to help. This is a much more accepting approach than what you might really be thinking ("I've *got* to get this child potty trained by September" or "This is taking so long, I must be doing something wrong"). Eventually the process will be over, but until then, give your child permission to get it wrong.

Not Interested in the Potty

If your toddler seems uninterested in the potty, it could be that she is not yet ready to start potty training. Doctors usually encourage you to begin the process anytime after age two (or even earlier if your child shows interest). If you notice some signs of awareness in your child, like announcing she has peed or pooped in her diaper, you can start easing into the process by simply encouraging her interest and talking about it. Here are some other ways to get the ball rolling:

- To generate excitement, show some potty videos and read potty books. Your child may want to go and try out the potty or toilet. Let the interest come from the child; don't force or coerce her to sit on the potty. Praise her for sitting on it fully clothed, if that's as far as you get. Too much praise can backfire. Save the flashing lights and parties for when your child is actually successful. In the trying-out phase, use toned-down language instead:

Wow, you're getting ready to learn to use the potty.
Great, you're learning to sit on the potty.
You tried the potty again. That's great.

- Put potties in designated spots on all floors of the house. It's best to have it in the bathroom, if you have room. Otherwise, put it on an uncarpeted floor. But don't keep moving potties around the house, as it's confusing for a tot in training. Once she is comfortable and willing to sit on it bare bottomed, then you can set a timer at regular intervals for "potty time." Let her stay on the potty for two minutes or more, if you can. A good timer is one that the child can see. You can chat a bit about what it feels like to sit on the potty, but don't get too involved. Give her a book or toy to help her stay seated. Eventually— that is, in a week or in a few months—she will go. If your child is in day care or preschool, the teachers should be starting the process for you. If this is not the case, then you'll want to start regular trips to the potty at home. If she refuses to sit on the potty, don't force it. You don't want to create a battle situation, because you can't win this one by force of will.
- At home, get into the habit of putting your (willing) child on the potty just before he goes to bed. At first you will probably get no results, but as long as he's willing to sit, keep it going. In time, this will turn into a very productive routine. If you know your child always has a bowel movement after breakfast, for example, make it a routine to sit on the potty after breakfast. For how long? About two minutes when you're first starting out.

- Let your child come into the bathroom with you to watch. Kids are riveted by what you do in there. Here's what you can say:

Soon you will decide to put your pee (or urine) in the potty, just like a growing-up boy.
Soon you will be ready to put your pee in the potty and then you can have new underpants like Daddy (or your sister/brother).

- Take advantage of warm weather. Let your child run around with nothing on her bottom. It will give her a chance to feel the sensations of urinating. Outdoors is a great place for everyone to relax and not worry much about accidents. You can say:

I see you put your pee on the grass.
Did you see the pee coming out? We can get some water and wash the spot.
That's OK; the rain will wash it away.

- After your child has shown comfort and willingness to sit on the potty regularly, be patient. Let her move forward at her natural pace. If you've seen no progress in several months, you might want to advance to the next step. Take your little one shopping to help choose underpants—the thick cotton kind. Then do a diaper countdown: explain that after the last one is used up, she'll be ready to use underwear. Wearing underpants for the first time is exciting for both of you. In the beginning, use a timer to set up regular potty visits at home, as mentioned above. We do not recommend diaper pull-ups for beginners, as toddlers often treat them like regular diapers. Better to use pull-ups after children become more experienced or for practice staying dry overnight.

- When children are sitting for potty time, keep it relaxed and don't hover over them. Find something else to do nearby, like wash dishes or tidy up. Let them have a book, toy, or comfort item to hold to keep them seated. You can read to them or offer a cup of water.

- You can tell your child that when he puts his pee/urine in the potty you will celebrate, and he can pick a treat or have a little party. What kind of treat does he want? This can help to initiate his first attempts. Sound like a bribe? You bet, and it's well worth it! (A sticker is much better than candy, but do whatever works.) It's important to bring about that first experience of success to get the ball rolling.

- And, of course, praise your child enthusiastically when he has success. But make sure you put the emphasis on your child:

You are so excited because that was your first time. You must feel really good about this.

Too much praise will teach your child that he has to pee to make you happy, instead of feeling proud of himself for doing it.

- If you are getting way more accidents than success with underpants, and your child is under three, put the diapers back on for a few days or weeks. Your child may not be ready. After age three, however, you will want to move your child along by keeping underpants on for longer periods of time. After age three, you can even go cold turkey on diapers if you are prepared to stick to your plan. Keep it low-key and low-pressure for your child. Keep your own frustration in check while you are cleaning up all the accidents. Do not talk about the potty all the time. In a few days, he should get the hang of it.

Are You Hesitant?

If you are unsure of how to encourage your child without pressuring her, your messages might end up sounding ambivalent and invite a "No" response:

> *Do you think you can go to the potty now?*
> *Will you go to the bathroom now?*
> *Want to sit on the potty now?*

Try to be a little more declarative and affirmative:

> *Time to go to the potty.* (Take your child's hand or shoulder to gently lead him.)
> *When the timer rings, it's time to sit on the potty.*

On the way to the potty, try to distract her by having a little discussion about something random or even the weather.

As Soon as They Get off the Potty, They Wet

This is a classic situation where your instincts tell you to try a little negative feedback. But scolding will only cause shame. Hold yourself back! Here's what you can do instead:

- At the next potty time that produces no results, keep your child's pants off, and try to let him play in an uncarpeted or gated area. Keep an eye on him. When you see him starting to go, whisk him over to the potty. Getting something in the pot will seem like a big success to your child. With bowel movements it's usually easier to spot your child standing very still or straining when he begins. Whisk him over to the pot. Once again, if he puts up a huge fight, don't force him to sit on the potty.

- Let your child feel the wetness. Don't be in a hurry to clean up wet underpants. Give her time to notice how uncomfortable it feels. You can say—with curiosity, not anger:

You decided to put your pee in your pants. I wonder how it feels?

Takes Diaper off All the Time

Taking a diaper off may be a strong sign that your child is ready for potty training. Indulge his urges by stopping diapers and introducing new underpants, as mentioned above. Be ready to handle accidents, but don't revert to a diaper unless your child is feeling very distressed. If you feel your child is not ready for underpants, but she still takes diapers off, fasten the diapers shut with duct tape when you really need them to stay on, such as overnight or in a setting where there is no bathroom, like at a concert. Keep in mind that a two-year-old who ditches her diaper is probably ready for potty training.

Starts out Well and then Backslides

Backsliding is fairly common during potty training. Since the process is usually not linear, the backsliding episodes can go on for days or months. The sense of regressing can be even more disturbing to parents than the unpleasantness of an accident. But wait, it might not be regressing at all. He could be testing out his autonomy by deciding for himself when to comply and when not to. If you are cleaning up two or three accidents a day, then bear with it. Most likely your child will swing back to his cleaner record. This is just the time when you'd be likely to turn up the frequency of trips to the potty, or more urgently coerce him to go. But these approaches will probably backfire. To my never-ending frustration, our children had the most success when we parents weren't even paying attention. Such is the power of autonomy in a small child. Ask yourself: Is the potty accessible? Can he pull down his own pants? That may be all you need to arrange for a particularly independent child.

In the meantime, as you tend to the messes, use some grin-and-bear-it language:

> *That's okay, you're still learning. We'll clean it up together.*
> *Next time you can decide to put your pee/poop in the potty.*

- Involve your child in the cleanup process, however limited. For example, she can help to wipe the floor or rinse out her underpants.
- If your two- or three-year-old child is having only accidents and no success all day, it may be time to put the diapers back on, for your own sanity. You may have to suspend training for a few weeks. Make it clear to your child what you are doing, and set a time to put underpants back on. For example:

> *I know you are still learning to use the potty. You are putting a lot of pee/poop in your pants. So now Mommy and Daddy are going to put your diaper back on. And pretty soon you'll be ready to try again.*

Depending on age and awareness:

> *When all these boxes are filled on the calendar, it will be time to begin learning again, and we will put your underpants back on.*

Until those days or weeks are over, don't bring up potty training or allude to it in any way. Don't say anything negative, and try not to show your disappointment—even if it's hard not to. In a few days or even a few hours, your child is likely to ask to have the big-kid underpants back. Try to stay the course with diapers for a little while, such as one whole day, or you may find yourself jumping back and forth as your child changes her mind every few hours. When the diaper period ends, always prepare your child in advance by saying, for example:

Tomorrow morning you are going to put your underpants back on.

- If your child was fully and confidently trained for a while but then backslides and demands diapers back, you can try a bit of gentle reverse psychology. But only do this at home, and only if your child is not struggling with other problems or changes at the time. The idea is to show the child that returning to diapers is like taking a step back into the world of a baby.

The baby part of you wants to wear diapers. That's OK. But there are certain baby things you need to do. Babies don't watch videos, and babies need to go to bed early. Playdates are for bigger girls.

Do not be vindictive or punishing; just play the part of a parent taking care of her baby. Your child may like the attention and go along with the role for a while, but pretty soon she'll remember the disadvantages of being a baby and may even ask for her underwear back.

If you are attempting this, do not tease or taunt your child for being a baby, for goodness sake. Act calm, serious, and respectful during this role-play. And don't attempt it if your child is having trouble with bowel movements because he may truly need the comfort of a diaper until his constipation is resolved.

Asks for Diapers Back

When a child in training asks for a diaper to be put back on, take him to the potty right away. He probably has to go. Try to keep him on the potty by offering him a book to read or toys to hold. If he stays on the pot for any length of time but doesn't go, then say:

You are really trying to learn.

Either put the underwear back on or let him walk around bare bottomed for a while, and see if you can catch him in the act. If he pees on the (non-carpeted) floor, you can say:

Oops. This time you put your pee/urine on the floor; pretty soon you'll decide to put your pee in the potty (and then you can keep playing instead of cleaning up).

If your child is pitching a fit about sitting on the potty and is very distressed about not having a diaper on (and can't be convinced to go around bare bottomed), put the diaper back on and assume your child is not yet ready for more progress. Things you can say:

This is hard for you to do. Mom and Dad are here to help you learn, and we know that you will soon be able to do it.

If your child insists on diapers in spite of your usual persuasions such as:

You've shown Mommy that you can put your pee in the potty, so you don't need diapers anymore.

You're growing up and getting bigger, and you don't need diapers anymore.

Then once again put the diapers back on, getting your child to help you if possible, saying:

You seem like you want to take a little break from using the potty. Let's put your diaper back on. We can put your underwear back on in three days and try again. (Or use another interval of time that feels right.)

A BIG GIRL NOW

It will be irresistible to say, "You're a big girl now; you don't need any diapers." In general, try to avoid labeling your child "big." Why? Because it will come back to haunt you, as when she retorts, "You said I was a big girl, so now I can stay up late and chew gum!" And you must admit, she's got you.

Also see "Starts Out Well and then Backslides" on page 101. If your child is asking for diapers only for bowel movements, see the next section below.

Urine Trained but Won't Poop in the Potty

Bowel movements can take longer to master than urinating. When your child is pooping in her underpants nearly every time, try taking a practical approach:

- If you can handle the repeated poop accidents, keep your child's underwear on during this shaky stage, in order to avoid going back to diapers. But if your toddler is having all accidents and no successes, and it's driving you crazy, go back to diapers.

• If your tot is asking for a diaper before a bowel movement, put the diapers back on, but keep a close eye on him. When you see him straining, whisk him over to the potty to finish. This is a good way to get him to see his own success. There might be some protesting, but if he puts up a huge fight, he is not ready to poop in the potty. Let him do it in the diaper.

• Tell (and tell again) the Poop Story. To ease the anxiety of the loss of their poop, draw a picture of the toilet, and explain that after you flush, the poop and pee go down the pipes and into the ocean, where the plants use the poop to grow, and the fish eat the plants. After you tell them this story, bathrooms will achieve a new level of fascination. (As a preface, your child may be interested to know that "Poop is the food your body doesn't need anymore. You have to push the poop out to make room in your belly for the new food.") Stories like these are effective from around age two and a half.

• Some children respond to potty calendars, where you affix a sticker for every day they poop in the potty, and then they get a small prize or token after a week or so. But these charts are tough to keep up with, so only initiate a calendar if you can be fastidious about keeping it accurate.

Been there. . .

Your child willingly sits on the potty, and after a few minutes, puts a little poop in it—to everyone's great excitement—only to deposit the rest in her underwear five minutes later. What do you do? Is it a success or failure?

Reward your child for being partially successful. Give the designated prize, if any. Then involve your child in the cleanup, as described on page 102.

Withholds Poop; Has Smears on Underpants

Been there. . .

Your child is wincing and gyrating, an obvious sign she's got a bowel movement brewing. You say it's time to sit on the potty and lead her over to it. She yanks away her arm and shouts, "No!" So you let her have her way and release her. Five minutes later she has poop in her underpants. In frustration you say: "Ugh! Lucy, I just asked you to go two minutes ago! The potty was right here, why didn't you go?"

You have every reason to feel frustrated by this situation. Try hard not to say what I said to my daughter above. Your anger and disappointment can make her feel ashamed and guilty. And a young child has no way to work through those feelings on her own. Say this instead: *You decided to put your poop in your underpants.* That's it, so simple. And you'll say it again and again, after each accident. Let this statement be the barrier between your child and your exasperation. Without being harsh, proceed to clean up with your child's help in a businesslike way.

There are several reasons why your child might stubbornly avoid bowel movements. Fear that it will hurt is the top culprit. Or there may be too much pressure to perform or a need for control. Younger children might also fear losing a part of their bodies. It is also possible that your child withholds because she gets a lot of attention around the accidents. If your child holds his urine in for a long time, nothing bad usually happens, except possibly wet pants. Not so for poop. If a child stubbornly holds in his feces, a problematic cycle can begin where the stool inside his body becomes bigger and drier, and he becomes constipated. The pain of constipation increases fear, which perpetuates the withholding behavior. In the worst case, his colon can get stretched, causing a diminished ability to contract and making it harder to push out the poop. Some stool will leak or squeeze out into underpants in spite of the strong effort to hold it in. This is a condition that can be very prolonged and stressful for everyone. Here are some signs of withholding behavior:

- You find poop smears on her underpants or diapers throughout the day, and you can see more starting to come out of her bottom as you wipe her.
- When a bowel movement does happen, the stools are not hard, which suggests he's holding it in by choice and is not constipated.

Here are some signs of constipation:
- A change in behavior: your child becomes grumpy, sleepy, or listless when a bowel movement is long overdue.
- A bloated belly.
- Loss of appetite. It's common for a child to skip meals when he's feeling backed up.
- Straining but nothing is coming out.
- Stools that are pebbly or hard.

You can address a withholding issue immediately by giving your child high-fiber foods and water at snack and mealtime. Here's a list of foods that have been known to make children "go":

Blueberries (frozen berries are cheaper and less messy to serve, and they can be eaten frozen because they are not too hard)
Dried fruits (raisins, apricots, cherries, pears, figs)
Mangoes

Papaya

Pears

Apple slices with skin on (for older children)

Fig cookies

Canned peaches and canned apricots

High-fiber cereal with milk (cereals with a dietary fiber content of
two to four grams per serving)

Make sure to serve these foods with plenty of water or watered-down juice to drink.

At the point where you even suspect your child is withholding, you should call your pediatrician and ask about prescription stool softeners that you can give your child every day in his juice to get him started again. Stool softeners are useful because they teach your child that pooping does not hurt. It may take a few tries before you get the right dosage on the stool softener. For example, if it seems like your child is having no improvement while taking the stool softeners, ask your pediatrician about increasing the dose. Or ask about lowering the dose if stools have become too loose.

If you are tempted to give your child an enema, stop and have a discussion with the doctor first. There are some children who are so turned off by their first enema that they are instantly cured of their withholding tendency. But giving enemas can cause an unpleasant physical struggle with your child that can set the stage for future battles and even more fear. In rare cases there can be a physiological cause of withholding behavior, another good reason to check in with your pediatrician.

It is infuriating for a parent to see stool starting to come out of her child's bottom just as the child is refusing to go. The poop and the potty are inches away from each other, but your child won't put the two together. This is a prime time for you to vent your frustration, but once again, try not to. Do not force your child to sit on the potty until he poops. We made this mistake with our first daughter and she became more and more resolved not to poop. Our battles with her dragged on for over a year! Do give your child back his diaper if it's the only way he feels safe to have a bowel movement. Wait a period of time and then casually initiate the training process again.

Reality Check

A serious roadblock is the last thing you need in your mission to potty train your child. Withholding issues should be addressed immediately. If your child is having this problem, remember it is just one more bump on the long and agonizing road to a completely trained child. You might also consider whether your child is enjoying the attention, albeit negative, he gets when he has a poop accident. If you think there might be too much hoopla around these accidents, try not to react so much during the discovery and make cleanup a lot more boring by not lecturing. And, as always, enlist your child's help, even minimally, in the cleanup. Potty training might be one of the biggest challenges you have as a parent, but eventually your child will be trained. Most kids are trained by age three, but some are not out of the woods until age four. (After age four it gets a lot more complicated—try not to go there.) We may never know the reasons why a child can take so long to get it, but somewhere along the way they do. As helpful neighbors like to say, "No child ever went to her prom wearing diapers."

Will Only Have a Bowel
Movement at Home or School

Give your child and yourself a break here. I bet most adults would say they enjoy their bowel movements better in the comfort of their own toilet, too. If your child is pooping regularly, but is just picky about the location, consider yourself lucky. Give her plenty of op-portunities to go, wherever you are, and accommodate her as best you can by bringing along her comfort item to hold—a toy, book, cell phone, or whatever has worked in the past. Let your child see you use the unfamiliar toilet first. Eventually she will take the bold step of going in a foreign place.

ACCIDENTS ALL AROUND

During potty training, accidents can become the bane of your existence. They seem to go on forever, and a number of possessions can get ruined—mattresses, couch cushions, car seats, and even other people's rugs—depending on how long your child takes to be fully trained. Always, invest in waterproof mattress pads and, if needed, slipcovers for your furniture. Acquaint yourself with how to remove the cushion on your child's car seat with your eyes closed, because you'll want to be able to whip it off in a pinch.

Needs Overnight or Naptime Diapers

Before you start taking away bedtime diapers, make sure your child has mastered naptime dryness first, meaning she can take naps in her underwear with only occasional accidents. In a good preschool, the teachers start this process for you. If your child starts at home, just make sure you have a plastic cover on your mattress. Children are very proud when they wake up from a nap with everything dry, and you should make sure to offer praise:

You stayed dry the whole time you were napping. You must feel really good about that!

Before taking away bedtime diapers, discuss this milestone event with your child. (She might even initiate the process herself.) Your first job is to make sure her mattress has a plastic or vinyl cover on it. Take her to the potty before turning out the light. Put a laundry basket in the room for wet clothes, along with a towel and a potty. (If the potty is in the bathroom, make sure to turn on the night-light.) You can explain that if she gets wet, she can put the towel on her bed to sleep on, in the hopes that she will be able to go back to sleep after an accident. Chances are, though, she will wake you up the first time she wets during the night. Then what? Minimize your intervention. After all, it's the middle of the night. Change her underwear and put a towel down on her bed for her to sleep on. In the future she may learn to do this ritual on her own. Save the real cleanup for morning.

It takes a while for a child to master overnight dryness. If you are changing sheets every morning, put bedtime diapers back on, for practical reasons. Return to this issue at some later date, or when you and your child think she is ready to try again. When you return to bedtime diapers, tell your child:

Learning something new takes time. Let's put your diapers back on at night. You can try to sleep in your underpants a little later, when you feel ready again.

Reality Check

As if the frustrations of potty training weren't enough, the other thing that dogs us is peer pressure. We see other kids who are potty trained and we get a little panicky about our own child. How many times have we heard a proud parent report how her baby was trained before age two, or trained in three days flat? It can happen, because kids come in all kinds of temperaments and take different amounts of time to get in tune with their bodies. (Think of the coordination it takes to ride a bike.) Sometimes I wonder if my husband and I had *anything* to do with training our two-and-a-half-year-old triplet daughters. Bevin got trained in a flash in about four days. Today, one full year after training began, Josie is still not out of the woods and struggles with bouts of withholding bowel movements. Lucy "got it" two months after Bevin, and immediately said good-bye to diapers forever, whereas the other two, now age three, still wear diapers or pull-ups at night. Three different children, three different time frames.

Potty training makes us feel like we're in limbo: it's a messy, anxious place to be and we just can't wait until it's over. Keep reminding yourself that your job is to be—rather, act—calm and accepting about the whole process, however long it takes for your child to be trained. It's a small amount of time compared to a lifetime of continence. A year from now, you will hardly remember the messy details that keep you running around today. By then the next challenge will be underway!

CHAPTER 6

Fighting

We grown-ups fight with our words and our cunning when we have to. Little children use anything at their disposal: fingernails, feet, teeth, saliva, hard objects. Being a referee (your other job) requires so much repetition you despair that anything is getting through your child's little head. But if you respond to a transgression calmly and consistently every time, it will sink in. Will you sometimes feel like a windup toy? A talking, walking robot breaking up the same fight over and over? Oh, yes. Remember all the repetition you needed to learn a foreign language? Well, just tell yourself you are teaching your kids a foreign language, too, the language and actions of dispute resolution. After all, you are the greatest teacher in your child's life.

Little kids sometimes fight with their friends, but nobody fights like siblings. They clash more because they are always together, and they feel safe enough to let it all hang out. Indeed, siblings are on a playdate that never ends. We often don't realize that they need space away from one another. We expect our children to learn to get along, without recognizing that each child has a certain capacity to be civil until she simply needs a break. Thankfully, as children get

older, the physical aspects of fighting will lessen (as the verbal spar-
ring increases).

I used to think fighting was unacceptable, and I tried to deliver a
strict consequence whenever someone got physical. I figured it was a
parent's job to prevent her kids from becoming wild animals. Not only
did I exhaust myself as I tried to nip every bad behavior, but it became
clear to me that, in the case of everyday disputes, scolding (*Don't ever
push him again!*) was not successfully changing behavior. I soon realized that fighting was here to stay—for several years, anyway.

That doesn't mean parents should do nothing. The best we can do
is teach our children conflict-resolution skills—that is, encourage
kids to talk (or complain) to each other and teach them different
ways to solve the problem. So instead of seeing myself as the police,
I now think of myself as a coach, encouraging my kids to settle their
own disputes. It doesn't work smoothly every time, but I have seen
more positive results overall. Don't get me wrong, there's always a
time for scooping up your child and taking him away when things
have gone beyond the pale; or imposing a plan when she refuses to
cooperate. But there's an underlying benefit to the "help them solve
their own problems" approach. Child development researchers believe that children learn important social skills, confidence, and autonomy when they are given a chance to work out their problems,
rather than having an adult impose what's right and wrong—in other
words, when a parent "thinks" for them. That means we parents have
to resist the urge to fix the situation so everything is equal and just.
In nonviolent disputes, children do just fine without an adult hover-
ing over them. Several studies have shown that children actually take
responsibility for their actions and generate their own solutions more
often when an adult is absent. Even the little ones.

One final note. As you're playing referee, you may be tempted to
get your child to say, "I'm sorry," each time she hurts someone. Be

careful not to rely on this phrase to solve problems. Two- and three-year-olds will easily pick it up and parrot it, because it offers a quick way of getting out of trouble. Indeed, using this phrase removes the need for your child to take a more constructive route. She won't really understand the importance of apologizing until she's closer to four or five years old. Rather than coach little ones to say the words, it's better to let them see you use "I'm sorry" in the right context.

General Rules of Thumb for Nonviolent Disputes

1. When you witness nonviolent conflicts, hang back and see if the children can work out their own resolution. It doesn't matter if it looks fair to you, as long as the participants are satisfied.
2. If you get recruited to help, encourage the children to work it out themselves. Even children as young as three have been shown to come up with their own resolutions if given a chance. If they get stuck, offer suggestions.
3. Two-year-olds should also be given a chance to come up with ideas to solve the dispute. However, they will get stuck more often and will need coaching and helpful language from parents.
4. Finally, if children are waging an out-and-out war, and are too crazed to listen, you must step in and impose a plan. If, for example, the children are fighting over a toy, separate them, set a timer for taking turns, or confiscate the item in dispute. Be the parent; lay down the plan.
5. Avoid taking sides whenever possible.

General Rules of Thumb for Violent Disputes

1. Separate the children and take away any "weapon" that may be involved.

2. After a few moments, encourage both children to talk or share their feelings. Have them take turns talking. (You can suggest appropriate words or emotions.)
3. If one or both of the children are too upset to listen, take each away for more calming-down time.
4. Ask the children if they are ready to go back and play or if they need more time to talk about their issue.

Pulling Things Out of Another's Hands

Possessions, possessions. Who owns what, and does it matter? It does. However, you should make it a family rule, and write it in your Family Policy Book (see page 36), that no one is allowed to pull things out of another person's hands. It's a simple, straightforward rule, like "No biting," that never changes.

There are two kinds of conflicts: those you see with your own eyes, and those you don't. However, even when you think you have witnessed the event, you might not have seen the whole thing. It is very hard to determine what the initial "irritation" was and how the sequence of events unfolded and escalated. The only way to play it safe is to stay neutral and avoid making judgments.

If you witness your child pulling or grabbing something from another child, you must intervene.

Alex, we do not grab things from other people.
You feel that you should have the truck now, but it's Jerry's turn to have it. Let's give it back to him.

Most likely, Alex will not give the item back. Then you, the parent, must pry it from his hot little hands and return it to its owner. First, though, give your youngster a count.

You have to give it back to Jerry now. And if you can't do it, Mommy will do it for you. I'll count to five. One, two, three. . .

If he won't respond, then don't yank it away, of course. Take it away in a grown-up way—gentle but firm—and acknowledge his feelings.

You really, really want the toy right now, but it's Jerry's turn. Let's find something else to play with until it's your turn. (If needed, set a timer.)

If after being corrected, your child is still not being civil, take him on your lap or into a separate room until he calms down.

Here are other ways of managing the process of taking turns:

Let's ask Jerry if you can play with him. Encourage your son or daughter to ask the question. If the friend says yes, you might have to give your child a little jump start to involve him in play, by asking a question or pointing something out. If the friend says no, respect that answer and try another approach, including simply redirecting to another toy.

Let's ask Jerry if you can have a turn when he is done. If yes, redirect your tyke to another toy or activity until it is his turn.

If your child is really angling for that toy:

Jerry, how much time do you need for your turn, five or six minutes? For older children, suggest five or six minutes. For two- or three-year-olds, suggest two or three minutes. Or hold up your thumb and index finger to indicate a lot or a little time. Let the child choose, and then set the timer.

If Jerry wants a lot of time, say:

It looks like Jerry has a plan right now. Why don't we:
Come back in fifteen minutes to see if he's done.

Write your name on a list for the next turn. This is especially useful when you have multiple kids clambering for a turn. Write the names in order of turns on a sticky note and post it in a visible spot.

While your child is waiting, suggest something else he can do. If he howls because he wants the toy right now, let him express his frustration in another room. Tough luck and tough love: you cannot coerce or force the other kid to turn over the toy at that moment. After the timer rings (or other time frame has expired), it's appropriate to encourage the holder to relinquish the toy.

You may also suggest:

> *Why don't you try to make a trade?* (If the other child doesn't go for the trade, don't force it.)
> *She doesn't want to trade right now. Let's go find another puzzle for you.*

Following particularly sticky interactions, it's useful to have a debriefing chat with your child after some time has elapsed. (Best for four- and five-year-olds or tots who have more developed powers of comprehension.)

> *Let's go over what happened in there* (very briefly). *What are some helpful things you can do next time this happens?*

Been there. . .

You're making tea in the kitchen when you hear your two children screeching at each other. A fight is brewing. When you enter the living room, they are having a tug-of-war with a pair of dress-up shoes. Who had them first? When you ask, each turns red in the face trying to convince you, "It was me!" You have a strong hunch your oldest had the shoes first but you can't be sure. How do you respond?

I fantasize about putting video surveillance in every room, so when there's a fight we can replay the tape to find the real instigator. I will have to keep dreaming. We can't have our eyes on our children constantly when at home, since we're supposed to be involved in other parental duties like making dinner and washing laundry, to name a few. When you are late to the scene of the crime:

Do not argue or interview. This is so hard to avoid, since we all think we can interrogate the truth out of our child.

Take the disputed object away and say:

I wasn't here to see what happened. It looks like Benny wants the truck and Sarah wants it, too. How are we going to solve this problem?

The children may suggest setting a timer. Good idea! They may suggest playing together. Another good idea!

A child may demand to have it back and nose-dive onto the toy in your hand. Give a count, before taking her away to another room, or to your time-away room, until she calms down. She forfeits her chance to have the first turn.

If you are certain that A had it first, give that child the first turn. Set a timer for ten or so minutes, depending on the age. When it rings, child B gets a turn.

Most likely you will not know who had it first. In that case, flip a coin to see who gets the first turn. Be sure to explain what you are doing before you flip it. Another option is to have the children pick a short straw, if you have any handy. Or make a can with just the right number of Popsicle sticks in it, but one of the sticks has a colored mark at the bottom. Keep this can next to your timer.

What if. . .

One child really did have the object first and did nothing to provoke its being taken (but you don't know this because you weren't there)?

When you confiscate the object, you are taking away the toy for the second time, and it doesn't seem fair to punish someone by taking away his toy twice. Unfortunately, life is not fair, and this is the best you can do, since you were not there to witness the event. You can say:

I'm sorry; I did not see how the problem started. I don't know who had this toy first. How can we solve this problem?

If no suggestions are offered:

The only way I can help you is to set a timer so you can take turns.

If faced with lots of protesting and charges of unfairness, you can say:

Today I will give Benny the first turn. Next time that I have to help you, I will let Sarah go first.

Write this batting order down and stick it on the fridge, because you will never remember it the next time the situation arises. At the next unwitnessed dispute, take the object away and refer to your handy sticky note.

What if. . .

Even after various resolutions have been brokered, fights keep breaking out over the same toy?

Take the toy away for a half hour, an hour, a whole day, or even a week if necessary. You may also take the precious object away for the duration of a playdate, and redirect the children to other activities.

Disputes over Ownership

Been there. . .

Your child has been doting over a particular teddy bear all day, taking it for walks, dressing it, talking to it, playing house. Some time in the afternoon, she abandons it on the floor. Her big brother comes along and picks it up, as siblings will do. She explodes, insisting that it is hers. Her brother is indignant and will not give it up. The situation becomes an ethical dilemma for you, the parent. Should you immediately give it back to the child who was so attached to it? How was your son to know it was off-limits?

Make it a family policy that whoever abandons a toy on the floor or other public space is telling everyone else that he is all done with it. In the case where a child is very invested in the toy, set a timer to give the newcomer a turn first. When it rings, you can return it to the child who is very attached to it. Say:

Betty, when you put the teddy on the floor, it tells us you are all done with it. Owen thought you were all done with it. I'm going to set the timer to give Owen a turn now. When it rings, you can have it back.

Shared Toys vs. Individual Ownership

If you have multiple children, you should distinguish toys as family toys or as a particular child's possession. It is very useful to put an initial on an ownership item, because weeks from now you may not remember whose it is. (If you have more than two children, you will forget within hours.)

Use a Lock Box

Well, maybe it doesn't lock, but a personal treasure box is a good place for a child to squirrel away toys or objects that are off-limits to others. Whatever the container—a plastic bin or large shoebox or basket—make sure your child can open and close it by herself. She can store it under a bed or in a closet when not in use. Inevitably, the box will overflow. What was once a sweet, personalized storage box will spill over into a paper bag, a cardboard box, another cardboard box, and several nearby vessels. But you should try to keep it to one box. Your young child cannot understand the concept of limiting possessions. This is where a parent must make the tough decisions. You can try to enlist the help of your child in deciding what stays and what goes. For example:

Take out some items she hasn't used in a long time.

Let's make room for your newest treasures.
Let's pick out ten toys you want to play with and keep in your box.
   We'll put the rest away.

OK, so where does the rest go? Recycle, throw out, donate, or store it away in limbo (yet another box, hidden out of sight, the fate of which you can decide much later). Odds are she'll want to keep everything. Then you must make a unilateral decision to store some items in limbo. (For storage ideas and ways to help your child clean her room, see page 228.)

Pushing, Pinching, Hitting, Kicking, Scratching, Pulling Hair

Although anguishing, these are all normal acts of childhood frustration. A small person's self-control is not developed yet, and two- and three-year-olds haven't mastered all the language they need to communicate their state of mind. Your child will develop skills over time, with your help. Until then you can respond in the following ways:

For younger children (two to three years old):

If desired, you can turn to the "recipient" and say, *Are you OK, honey? I'm sorry you got kicked.* That's all. Don't make a big deal of it, or it could encourage her to overdramatize her "injury."

Then take your child aside, get down to her level, and talk to her. Keep your voice calm but serious.

We don't kick other people. Kicking hurts!

Or

I noticed you were angry and you pushed your friend.
You're just learning to stop yourself, and I can help you.

Redirect your child to another activity or toy. Don't come down hard on him; otherwise your child may start to enjoy the negative attention. If he wants something that another child is playing with, bring him to that child and gently say:

> *Let's ask this boy if you can play, too.* (See if your little one will ask.)
> *Do you want to ask, or do you want me to?* (Some children will need this support.)
> *OK, maybe you can stand right next to him. You can play with the red train and he can play with the blue one.*

Be brief, simple, light. Disengage and let them play.

For older children (approximately four to five):

By now, older children should know that pushing or kicking is inappropriate behavior. Just lead them aside so you can talk. There is no point in scolding. In these situations, children respond better to neutral reactions from an adult. Some things you can say if and when your child is ready to listen:

> *It seems like you were so angry with your brother that you resorted to pushing him. What are the things you can do instead of pushing when you get angry?*
> *It seems like you were so angry you couldn't say what you wanted to.*
> *I bet you are really sorry you pulled her hair. What can you do the next time you get angry?*
> *I know you are ready to learn what to do when you are mad.*
> *You're the kind of kid who can learn to use his words, instead of pushing. I know you're working on it.*

What if the aggressive behavior becomes a pattern? See "Reality Check" at the end of this chapter.

Your are on the phone making a doctor's appointment, when your three-year-old runs up to you howling that her big brother pushed her down. You weren't there, of course, so how do you know what happened? Did it all start when your three-year-old knocked down his tower? How should you respond?

First, briefly comfort the hurt one. Then turn to both of them and say:

Do you two want to talk about it, or do you need some time away from each other? (Remember this line, because it will prove to be useful in so many situations.)

If they are both acting civilized, listen to what each one has to say. You can repeat what they say so they know you understand:

It sounds like Betty knocked down Owen's tower and then Owen pushed her down.
Do you need some time away from each other, or can you make a plan together?

Or

I really don't know what happened, but I can help you by giving you some time away from each other.

Or

Betty, can you please help Owen rebuild his tower?
Owen, can you tell Betty how to help you?

If Betty says no, then her consequence is to lose the opportunity to play with the blocks for the rest of the day, or to play in a different room. You should state this outcome explicitly.

What if Betty says "I don't care!"? You can say evenly: *You don't care. I do. So this is what I will do to help you learn. You may not play with the blocks for the rest of the day.* Say this only once—don't get into a back-and-forth. If faced with more "I don't care's," respond minimally or not at all: "*Mm, hmm, OK,*" and leave it at that. Uphold the consequence for the amount of time you choose.

Repeat Offenses

What if. . .

Your child becomes a repeat offender? She's on a little rampage today, pushing or hitting siblings or friends, or knocking down other kids' projects.

Take her hand and bring her over to a pile of pillows or even a wall, and give her a place to safely push/kick/pull/hit. Be encouraging rather than punishing:

> *You've been pushing a lot today. Let's get those pushy feelings out of your system. You can push this wall because it doesn't have any feelings. Friends (or brothers or sisters) do have feelings, and it hurts them when you push. Push, push, push! Get those feelings out of your system. I bet it's not out of your system yet, let's push some more.*
> *Do you think they're out of your system? Great.* (You get the idea.)

Bring her back and arrange something quiet for her to do, like drawing or play dough.

She goes back to pushing/kicking again?
Bring her back for more pushing at the wall or in the pillows.

I really want you to do more pushing, as hard as you can. You can't hurt that wall/pillow. I can't let you go back with your friends until you get all that pushing out of your system.

When she says, "It's all out of my system," tell her:

I want to make sure you really have those pushes out of your system. Just push some more pushes out on the wall.

Your child has been pushing and pinching all week long in the same situations? For example, every time her big brother takes out the trains in the playroom, she starts pushing. Or every time your child joins the neighborhood kids at the playground, she ends up pinching someone?
Have a talk before the next situation:

I noticed that every time we go to the playground you push other kids. So I am going to help you stop doing this. Every time I see you trying to push, I am going to tap you on the shoulder. That means stop.

Do a little role-play or rehearsal at home. If this tactic doesn't work in the field, you can give your child a time-away on your lap or by your side for a few minutes. If she doesn't calm down and decide to cooperate, it's time to pack up and leave. A good consequence now is to make the playground off-limits for one or two days.

You really like to go to the playground, but we can't go when you decide to pull hair. We'll try again in two days.

Mark it on the calendar and show your child what you are doing.

Biting

Around age two many toddlers start to cut molars, a process that can be aggravating to them. They may have a physical need to bite. Teething rings are not passé; always give your child something safe to bite.

If your child bites another child, quickly take her away to a chair or a different room. Tell her (firmly):

We do not bite people. Biting hurts!
If you need to bite, you must bite this chew toy instead. (Or use a plain bagel or a peeled apple.)

Keep in mind that at age two, children quickly learn that biting can be a way to get your attention. If you sense your child is doing this, you may have to respond with a downplaying or "loss" of attention. Bring your child to a neutral, safe place, but stay aloof. Don't cuddle, engage, or lecture. This way, you won't be rewarding your child with your excited response.

On rare occasions, a four- or five-year-old might bite a sibling. Give the older child something to bite as well, even a baby chewing ring. Ask her what she can do to express her anger the next time, instead of using her teeth. If she doesn't know, give her some suggestions, like asking a grown-up for help. (See page 159 for ways a child can learn to express anger.)

To recover from a traumatic biting experience, have your child take an ice pack to the victim and check on how she feels. Your child can learn about consequences from looking at the bitten area and seeing the sad expression on her friend's/sibling's face. (Note: A two-year-old usually does not understand empathy yet.)

Sometimes a biter is very shaken and ashamed by the experience of hurting another child. Give the biter some time to recover before you enlist her in the recovery process. In serious cases, you may even have to wait a day or two until your child has regained some self-confidence. On the other hand, if the biter is not acting a bit remorseful, engage him immediately in the recovery and checking-in process.

Been there. . .

When my three-year-old daughter bit her best friend, we were mortified to see the full set of teeth marks imprinted on our little neighbor's cheek. We couldn't even discuss the incident because my daughter would clam up. She was clearly worried and upset about her actions but was too young to know how to handle her feelings. I called the family to apologize. A couple of days later, my daughter brought a bag of frozen blueberries and some flowers to her friend. (*What can we bring to Miriam to help her feel better?*) My daughter was still shy and ashamed to talk about the incident, but she willingly made the gesture and got to see her friend's injured cheek. There was no need for any adult to put words of apology in her mouth. That was enough. She learned something about the effect she had on her friend.

Tattling

> **Been there. . .**
>
> You have spent a long time teaching your four-year-old what she can do when she's angry instead of clobbering her sibling. One of the options she likes to use is to ask a grown-up for help. But now, several times a day, she comes to you complaining that her little brother pushed her. Her brother hit her. Her brother pinched her and took away her necklace. Her brother called her a poopy head. Shouldn't she be praised for not fighting back? Should you keep intervening at every complaint, so she doesn't resort to being physical? Have you created a tattling monster?

Ask yourself this question: is my child really looking for help with a situation, or is she trying to get someone in trouble? Does she have the skills to handle the annoyance by herself?

Let's take the first scenario: she is distressed by someone else's behavior and wants help. What to do:

Words, Name Calling, and Lesser Offenses

If the chief complaint is name calling or an unkind comment ("Dad, Jimmy said I look like a boy!" "Mom, Jenny said my shirt is ugly!"), try not to react much. Encourage your child to handle the situation on his own, as much as possible. When you are facing a litany of minor complaints, you can use one of my favorite responses of all time:

Boy, that sounds really annoying. Did you tell her how you feel?

It's versatile, yet sincere. In some cases you may want to accompany the child back to the scene to help her deliver her message. But usually you don't have to take any action. Here are some alternative responses that can be helpful, depending on the situation:

For younger children:

(Within earshot of the name caller. Firmly.) *You didn't like it when Josie called you "stupid," and you know what, I didn't like it either. I hope she will soon learn not to say "stupid."*

Mm, hmm. (Nod.) *OK, I hear you. That word really annoyed you.*

Did you tell her you don't like it when she says that?

Did you tell her you don't want to play with people who say mean things, and walk away?

What are some other things you can do?

Remember, you can always say, "Sticks and stones can break my bones, but names will never hurt me," and then go find something else to do.

For older children, hold up your hands in a shrug, and ask:

What do you think you can do when this happens?

Why do you think it started? It takes two to tango. (Ask her if she knows what that means. If she doesn't, you can explain that it takes two people to have a disagreement.)

I'm sure you can decide what's the best thing to do.

You are the kind of girl who can figure out what to do.

What if. . .

You catch the perpetrator (your child or someone else's) in a verbal attack?

- Say to the child firmly: *Hold on! There is no name calling in our family. Can you please think of different words to use to express your anger?*
- If your young child is name calling, explain that when she says, "You are a dumb head," it makes her sibling or friend feel sad, and that friend might decide she doesn't want to play with her anymore. (You can explain this to older children, too, but they probably know this by now.)
- If your child continues to verbally taunt and name call, give her a time-away for a certain number of minutes (usually the same as her age).
- In many cases it may be appropriate to encourage a youngster to ignore a name caller who is very persistent, as in: *That's not a friendly thing to say. You don't have to be near him; just walk away.* There's no better way to extinguish a behavior than rendering it ineffective.

What if. . .

The tattling continues to the point where it is getting ridiculous? It's obvious that your child is on a kick to get her sibling into trouble. The response should show your child that tattling for the purpose of getting someone into trouble has consequences too.

- Separate them.

It seems like you are both annoying each other today. You both need a break from each other. For the next hour you, Tommy, will play in the living room, and you, Olivia, will play in the kitchen. (Keep them in separate rooms for whatever length of time makes sense, but long enough so they notice.)

- Give each a separate time-away.

If it continues and your children are locked in a cycle of taunting, teasing, and tattling, give each a time-away.

It seems like you are annoying each other and complaining a lot. I can see you both need a time-away.

Injury Complaints

Been there. . .

Your two children are happily putting on a dance show in the playroom. You take this time to go to the kitchen and load the dishwasher. Ten minutes later, the younger one runs in crying and yelling that his sister pinched him. Should you go and question the big sister? Should you make a big deal of this, so your children understand they must play cooperatively? Remember, you weren't there to see what happened, and it takes two to tango.

Respond neutrally, as previously described. Here are a variety of responses you can use, depending on the severity of the injury.

"Mommy, Sarah pinched me!"

She did? Did she pinch you hard? Mm, hmm. Do you think you can go back and play or do you need an ice pack? (Have the perpetrator help with the ice pack, if possible.)

Or

Mm, hmm. I see. (Loud enough so that Sarah can hear.) *Bobby, you do not like pinching, and neither do I. Is there something you would like to say to your sister?* (Remember, you don't know which child started "pinching" the other first.)

What if. . .

Your child demands that you give her sibling a time-away, or at least take her away?

> *Mommy and Daddy make these decisions. I think you're the kind of kids who can fix this problem together. Now, do you think you can go back and play, or do you need more time apart?*

Or

> *If you are uncomfortable playing together, just stay and play beside me. (Bring your toys over by me and play.)*

What if. . .

Someone really crosses a line and harms another child?

If there is physical evidence—a red area, teeth marks, a scratch, etc—have the perpetrator help the victim with an ice pack or Band-Aid. Don't expect a two-year-old to fully show empathy yet. Think of his actions as helping to correct or clean up a mess. As he gets a little older, you can point out how the hurt person is feeling—but make sure you keep your tone of voice under control.

Your first reaction should be to use a firm "I'm in charge" voice:

> *Never scratch someone!*

Help or encourage the child to deliver the ice pack or Band-Aid. Then soften your voice to continue:

> *Tommy, you scratched your sister and that hurts her. It's not a good time for you two to be playing together.* (Set them up in different places with different activities. Most likely they will want to drop the incident and just keep playing together.)

Or

> *This is the third time you scratched your sister. Scratching hurts. Here is an object you can scratch. And for now, you two will have to play separately.*

Or, try one of these:

> *Jane has so many tears. How do you think she is feeling?*
> *Jane's face is going like this.* (Demonstrate.) *How do you think she feels?*
> *This spot looks very red. Do you think that it hurts?*

Bring them together to talk about the incident (the older the child, the better this works):

> *You two need to talk about this.*
> (Huddle them with your arms.)
> *Let's take turns. Tommy, you go first.*
> (After each has had a say, repeat it back.)
> *It sounds like Tommy was sitting on Jane's skirt and wouldn't get off, and Jane got really angry and punched him.*

(Pause for any response.)

Jane, I bet you wish you hadn't hurt your friend. Is there another way to get Tommy off? Is there a way to solve this problem without punching? What could you do instead of punching?

(If the child cannot answer, give suggestions.)

How about if you say, "Please get off my skirt now"?

Do you need some time apart, or are you both ready to play again?

For Older Children Grappling with Tattling

Explain that when he sees a child who needs help or might be in danger, he should call a grown-up for help. That's not tattling. For example, if a friend is stuck on top of the monkey bars and can't get down, or if a sibling is playing with matches that might start a fire, then he should tell a grown-up. Tattling is when you tell a grown-up what your friend or sibling did just to get her in trouble. Give examples. ("Daddy, Marcus won't put his toys away!" "Mommy, Cindy is taking the balloons out!" "Daddy, Jimmy is getting toothpaste all over the sink!")

Reality Check

We keep our own temper under control all day long. But the sight of one child hurting another is enough to unhinge us. The audacity of a child who commits the same transgression after you have calmly and firmly explained the rule a thousand times would push anyone's buttons. But be assured that every time you stop a physically dangerous behavior and teach an appropriate alternative (or give a consequence if necessary), your child is learning. It feels like a long, slow process, but you can't back down. Progressively, your children will learn new problem-solving skills and apply them in more sophisticated ways as they get older.

It's common sense for a parent to stop a child who's hitting or biting. But what about stopping antisocial behaviors, like when a child messes up another's puzzle or knocks down a tower? It's hard for a parent to sit back and be mellow when her child hurts someone. But we have to be more easygoing because we will never be able to eradicate conflict. The best we can do is teach our children the skills to manage it. Sometimes, however, we get confused about when to teach, and when to really put our foot down.

Here is a story that illustrates this confusion. This scene occurred in the toddler area of a children's museum. I was reading on a nearby bench as my two-and-a-half-year-old son, Cian, was playing with trains on the train table. A little girl his age came over and pushed him out of the way so she could play. Cian fell down on his bottom, and then got back up to play. Before I could register what was happening, I heard a loud voice yelling, "That was not nice! That was really not nice!" The girl's mother came stomping over, picked up her daughter, and planted her in front of my son. "Now say, 'I am sorry I pushed you down!'" The girl repeated it. The mother continued. "Say, 'I'm sorry, I forgot I was not supposed to push!'" The girl repeated it to my son. "OK, now a time-out!" The mother whisked her daughter onto her hip and marched away to another section of the room. The girl was screaming. A few minutes later, the mother looked up from her crouched position to someone who was presumably her own mother and shook her head in exasperation. "This is not working! We should go."

Wow. I could barely believe that a mini case study in what not to do had just presented itself to me. That mom really could not tolerate antisocial behavior in her little girl. Did she think I expected her to punish her daughter for knocking down my son? Would she have acted so hard-nosed if she were just at home with her kids? I don't like to judge, but her child was just two and did not appear to be wild or out of control at that moment. Pushing behavior comes with the territory. The point is that little girl lost her chance to learn how to ask Cian if she could play with him.

So, are there any concrete rules about when to crack down and when to teach, redirect, encourage, and make suggestions? I think yes. This sounds crude, but it's practical. When your child is being really horrid, and won't listen or cooperate, remove him from the scene for a time-away or cooling-off period. If he's attentive, discuss alternatives he could have used. Once he is calm, quietly bring him back to what he was doing before the meltdown. It sounds so obvious, doesn't it? But making these moment-to-moment judgment calls is perhaps the most challenging part of our jobs.

On a developmental note, if your child seems to be locked in a disruptive or aggressive pattern that doesn't seem to evolve or change over time, it is natural to wonder if he has crossed a line from expected behavior to something more problematic. If your child's behaviors follow him as he gets older, interfere with his social relationships, or affect other family members' behaviors, then it's time to ask a professional for advice. First consult your pediatrician, as there may be subtle physical problems that can contribute to a child's aggressive behavior (these include sleep disorders, hearing or vision problems, undiagnosed infections, or mild delays in motor or verbal development). A valued preschool teacher, counselor, or family therapist can also help you step back and examine the underlying causes of the behavior pattern and create a strategy to help your child.

Jealousy

The indignation of being displaced by another sibling—older or younger—can set off angry, aggressive, and defiant behaviors in young children. Above all, kids need understanding at these times, and guidance on how to deal with yet another bewildering emotion. Children can't control their feelings of jealousy like they can learn to stop hitting, for example. Adults have a hard enough time understanding their own jealousy—it's a feeling that we must manage all our lives. Parents have to keep in mind that yes, jealousy can bring out the worst in a child, but that it's extremely important to be understanding and empathic at these times. The flip side is that you should not give in to the disruptive/jealous child if that means abandoning the child you are with first. If you do, then your jealous child has won, and you have not helped her manage her emotions. Whether you end up diffusing the anger or giving a time-away, always try to acknowledge your child's feelings first. Here are some ways to empathize with a jealous child:

> *I know it's hard to be home with your baby sister because she takes up all my time.*
> *Sometimes it's really hard to be a big brother when you have to wait your turn to play.*
> *I understand you feel left out because I am always with your little brother.*
> *It's OK for you not to like having your older sister around, but she's part of the family, and we love her like we love you.*
> *I bet you feel really frustrated when you can't have Daddy right away.*
> *It doesn't feel fair, but it's Bevin's turn now.*
> *When I was a little girl, I used to get so angry when my older sister came home from school. . .*

To diffuse the jealous child's anger, suggest and practice using language:

You can ask: "Mommy, when will you be done?"
"Daddy, when can I play with you?"
"Mommy, can we play soccer when you're done?"
"Daddy, when can I have a turn?"
"When are we going to go outside?"

Jealousy toward a Younger Sibling

Been there. . .

Your two-year-old seems to require a lot of your attention. The minute you stop moving, he is right by your side, climbing into your lap, pressing a book into your hand, or trying to steal a bite of your food. Your five-year-old, at the same time, has been hounding you to start a project with her. She gives up and starts pushing objects off the table. Suddenly, almost everything is bugging her. She refuses to pick up the stuff she's thrown, and worse, she's starting to destroy one of her own pieces of artwork that she labels "ugly." How can you scold her for her behavior when you know she deserves your attention, but it's impossible for you to deliver it?

If the jealous behavior is an isolated incident, here are some actions you can take after acknowledging the jealous feelings:

- Always spell out for your child why you can't be with her right now. You might feel like it does no good, but it's important to say it because it will help your child understand why she is waiting. Sometimes a small child will actually understand and accept a rational explanation.

I can't play with you right now because I have to give your sister a snack. When I am finished, I will help you.

I can't play with you right now because I'm having "special time" with your sister. When I am finished, I can read you a book.

You really want me to do that puzzle with you, but right now I have to change your brother's diaper. When I am finished I will play with you.

- If possible, give a discrete time when you will be ready to play. Set a timer if needed. Then try to ignore any complaints to the best of your ability.
- To diffuse a situation, find an activity that both children can do with you or near you. (Do not do this if you are in the middle of alone time with a child.) For example, read a book with one child on each side, or offer them kid scissors (starting at two-and-a-half to three years old) and magazines to cut up on the floor. If your frustrated child balks, tell her she needs to cooperate, or find something else to play with by herself.

Mommy is taking care of two children today, Betty and Owen. And we have to play all together.

- Take out some toys-in-reserve (see box following page) for your child to play with until you are free.

If your jealous child becomes really horrid, give her a five-count warning. If she doesn't stop, pick her up and carry her to a gated area or another room with a book or toy. (This is not really a time-away, since we're offering something fun for her to do while she waits, and we are trying to be understanding because jealousy is not something a child knows how to control.)

TOYS-IN-RESERVE

Toys-in-reserve are items that are not in regular circulation around the house. They are toys that your kids are not (yet) bored with. Keep them in small labeled bins that you hide, but not so far away that you don't feel like getting them out. If possible, keep each activity in its own separate shoebox or small see-through bin. Here are some suggestions. (Note: These toys are for children who don't regularly mouth anything other than food. Before choosing the reserve toys, make sure your child is competent using them first.)

Extra large bolts and extra large wing nuts

Pipe cleaners

Puffballs or pom-poms (colorful fuzzy balls sold at craft stores)

Etch-A-Sketch

Floam molding beads (it can't stain your furniture)

Spiral ball chute and balls

Mr. Potato Head

Magnets

Gumby figures: twisty, bendy, stretchy figurines

A pocket folder containing a special eraser, pencil, fancy notepad

Figurines: trolls, animals, cars, soldiers

Colorforms (or other brand of plastic cutouts that can be arranged on a background)

A puzzle that your child can do without help

A tiny kids' watercolor palette and paintbrush, plus tiny cup of water for painting

Special Time

If jealousy is part of a lasting pattern or phase, you'll likely need to make some changes to your routine that might at first seem far removed from the episodes of jealousy. In short, increase the time you

ENGAGING ACTIVITIES TO SET UP

These ideas require a little more preparation and supervision, but can be effective in occupying your child for those times you really need a breather.

- Give your child a kids' tape player and recordings of you and your spouse reading stories or singing. This requires you to do some advance prep and your child to have some familiarity with the tape recorder.
- Your child can stand on a stool or chair at the sink washing plastic dishes or baby dolls in soapy water. Cover the floor with lots of towels.
- Allow your child to watch approved short videos. (Not movies, just short educational ones. See page 305 for a recommended list.) Use videos sparingly. Why? It's all too easy to eliminate a bad behavior by hypnotizing your child with a video. A video robs her of the opportunity to learn to entertain or occupy herself—even if the learning process evokes moans and complaints. You also must be careful that your use of a video does not reward bad behavior. It's safer to use a video—occasionally—when you anticipate a tricky situation rather than give a video after the whining, hounding, and hectoring has begun.

spend alone with the child who has jealous feelings. Introduce regular, repeating "special time" with him. Here are some parameters to follow:

- For parents who work full time, it should happen every day for at least fifteen minutes. If you have a more flexible schedule, you might set it up for three times per week for a longer duration. This regular pattern will give your child a sense of when she can expect to be alone with you. It will also reinforce that she is, indeed, worthy enough to have you all to herself.

- Special time involves you and your child spending time together, nobody else. It does not include taking her to dance class, running errands, going on playdates, or meeting a group of friends at the playground. While these outings can be a lot of fun for both of you, they are not intimate enough to be considered one-on-one time.
- Whether the time is spent at home doing something quiet, or an outing to a zoo, the important thing is that you both have uninterrupted time to talk.
- Ask your daughter what she would like to do during her special time. If you're watching multiple children at home, she can pick an activity to do with you at home while a smaller sibling plays in a gated area or playpen. If you both want to go out of the house, anticipate your trip by arranging for other adults to stay home.

How long should you continue special time? Until your child decides he doesn't want or need it anymore. He will let you know.

Jealousy toward a Baby

Children often feel bad about having negative feelings toward a new baby sibling. When preparing a child for the newest member of the family, it's important not to oversell how wonderful it is to be a "big sister." From a child's perspective, it often doesn't feel good at all.

- Acknowledge the hard parts of being an older sibling.

I bet there are times (or will be times) when you really don't like the baby and wish she weren't here. That's OK. You don't have

*to like her all the time. But we all have to respect that she's part
of the family.*

Some days you're going to wish the baby were not here.

*I bet you wish you could go back to your life before the baby was
born. I bet you liked it better when she was still in my belly.*

*I remember when I was little and my baby sister was born. I got
really grumpy, and Grandma says I wouldn't talk to the baby
for five days. . .*

- Always remind your son or daughter that you have enough
  love for all your children.

*I have a special place in my heart for you, and for everyone in our
family.*

*Mommy loves you even when she is nursing the baby. When I
nurse the baby, I like it when you sit right next to me and cuddle with your doll . . . look at a book . . . draw a picture in
your notebook.*

- Buy your older child a baby doll of his or her own. Depending
  on the age of your child, and regardless of gender, get him a baby
  stroller, clothes, little dishes and bottles, and blankets for swad-
  dling. The concept is that your child can model what you do
  with your new infant by being in charge of a baby of his own.
- Make your child feel that being an older sibling is very special
  by giving him specific jobs to do that only a growing-up boy can
  do. Some ideas include helping to set the table, helping to get
  the recycling ready, or helping Mom or Dad with a fix-it project.
- Give him certain but limited baby caretaking activities to do if
  he is interested. Some ideas include collecting the diaper and
  wipes, putting a blanket on the baby, holding up pictures for

the baby to see, or singing. As the baby gets bigger, the older sibling can play musical toys, tell him stories, and give him stuffed animals and rattles.

- Show him safe ways to softly touch his new baby sister or brother. Tickling, holding hands, touching feet, giving gentle kisses. Do it together until he gets the hang of it. If you find him being too rough, redirect him to one of the safe ways of touching.
- If you think your child is acting out because he is bored, give him some toys-in-reserve, a tape player with a story on tape, or even an approved short video that he can watch while you are tied up with the baby. (Use videos sparingly, and make sure they have educational content. Decide in advance what your family policy is regarding the amount of screen time a child may have per day. See page 305 in the Ongoing Adventures section for video suggestions.)
- When time permits, reminisce about when your older child was a baby. Pantomime how you cared for her, by holding her in your arms and rocking her. Pretend to feed her, burp her, and change her diaper. Your child will love the chance to be playful with you, and be comforted by the idea of having been there, done that.
- Above all, you have to keep your new baby safe. Older siblings are unpredictable and should be supervised at all times during the early, critical stages of adjustment to a new baby.
- Most important: make a schedule for you and your older child to have "special time" as explained above.

Jealousy toward an Older Sibling

Toddlers get jealous, too. Their buttons can get pushed when they see you doing something especially toddlerlike with an older child, like cradling your eldest in your arms or tickling her. Of course this does not mean you should curtail your show of affection. To the best of your ability, never abandon what you are doing with one child because a sibling is jealously acting out for your attention. It will make the first child feel unimportant, and reinforce the other one's strategy for getting his own way (i.e., by screaming). There are ways of calming or distracting the little tyke who is pushing, yanking, shoving, or complaining. And, yes, sometimes it might mean having to ignore her for a few moments until you are done.

- If your child is calm enough to listen, acknowledge his feelings first. Pick a discrete time when you will be through and set the timer if that has worked in the past. *I am playing with Becca right now. I will play with you in five minutes.* Then you can benevolently ignore her for a few minutes, as you tune out the whining.

Always spell out for your child why you can't be with her right now. You might feel like it does no good, but it's important to say it because it will help your child understand why she is waiting.

I can't play with you when it's your sister's homework time.
I can't play with you right now because I'm having "special time"
   with your sister. When I am finished, I will read you a book.
You really want me to do that puzzle with you, but right now I
   am helping your brother with his project. When we are finished I will play with you.

- If you don't know how long you will be, take out a box of toys-in-reserve (see page 144) for the complaining child to play with.

- Your first instinct may be to involve both children in your activities. That's fine if both of them agree, and you're not having alone time or "special time" with one child. If your affection can be shared among children, then you can try alternating giving tickles and hugs.

- If nothing is working, put the disruptive child inside a gated area with some toys-in-reserve. Tell her you'll be back in two or three minutes. If she hollers, let her go for a few minutes. If you sense the crying is out of anger or protest, you do not have to intervene. If she is feeling pain or real fear, then take her back out. At the next disruptive act, give a three or five count before returning to the gated area.

- Note: This is not a time-away. You are helping your child deal with feelings of jealousy by learning how to wait and find something else to do. It is a much different response than, say, giving a time-away to a child who has pushed his brother down for the third time. When it comes to jealousy, give your child a lot of slack . . . and understanding. But don't abandon your plan with the first child, or you will set the stage for more petulant behavior.

Been there. . .

At bedtime, your two-and-a-half-year-old can't bear the sight of you tucking in and cuddling with your older child. Your spouse is out of town, so you've got no backup. Your little one screams, and tries to pull you out of the bedroom. You try to involve him in the cuddling, but he refuses. He won't stop howling. It's not fair to disrupt your daughter's peaceful bedtime routine because her younger brother wants all the attention. Is it?

It's not OK. Every child deserves a few minutes of undisturbed cuddles with you before the lights go out. If you see a pattern of jealous behavior in your child in certain repeating situations, you can try to anticipate it and head it off the next time:

- Give your younger child a special task to do during these tricky times. For example, at bedtime, give him a stuffed animal or baby to carry and tuck in its own bed (perhaps a shoebox) while you are putting your other child to bed. Your younger child can even follow you around holding the "baby," or play in the hallway as long as he doesn't interfere with you. Explain a few hours in advance what you'll both be doing.

Ugh, the Noise!

We now know it's useful to let kids argue, bicker, and work out their own difficulties. But when the noise level gets out of hand, your poor head is begging for relief. When your children's arguments become unproductive—like when they shout each other down—it's time to offer some help. There are also times when happy children make noise. Being goofy and silly can whip up some serious noise levels, too. When it ceases to be music to your ears, you can intervene a bit, or remove yourself, depending on the circumstances.

- The talking cup

It doesn't have to be a cup, but it's great to have a tangible object for children to hold while taking turns talking. Whoever holds the cup gets to talk, and everyone else has to listen—interrupters must be reminded of this rule. Because I don't carry this object with me all the time, I often designate a new talking something as I go along, like a sock, a shoe, or other object I find in the glove compartment (an air gauge works well).

- Hand signal

You can't yell at your loud youngster to be quiet; that's just bad form—not to mention impossible for your noisy child to hear. You can teach your children that when you cup a hand over your ear, for example, it means they need to lower their voices. *Too loud. The noise is bothering me.* If they stop responding to the signal, you can issue a lower-level consequence, like making them leave the room.

- Use a quiet voice

Don't answer your child using the same volume; switch to a deliberately quiet or whispering voice instead. She'll have to quiet down in order to hear you.

- Who's being annoyed?

It's nice to let your children be children and get as loud as they want. But there are limits. If you are out in public and their noise is really distracting and interrupting other people, you obviously must intervene. Simply put, if a child can't lower his voice, he must be taken outside or away from the area to spend a few minutes with an adult. If a group of children is having a hard time cooperating, it's time to pack up and go.

- Indoor/outdoor voice? Nah.

We don't like this phrase much, because it's full of contradictions. Kids will always find the exception to the rule. There are times when you are outside and you are asked to be quiet, and vice versa. You might try using a "conversation voice" versus a "loud, yelling or screaming voice."

> *Can you tell me in a conversation voice?* (To set a good example, keep your voice normal and "conversational" when saying this.)
> *You're using a yelling voice and it's bothering me.*
> *I can't understand because your voice is screaming.*

- Take me away!

If your kids are safe, feel free to remove yourself from the room when the noise level gets out of hand. If anyone asks where you are going, say the noise is bothering you and you can't concentrate. So you need some time away.

- Tape-record the noise fest

Record a particularly loud session and play it back to your child or children. Don't make judgments; just ask questions, such as:

> *Do you think it's easy to talk to each other (listen to each other) with so much noise?*

It's quite a learning experience for everyone!

Reality Check

Sometimes when we're in the thick of teaching and training our kids, we lose sight of the fact that our kids are dynamic, growing little beings, and in time, things will change. We work hard to set up a rule and teach everyone to follow it. And then one day they stop pulling toys away for a whole week. Was it because of our patience and determination? Or did they just grow out of it? Your instincts may tell you it's one or the other, but ultimately it doesn't matter. Give yourself credit for nurturing your child's new skills!

CHAPTER 7

Getting Really, Really Angry

The intensity of a young child's anger can really shock us. How can that beautiful face get so steamed up and red? The singsong voice become so ear shattering? Some kids have more angry outbursts than others; it depends on their temperament. It's hard to believe, but there are some children who are so mellow by nature they might have only a few outbursts in a month. Other more active, extroverted types might have them once a day or more. Whatever the personality, little tykes will at some point reveal the full glory of their anger to their parents or caregivers. It would be unnatural if they didn't.

Anger, Aggression, and Destruction

Young children are capable of the fiercest displays of anger and aggression toward peers, parents, siblings, and even material objects. It's astonishing to see the white-knuckled, teeth-baring postures our child can strike during an entanglement. But what about the urge to destroy something? In frustration, children might throw toys, tear up papers, knock over trash cans, or stomp on something to break it. In general, young children should not be punished for their angry outbursts. Ironically, they need empathy and redirection, not scolding, from a parent. (As in, *I can tell you are really angry. . .*) Anger is a normal emotion and a part of life. Self-control comes only after several years' maturity, patient teaching, and role modeling. If, however, an outburst has a destructive effect, a child should be expected to help repair or somehow make amends for the material damage when he calms down. The extent to which a child can help fix something she broke, for example, depends on age. (For example, two- and three-year-olds might need your help picking up the papers that were thrown on the floor, while a four- or five-year-old can likely do it solo.) Also, keep in mind that most children do feel remorse after they've done something hurtful, but they rarely have the language to express it. It's a good idea to acknowledge this feeling of regret.

What to do after a destructive outburst:

When your child has calmed a little, you might ask:

I wonder why you got really angry and decided to tear up your sister's artwork?

If there is a logical answer, get the children together, huddle them, and have them take turns speaking.

If there is no logical response, then you can say:

I see. But you may only tear up your own artwork, not your sister's.
  (Variation: You may only smash up your own toys. This water gun
    is something the whole family enjoys, and if you break it, we
    can't use it anymore. And you know what? You won't be able to
    either.)

If you are faced with a blank stare:

Your sister is upset about what you just did, and I am, too. (Say it in a firm but not yelling voice.)
I bet you wish that your sister didn't feel bad. Or: *I bet you are sorry you ripped that up.*
Let's figure out a plan to make it better.

See if your child has an idea of his own. From drawing a picture to offering a treat, you'd be surprised at the creative ideas kids can come up with. Keep your tone and demeanor neutral, businesslike. You don't want to make the consequence too exciting.

What if. . .

Your child offers to collect all the scraps of paper—for example—and return them to his sister, but you know that idea will just make the situation worse?

When a small child offers a solution, no matter how impractical, show him that you value the idea.

That's right, maybe you could give her back all the pieces. But what if she sees those pieces and it makes her sad because her drawing is all ripped up? Maybe we could give her a new piece of paper and some markers so she can try again? What do you think?

What if. . .

Your child sulks and broods and doesn't want to make an effort?

First, disengage from your own feelings of anger, and then take him by the hand. Say:

We are going to try to tape the picture together.

Involve your child in the repair: He can hold small pieces of tape on his fingers; he can smooth out the tape; or he can hold the paper fragments down on the table. Then accompany your child as he offers the fixed painting to his sister. (If he is too shy to confront her, don't force it; perhaps he can just tag along while you do it.)

What if. . .

The recipient of the peace offering ungraciously swats it away or dismisses it?
Just say to the first child:

Jody is still feeling very sad about her drawing being ripped up. She's not ready to look at the fixed drawing yet. Let's give her some privacy/time alone.

What if. . .

Your child wants to say, "I'm sorry"?
If it's your child's idea to say it, fine. But don't make him parrot words because it will not be sincere; it will just be a quick way for him to get off the hook. If your youngster uses the phrase on his own, having learned it from others, then he'll be more likely to use it with empathy. It's much better to teach him the consequences of his behavior by making amends somehow, than by teaching him a pat phrase to use when he does something wrong.
If your child is calm, address the angry outburst shortly after the incident:

Now that you see what happened, I bet you wished you had tried another way to tell your sister you were angry.

How to Express Anger

It is helpful to teach children alternative ways to show their anger. A great book to read to your child is *When You're Angry and You Know It.* It offers some of the following alternatives to going ballistic:

Stomp your feet.
Bang a drum or pillow.
Walk away.
Talk to a grown-up.
Say, "I am really, really angry" while stomping a foot.
Draw a picture of the person who makes you angry.

Perhaps you have some ideas of your own. Write them down in your Family Policy Book (see page 36) so you can refer to them when you need to. Act out some of these choices to show your child how it looks. Kids love it when you role-play.

Note: It's sometimes useful to pop in a new vocabulary word when you're empathizing with your child, such as*: I wonder why you got so disgruntled and decided to tear up the mask.* An older child may become curious about what disgruntled, or another word, means. Listening to you define it might give him insight to what he's feeling. Of course, a child who is flipping out won't find any words intriguing.

Remember that you, the grown-up, have unique ways of handling anger, too. When you suddenly find yourself in a frustrating situation, and your children are watching, it's a great learning experience for them to see you keep your cool. One trick that sometimes works is to verbalize your feelings out loud, or to the air, even if the kids can't understand it.

> *Mommy came to the repair shop to pick up the car because some-one told me it was ready. But now the mechanic says it's not ready. So now I am going to think about how to get us home. . .*

Approaches for Not-So-Angry Outbursts

For two- and three-year-olds, a little lightheartedness can work wonders:

> *Oops! What should we do with all the logs you dumped on the*
> *   floor?*
> *Let's put all the green ones back first. . .*

Or go over to where she has started playing:

> *Excuse me for interrupting. Lucy has to pick up the toys she threw down, and I will help her.*

Try to hold her hand and lead her over to the area. Start to pick up, and give her a discrete task.

> *You can pick up that blue one; there it is, right there.*

For older children, after they have calmed a bit:

> *Jason, I don't know why you threw all the toys off the shelf. Let's see if I can help you put them away.*

Your child refuses to cooperate?

For two- and three-year-olds, you can try to take their hand and put it through the motions of picking up. That's right; hold your child's hand as it picks up one, and then another item. *Let's pick these up together.* But drop this strategy if it is escalating into a physical struggle. Try some of the other interventions below.

- Tie the chore to the next event.

> *We will not start our snack until you help clean up the toys you threw down.*
> *We cannot open up the paints/take the balls out/go outside until you help me clean up.*

Or

> *You may not come to dinner until you help pick up the games.*

Try to keep an even tone, not accusing or threatening, and simply state the plan for the next activity. (If holding back a meal is not desirable, tie the chore to a different, but still immediate, event.)

Remember, when it comes to tidying up the destruction, you are not looking for a complete job, just a reasonable effort.

Don't hold out a consequence that is too far in the future, such as:

> *If you don't pick up the toys, you won't get any treats tomorrow.*

Even a five-year-old won't know what to make of that time frame, nor will she be able to connect events between the two days. This kind of delayed consequence weakens your credibility as a parent.

- If you're at home, you can remove him to a time-away room (with or without you) for some calming down until he is ready to cooperate.

If he still won't help clean up:

- Take away the items.

If your child is so defiant that she won't join you in picking up the area, bring out a cardboard box and place the items in it.

You decided not to help me clean up. Now you may not use these toys for the rest of the day.

Store the box away for a specific amount of time, depending on the age of the child and the preciousness of the objects. (For example, one day for two- and three-year-olds; and two or more days for four- and five-year-olds.) Ideally, you want him to notice the absence, but if a child has loads of toys, the absence of a few might not make a big impression. That's OK; do it anyway.

What if. . .

You are in a social setting when your child has a destructive outburst?

If you'd like, you can say to an adult nearby, within earshot of your child:

Judy, you know I love Tommy very much. But in our family we don't allow someone to tear apart a room.

Take him aside or to a quiet spot until he mostly calms down.

Tommy, it's time to pick up the toys, and I can help you.

Or

Here's the thing: I can wait five minutes, but I need these to be cleaned up so people won't trip.

If your child still will not participate, you cannot move on to the next activity. If he is still resisting, he is probably at the end of his rope by now. Announce that it's time to get ready to go home and let him see you packing up. He might change his tune and suddenly start cleaning up his mess. But if there is no improvement, you should end the playdate. When you get to the point where you announce, "We are leaving in ten minutes," you have to follow through, or else your future announcements will not be taken seriously.

At the time of departure, walk up to your child and casually take him by the hand as you say your good-byes. Once you are holding hands with your child, he's not as likely to run away.

The Extremely Angry and Destructive Rampage

Been there. . .

Your three-year-old is so frustrated because she cannot go to the playground that she starts tearing up the living room. She knocks over a chair and heads for another room, where she picks up a box of glitter glue pens and dumps it out. Then she picks up a block and throws it at you. Should you put her in a room by herself? Should you be the kind, understanding parent and say, "Remember what you can do when you're angry? Stomp your feet!"

Forget the wordy approach. There is no amount of reasoning you can do with a child in this advanced state of fury. Sometimes children can get out of control to the point where they can't stop their own body, and they need your help. At this point you may worry that your child will hurt herself or damage the time-away room, so something else must be done. Controlled physical restraint is in order. First, take a deep breath and get a perspective, as in, "Children do this sometimes. It's normal and doesn't mean she is a monster." When your child is out of control and destructive enough to hurt herself or others, create a "containment circle" by sitting cross-legged on the floor with your child squirming in your lap, and hold your arms out in a circle around her until she calms down. It's a technique that may be unfamiliar to you, but one that many educators learn in the course of their training. (For more information about this method, see page 289.) After the storm passes, calmly hold her hand and lead her back to the living room. Help her pick up the mess she made.

Reality Check

Some children are naturally intense and aggressive—nonstop balls of energy. Other children are docile and easygoing. Most are somewhere in between. Remember, there are many different kinds of temperaments that are considered "normal" for children. It's true that after age two, boys on average are more active and aggressive than girls.

But that's not to say there aren't exceptions. We all know girls who seem to bounce off the walls with energy, and boys who prefer to sit quietly and play with puzzles or look at books. But all children will have angry or aggressive outbursts at some point, and, by nature, some will be more inclined to have them than others. The tough question is figuring out if the aggression you see in your child is a normal part of his personality or a reaction to something going on in his family or social environment.

Sometimes you might notice a pattern to your child's aggressive outbursts. For example, do they happen when she's tired, hungry, in a transition, or when a sibling comes home from school or a parent comes home from work? Can you remember what happened at the time you first noticed the outbursts? Was there a change at home, at school, or with a friend? Perhaps your child is transitioning to three or more caregivers in one day. Her outburst could be a result of too many changes, or retaliation for not getting enough attention from a loved one. Because it's not always obvious what's going on in the moment, it's important that you do not overreact before carefully assessing the cause. (Sometimes you may not be able to determine the cause.) Don't let her anger beget your anger. If you can anticipate your child's anger, try to head it off by redirecting her to play with something new, for example, or by giving her some "you time" right away, or by keeping her separate from her siblings. We know, it's easier said than done.

Hits, Bites, or Kicks You

Did you ever feel like a human punching bag? When we remove our little Tasmanian devil unwillingly from a situation (or perhaps we are only carrying her home from a playdate), we are sometimes the recipient of punches, kicks, and scratches. Our big, soft, welcoming bodies must look like a great place for a child to release his anger safely. Does that mean we should just sit back and take it? Yes and no. We should not react against our child for lashing out at us, but it is absolutely necessary that we stop our child from physically hurting us. If a child keeps trying to hurt you, he is probably testing to see how competent you are as a parent. Children need to feel safe and secure, and they come to believe that they are when parents set reasonable boundaries and take charge. So, how do you respond physically to a wild child slapping and kicking you?

Without using undue force, catch your child's arms and turn her around so her back is toward you. This way, her flailing arms will point away from you. As described above, hold your arms in a "containment circle" while you sit on the ground cross-legged with your child squirming in your lap. This should help your child calm down in a few minutes.

<hr>

What if...

In the process of deflecting your child's flailing fists, you unintentionally hurt her?

Don't be too freaked out by this. Sometimes in the course of defending ourselves, our reflexes swat away a threatening arm and our tightly wound child falls down, for example. You might catch a child's legs as she lies on the bed trying to kick you, only to have her erupt in howls of, "You hurt me!" Knowing that you did not intentionally try to hurt your child should ease your conscience. Don't apologize or start blaming yourself. Just say:

When you kick me I have to stop you from hurting me.
(Firmly) *I will not let you hurt me.*

If your child makes a big show of accusations against you, you can say:

You like to say that I'm the one who's hurting you, when you decided to scratch my arm really hard.

If you feel that your anger caused you to exert more force than you should have, then take a step back. Give yourself some distance to get a new perspective on the situation. What can you do the next time to ramp down your emotional response? (See page 278, "Losing Your Temper, Keeping Your Cool.")

Talks Back

What to do about a sassy mouth? Or a fresh mouth, as my grandmother called it. When we were children, we might have been slapped. Thankfully, many people now know this is not the way to help a child learn and grow. When a child talks back to you, it is an invitation to spar with him. Don't take the bait. As much as you can, avoid getting into a back-and-forth argument with your child. You will never succeed in changing her mind through the force of reason, and, later, you'll feel kind of silly for thinking you could.

When your child uses an inappropriate tone of voice with you, tell her you cannot keep talking to someone who is speaking in a harsh way.

Child being very loud: "I told you I want to go first and you never let me!"
You: *Your sister was here first, so she gets to take her turn first. You can have a turn after her.*

Child, now with veins popping out of her neck: "No! I said
give me my turn now!"
You: *Oh, I don't like to help people who speak to me with that
tone of voice.*

Calmly move away or ignore her. The hard part is not engaging
with your child in an argument. If she doesn't get much attention for
talking harshly to you, she will be compelled to change her tune, or
pout, and either is fine.

Says Mean Things

If you haven't heard the following declarations yet, you probably will
hear some version of them before your child turns six.
"I hate you! You are the meanest mom ever!"
"I wish I had a different family."
"I'm going to run away and never come back."
"I wish brother/sister/parent died!" (Or had never been born.)
Every parent feels crummy upon hearing these words for the first
time. It doesn't necessarily mean you have done anything wrong. Setting reasonable limits with your children will sometimes evoke angry
verbal outbursts like these that are completely normal. Here are some
ways you can respond:

*Yes, you are really mad at me because I am making you pick up
what you threw.*
You really think I'm a mean mommy. (Nod.) *Mm, hmm. Now
would you please brush your teeth?*
*I know you are really, really angry with me. I understand. But I
am trying to help you get to school on time.*

Boy, you are really hating me right now. Can you please pick this up now/put your coat on while you're upset with me?

Your child likes to use the word "hate" a lot?
Acknowledge his emotion, but use a different word.

Are you feeling angry with Joey today?

Or

It sounds like you are really, really angry with your brother today. Is Betsy really annoying you right now?

An optional approach for older children: *We do not use the word "hate" in our family. We say, "I am angry." We really love our family and friends, but sometimes we don't like what they do, and they make us angry. So we say, "Daddy is making me sooooo angry."*

If a four- or five-year-old is really going to town with the "I hate you's," you can also respond this way: *"I hate you" is something you really like to say. But I don't like to hear it. I'll bring you to a special place where you can say it, and I don't have to hear it.* Lead your willful one casually to her room or other location.

Your child says mean things to friends, like:
    "I am never going to be your friend ever again."
    "I only like Sophie today. I hate Owen."

"You are not my friend."

"You can't come to my birthday party."

What you can say:

*You don't have to be best friends all the time. But everybody has to
be friendly.*

*You may think whatever you want to think, but (in our family)
you may not say things that can hurt a friend's feelings.*

What if. . .

Your child says mean things to a stranger or new acquaintance?

"I don't like you. Your face is ugly."

"You're stupid!"

"You're fat."

Use your first encounter with these unsavory remarks as a chance
to educate your child.

First you can say to the adult: *I'm sorry. Lucy is still learning about
good manners.* Move away or excuse yourself. Then right away, take
your child aside, or have her sit on a chair, while you tell her in a firm
and serious voice:

*You might think that lady is ugly, but you may never tell her that.
    It can really hurt her feelings.*

I never want you to say unfriendly things to the people we meet.

There are some behaviors that go beyond the pale. And saying
awful things to a stranger is high on the list. Your child might not
fully grasp this social etiquette until age four or five. If the behavior
persists, nip it in the bud. Leave the store immediately, disallow your
child to come to the store with you for a certain number of days, or

cut out the next activity you are going to—these are just a few examples of sensible consequences that are not too far removed in time from the actual behavior.

Uses Offensive Words

How do small children even learn bad words? In two ways:

- They imitate the words they hear.
- The words get reinforced by the way adults react to hearing them. Using unsavory words is a powerful tool for getting a parent's focused attention, even if it's negative.

The single most effective tool you have to eradicate bad words is to not react to them when you first hear them. That means no sucking in your breath and pouncing on your child with "What did you just say?" or "Where did you hear that?" A two- or three-year-old will not be able to understand why we don't use certain words. When a toddler starts to mimic a bad word, the best you can do is ignore it. Don't react. This is the earliest, and best, solution. The same applies when a tot sticks out her tongue at you.

If a strict regimen of ignoring doesn't work with an older child, take your child aside and tell her in a firm "I'm in charge" voice: *We do not use those words in our family.* Don't lecture or talk too much about it, or you will give the bad word too much importance.

If your older child continues to use bad words, find an appropriate consequence. For example:

> *When you say these words I can't let you have friends come over. I want your friends to feel comfortable and they don't when you use those words.*

Sounds like you want to say those things, but I can't let you say offensive words. You have to go somewhere else. (Redirect her to another room or activity.)

"Offensive" is a good word to have at your disposal. At some point, you can explain what it means to your child.

<hr>

What if. . .

Your child catches you swearing?
Acknowledge what you did and that it was wrong.

You're right. Mom just used a word that's not kind. I made a mistake; I'll try not to do it again. (Try to avoid the word "bad" because it can make something sound forbidden and therefore enticing.)

If your child starts chanting your word gleefully, ignore it.

<hr>

What if. . .

Your child hears a bad word in a movie, or elsewhere, and repeats it?
Right at the moment you might say:

I am really glad we don't say those words in our family.

<hr>

Been there. . .

Your child is playing happily with other friends at a birthday party. Suddenly, the interaction takes a turn and you hear a volley of "You're a poopy head!" "I am not a poopy head. You're a stupid head all the time!" No one is hitting each other, but both kids are wearing grumpy faces. Do you pull your child aside and correct her? Should you give her a time-away? Should you apologize on behalf of your child?

If your child finds his own "toddler swear words" to use, then you should be grateful he is using them, and not some ugly grown-up version. Kids need words they can use aggressively. Most likely she did not get "poopy head" from her parents, but rather from other children. This means it will be extremely hard to eradicate at this stage. In the case of siblings fighting and arguing, you can simply do nothing or, if recruited to help, encourage them to work it out. But if you are in a social setting, such as a birthday party or playground, you might feel the other parents expect you to act.

If you act, do it mildly. Get down and tell your child:

How can I help you and Becky?
Do you need to take a break or do you want to keep playing?

Note: when your youngster is closer to age four or five, you can explain that she can call things "poopy" or "stupid" but not people, because people have feelings and things don't.

What if. . .

You and your spouse can't help yourself? You use bad words. That's just who you are?

First, you can do better! Being a parent necessitates that you rise to a higher calling—that of being a good role model. So figure out something else to say when you are miffed. Sugar! Crumbs! Drat! Darn it! For goodness' sake! Good grief! Jeez, Louise.

Second, you can try to explain to an older child that a particular word is something only grown-ups use, and they only use it in frustration but never directed at people. They "say it to the air." Children are not allowed to use that word. This approach may work for older children, but it is unlikely to work for younger ones. If parents use swear words at home regularly, it should be expected that children will use them, too. How can you give a small child a punishment for using words that he hears in his environment? It won't make sense to him—and it shouldn't make sense to you either.

What if. . .

You are out in public and your child swears at someone?
Address the person while your child listens:

I'm sorry; Joey is still learning which words he can and cannot use.

Or

I'm sorry; Joey is still learning that we don't say offensive words to people.

If it's the first time, pull him aside and say in your firm "I'm in charge" voice:

You may not say offensive words.

If you are dealing with repeat behavior, decide on a logical consequence, such as taking him home because his choice of words is offending others.

What if. . .

Your child regularly calls you a "stupid head" every time she gets mad at you?

A pattern of calling you a name is more than just a heat-of-the-moment slur. Disrespectful words should be stopped. Say firmly: *You may not call me names.* Then proceed to a time-away for the same number of minutes as her age. Remember, the first time it happens you can try to ignore it, but if it continues, use a firm voice, and tell her you don't like it.

That's a word we don't use in our family.
It seems like you want to say "stupid head" all the time. When you use that disrespectful word, I will ignore you.
If you want to say the word "stupid head," you can say it inside your room, where you won't offend anyone.

If the behavior persists, give a time-away.

Reality Check

Angry outbursts are a natural part of life for the toddler-plus age group. However, you should notice your child's flare-ups becoming less frequent—but not necessarily disappearing—as she gets closer to age five and you start to see those long-awaited signs of self-control. Until then, we are really put to the test as we manage all those seemingly illogical eruptions of anger and frustration. And as we face that wave of anger, what are we to do? Oh yes, stay calm. Remember, even if you are angry inside, you can fake being calm if you have to.

If, after all of your efforts, your child is having repeated outbursts in various settings (preschool, home, playdates, grandma's house) and it has been going on for more than a couple of weeks, you should discuss your concerns with your child's teacher or pediatrician. There could be any number of culprits: changes or losses in your child's life, unpredictable events, or difficulty going through a developmental phase like toilet training or verbal fluency.

Given the recent trend in medicating very small children for behavioral problems, it's important for parents to try every other means of addressing a child's behavior before resorting to drugs. Your pediatrician can (and should) be your ally in understanding your child's behavior, especially in the context of your particular family structure, and can offer referrals to specialists if needed. Don't accept medication for your child's "behavior problems" without a second, or even third, opinion from a child psychiatrist. Ask your insurance company for referrals to cover second opinions in mental health.

CHAPTER 8

Manipulators and Clever Cons

To get what they want, children are capable of undermining you in clever ways. What is the difference between insistence and manipulation? The key is to look at the overall pattern of behavior. Does your child really need what she is demanding right now (something you have reasonably denied), or is she just trying to figure out how she can get the best of you? When you start to feel like you are being manipulated, then most likely what is happening is that your child is testing the limits of his power. What is Mommy's breaking point? How can I do what I want, even though I was told no? You can expect an alert child to find all the loopholes and buttons in your adult armor. If you find yourself in this situation, somewhere in the back of your mind, give your child credit for being an astute observer and experimenter.

Prefers One Parent over the Other

Been there. . .

Because your spouse works long hours, you are the primary caregiver for your child. When the weekend comes, your husband naturally wants to spend some time with his two-year-old but encounters resistance. When it's time to go to the playground with Dad, your son cries and clings to you. Your boy looks so distressed; you decide that it's better if the whole family goes out to the playground together. You find yourself making this same decision week after week. Will a two-year-old grow out of this behavior? Shouldn't you support his choice to be where he feels secure?

It's important for a child of any age to spend one-on-one time with each parent on a recurring basis; for example, every Saturday and Sunday morning one parent takes a child to the playground. Or perhaps Friday mornings is the time for Mom or Dad to bring their daughter to feed the ducks. If you keep giving in to a child's preference for one parent over the other, you're preventing the opportunity for him to form a much-needed bond with his other parent. If the parent he's resisting is a permanent presence in his life, he'll quickly adjust and come to enjoy the outings if you follow through. The first one or two times you hold the line might evoke crying and protest, but if both parents act cheerfully and decisively (much like the attitudes to adopt at school drop-offs), the child will not pick up on the underlying anxiety and should recover fairly quickly. If a child does not settle in within a couple of weeks, there could be a bigger issue in play. You can seek professional advice to help you figure out the possible explanations for your child's feelings toward his caregiver.

Your child insists on having Dad do bedtime every night? Having Dad help her get dressed. Having Dad drive her to school. And if she doesn't get her way, she hollers and cries and makes such a big racket that you give in.

This scenario shows a classic example of manipulation. Not the premeditated, nefarious kind that adults are capable of. Rather, it's a clever solution to a problem. A child wants something that her parents won't give her, so she behaves in a way she knows her parents can't bear. They want her to stop being a pain, so they give in to her wishes. It's a tactic she can use anytime she doesn't get exactly what she wants. How to curb it? If the demand for one parent is getting out of hand, you must stop giving in to her demands. Can you compromise? Yes, depending on whether or not the compromise erodes an important boundary your child is still learning. Compromising is not the same as giving in (see "How Much Should You Negotiate?" on page 269). If you have reached the point where negotiation, compromise, and ignoring have all failed, pick up your little protesting one and take her to the time-away area until she calms down. She will probably change her tune before you arrive at the location and let the other parent read her a story at bedtime.

Here's a practical solution: For children age three and older, make a calendar showing when it's Mom's or Dad's turn to do bedtime. Then do your best to calmly but firmly uphold it.

It's OK, and in fact quite normal, for a child to switch back and forth between "favorite" parents. But if she continues to favor one over the other exclusively for more than a few months, you and your spouse should give her opportunities to spend time with the "less favored" parent, in spite of her protests. Sorry, you won't be able to avoid the scene where parent number two carries a kicking and screaming child out the door to the playground. But, as mentioned above, if the parent is consistently loving and present in her life, she should get over her resistance fairly quickly. Future outings will be more enjoyable and it will be great for the relationship if regular one-on-one time continues. When you are setting a limit like taking a child out the door (over her demands to be with the other parent), it's important to be cheerful and playful and not act like the rejected parent, even if you feel like one.

Remember, bonding with a child is not about going on outings. If you have been away for a long time or simply want to make inroads with your child, take a low-key approach, letting your child "warm up" to you. Don't be overbearing: *Becky and Daddy are going to have fun today, aren't we Becky?* If you come on too strong, your child will retreat. Be casual. Sit on the floor and play with some toys—by yourself. Don't browbeat your child to join you. If you look like you are having fun, you will attract children (a lesser known law of physics). Get down to your child's level and have conversations with her. During the day, check in with her as she plays; get down on her level and ask her some lighthearted questions about what she's doing, or make appropriate comments, like *Wow! That was a tricky puzzle. Are you the baby's mommy, or are you her babysitter? How do you take care of her when she wakes up?* As you are playing together, don't forget to give hugs and squeezes. Sounds simple, but it's surprising how many well-meaning parents forget to slow down and just play without directing the activity toward a desired outcome.

Plays One Parent off the Other

Been there. . .

It's about twenty minutes until dinner. Your daughter asks if she can have some cookies, because she is *soooo* hungry. Not right now, you say, but she can have some carrots or cucumbers as an appetizer. You don't want her to fill up on cookies because dinner's just about done. You tell her you've decided that everyone can have cookies after dinner. She walks off sulking and groaning. While the dinner's cooking, you take out the trash and recycling. When you get back inside, your daughter is standing in the middle of the kitchen with a little bowl of cookies. She looks up at you plainly and says, "Daddy said I could have some."

How dare she go behind your back? This is not OK. Should you take the cookies away? Wait a minute; your spouse is the one who should get a time-away!

No, don't take the cookies away—she gets them this time. Here's something you can say:

I see. Today Daddy had another opinion.

As much as you want to reprimand a little child for circumventing your authority, this is not a concept she will be able to fathom until she is beyond age five. After all, both her parents are authorities, right? It's not her job to check that both of you are in agreement when she makes a request. The best you can do is get yourself and your spouse on the same page when it comes to the rules. You should both agree to check with each other if a child is asking to bend the boundaries or rules a bit (or if you are not sure what they are), so that you don't get caught in a contradictory situation. That means each spouse has to get used to saying, *I'm not sure about this. Let's go talk to Mom/Dad.* Being in sync requires awareness on the part of each parent, and a mutual respect for the family policies that have been established. Occasionally parents will rule differently, and it's not the worst thing that could happen. Parents are human, too, and are allowed to disagree. They should follow up their disagreement, whenever possible, with a resolution. It's fine for children to see parents successfully working out their disagreements out loud, but in a civilized way.

What if. . .

Your child has really made a talent out of going over your head when you say "No"?

Then she is probably clever enough to understand when you have caught on:

I notice that when I say "No" about something, you quickly go to see if Dad will say "Yes."

Or

You like to trick me so that you get what you want. But we know; Daddy and I know.

Sometimes that's enough. Don't lecture her or tell her how angry that makes you. Just try to do a better job checking with your partner.

No family functions perfectly, and there will always be times when you and your spouse are not in sync or have differing opinions about what is best for your child. The key is to bring about compromise between the two of you. We know all about this; we're adults, right? Well, sometimes anger and resentment can get between two well-intentioned parents. Allow for some anger and aggravation in your relationship, but never stop talking to each other.

There also may be a subtler imbalance going on between two parents. It is common to the point of being a cliché that one parent turns out to be more lenient or more of a pushover than the other. A parent might even be able to recognize this in himself. To have one parent setting all the limits and the other parent avoiding them is a very bad situation—and extremely confusing for a child who is caught in the middle. A young child must have consistency in her life in order to feel safe and secure. Both parents must uphold boundaries and show affection; they must not take on the good-cop/bad-cop roles. If they do, relationships will be lopsided, and inevitably parents will start resenting each other. If you feel the situation between you and your spouse needs some realigning, schedule some time to have an uninterrupted talk. If that doesn't work, encourage your spouse to see a family therapist or counselor with you. Parenting is hard enough, and it puts a lot of pressure on adult relationships. There's no doubt that raising kids takes time and nurturing away from a marriage. To survive, partners must see their relationship as something that needs constant effort and constant care.

Provokes You

There will be some little thing—or maybe a big thing—that your child will discover that drives you mad when he does it. And he will find it entertaining to watch you become unhinged. Maybe it's climbing behind the couch to escape your reach, or pulling out the curtain hem. This particular behavior is not the curious exploration that children do all the time, but rather a pattern of acting out in order to get your attention. It occupies a special subcategory of pet peeves, and a parent knows it when he sees it.

What is going on? Your child probably needs more of your attention, or is testing you, or both.

• Needs attention

Sometimes when a child feels left out of a parent's life, or is hungry for affection, she will do something that is guaranteed to attract her parent's undivided attention. Does she want more hugs, cuddles, acknowledgment, encouragement? Does she feel like all her interactions with you are hurried and bossy? Well, the civilized way of getting her needs met is not working, so why not try a more inflammatory approach? If this sounds familiar, it might be time to chill out, ignore the other demands in your life for a while, and rediscover that bonded feeling with your child. Take a walk together or read a book as you cuddle. There are countless ways to do it. (Read more about quality time on page 292.)

• Testing you

He knows when he makes you angry, because he sees it in your body and hears it in your voice. But just how angry can he make you?

Can he make you so angry that your head will explode? Does he have the power to drive you away? Seriously, a kid wonders about these things. In order to feel secure in the world, he needs to believe you are never going to abandon him, no matter how horrid he is. Here are a few things to remember:

No matter how beastlike your child is acting, he needs and wants to be contained. Don't abandon him. Stay nearby but don't give him much attention for this behavior. Don't reinforce a child's image of herself as a bad person. Refuse to be convinced! Refrain from using ultimatums or plays on self-worth, such as: *You were so good this morning at breakfast; what's gotten into you? That's it, no playdate for you tomorrow.*

Act indifferent, cool, aloof. Stop demanding that he do something. If an object is being destroyed, calmly take it out of his reach. Don't chase him. Wait until he comes around on his own. If he doesn't get the reaction that he wants, he will become bored and stop. When he comes out of it, don't talk to him about it or lecture him. Just move on to the next thing.

Makes Demands and Bosses You Around

Where does a child get the idea she can turn us, her dutiful parent, into her servant? Can't you just picture your child wearing a robe and sitting on a throne bellowing, "Get me more juice!"? Ah, the egocentric world of a tot. One logical consequence of making a demand is that a self-respecting parent will not provide the service until he is spoken to in a different tone of voice. Here are a few ways to address those audacious little demands:

For younger children, always model the way you wish he had asked the question:

Child: "I want some cereal!"

Parent: *May I have some cereal, Mommy?* (Mom gets the bowl.)
Child: "Open the door right now!"
Parent: *Oh, Daddy, can you open the door, please?* (Dad opens
the door.)

For older children, you can teach them the difference between a
"request" and a "demand." Give a few examples, and ask them to
take a turn creating some. Ask them if they can tell the difference between the two. Tell your child that you don't feel like helping someone who makes demands because it doesn't feel friendly. Predictably,
the next time your child wants something, she will again demand:
"Give me a piece of cheese!" And you can say:

*Is that a request or a demand? Because I don't like demands/I don't
like helping someone who makes demands.* (Try saying it pleasantly.)

Don't fill the demand until it's put in the form of a request. Praise
your child for asking politely:

I like the way you said that!

Reality Check

To use the word manipulative to describe a two- to five-year-old child
is rather unfair. We may feel manipulated at times, but a child of this
age is simply trying to figure out the limits of his relationship with you.
"Who's the boss?" is a question that gets played out repeatedly, in various scenes and dramas. Who are the real manipulators? We, the parents, are. Our challenge is to reaffirm through our actions and
empathy that we are, indeed, the boss. Just not in so many words.

CHAPTER 9

Travel Survival

Traveling with young children is all about survival through entertainment. There are only a few instances when parents are truly obligated to entertain their children: when they are sick; when you make them wait for you in a boring place like a doctor's office or hair salon; and when you take them on a long trip.

The Essential Backpack

No matter what form of transportation you use, a well-equipped backpack will keep even a two-year-old occupied at intervals throughout your trip. The following is an extensive list of little toys that have been shown to keep a toddler's attention for at least . . . five minutes. You will never be able to find all of these items at once, but you can find a subset based on your child's interests. If you travel by plane, remember to pack very light items. With air travel it's important to get the weight just right, or your child will ask you to carry it. (It's a great scene—your kids proudly marching across the airport wearing their backpacks.) Once you have the right balance of stuff inside, a backpack will be a great focal point for your little one throughout the trip. If you travel by car, you have more flexibility with the weight of the backpack.

Little toys (can be found in boutique toy stores, chain toy stores, pharmacies, big grocery stores, dollar stores, or arts and craft stores):

- Small spiral notepads and pencils
- Stickers of all kinds, and sticker books
- Tiny markers, colored pencils, or pens
- A chunky plastic pencil (or pen) that contains a rainbow of colors (You press down a lever to select a color. Most suited for the three and older set.)
- Tiny windup animals that hop
- Stretchy lizards and frogs
- Travel Magna Doodle screens or "disappearing" tablets that you draw on with a plastic stick
- Balls or animals with suction cups
- Rings and necklaces
- Cars and trains
- Miniature dolls with different genders/occupations
- Pinwheels
- Play foam (Like clay but made of tiny spongy balls that stick together. It's not as messy as play dough.)
- Silly Putty (Kids love picking up newspaper print with this plastic clay. Throw it away when it gets dirty.)
- Small hand-held video games (If your older child has the dexterity, go for it.)
- Personal music player with headphones (Program your iPod or MP3 player, if you have one, with both new and familiar songs and stories your child will enjoy. Store it in your own backpack instead of subjecting it to your child's.)

Especially, but not exclusively, for two-year-olds:

- Little cups or boxes that can be opened and closed repeatedly (For example, an empty play-dough container. Tots love to fill and empty containers.)
- Pinwheels, small ones
- Small interactive books with flaps
- Any small toy with a button to push, or with other safely moving parts

In the Snack Department

It's a great idea to pack a little snack and drink in your child's backpack, as long as it doesn't get too heavy for her to carry. It might be a little Ziploc bag of crackers or half a PB&J sandwich, and a sippy cup or juice box. It gives your child the freedom to have his own picnic when he wants to.

The Delights of a Lollipop

Whoever invented the lollipop was a genius. There is no other diversion, besides a good video, that soothes and occupies children better than a lollipop. In our family, we reserve them for special occasions, like haircuts, birthdays, and long trips. Keep the waxed paper wrapper, because your child may want to stop and start at various times. One of my daughters once stretched out eating her lollipop for six hours on an overseas flight, as though she were taking care of a prized possession. It was something she turned to when things got boring. Whether to pack lollipops in your child's backpack or keep the stash separate is your choice. (In the natural foods section of your grocery store, you can find lollipops that are sugar free or made with all-natural ingredients.)

Especially for Airplanes

If you are lucky enough to have a plane with a video player embedded in the seat, you may just have smooth sailing. You are still the parent, so you get to censor any inappropriate TV program. At different times, kids will love to open their little tray tables and spread out the toys in their backpacks. They can even have a little picnic with their snacks.

Inside an airplane, most parents would do almost anything to keep their child from showing his beastly side. You feverishly offer lollipops, chocolate, your wallet. (Hey, if an apple and granola bar work, no need to go to extremes, right?) Sometimes kids get so strung out on airplane rides that what they really need is a drink and a soothing blanket. But before they agree with you, they often must make a requisite amount of ear-piercing noise. Two-year-olds are just phasing out of the intense energy of an eighteen-month-old, but they can easily shift back into overdrive. Here are some ideas for when you desperately need to occupy your two- or three-year-old:

- Take a walk up and down the aisle. (Chances are you've already done this fifty times!)
- Let your child play with ice in a cup. Just be careful he doesn't choke on any large cubes.
- Help a two-year-old use a pen, under your supervision.
- Go to the bathroom and wash your hands. (A toddler interprets this as "play with water.")
- Play some hand games, like "This is the church, this is the steeple. . ." If you don't know any, see the Ongoing Adven-

tures section on page 304 for several good books you can consult in advance.

- Bring out your hidden supply of novel toys: anything truly novel will do. Suggestions include any item on the above list that is not already in your child's backpack. Or how about a ball that lights up when you shake it? No noisemakers on an airplane, though. This is also a good time to try out your personal music player programmed with child-friendly music. The older a child is, the longer she will tolerate the earphones.

The Worst-Case Scenario

If your child is absolutely inconsolable and causing migraines in the passengers around you, carry some foam earplugs in your bag and offer them to your neighbors. If you have the cash, you might even buy them a drink! (Before long, they might even find your little ones charming. . .) Come to think of it, carry these two things in your bag: earplugs for the neighbors, and some ibuprofen for your own pounding head. After any long trip with young children, you and your spouse should try to find time to give each other a quick massage in those tight, tense spots, especially the head, neck, and shoulders. It will help you sleep better.

Especially for Road Trips

Overnights

If you can break up your long trip with overnight stays in a hotel, try to do it. Not only is it exciting for kids to sleep in a hotel, but also going to bed near a regular bedtime will help avoid cranky behavior the next day. Yes, you will break your rules about everyone sleeping in his own bed, but it's a new environment and your kids need to be close to you. When making the hotel reservation, try to request a small fridge for storing milk, drinks, or fruit. Some hotels or motels provide them free of charge.

Pillows

Don't forget to pack a pillow inside the car for your child to rest his head on when he starts nodding off. There's no better way to avoid that awful crooked-neck position you glimpse in the rearview mirror. Don't try to use a jacket for your child's head; nothing substitutes for a pillow. She'll stay asleep longer if she is comfortable and cozy in her toddler seat.

Backpacks

You can liberally fill your child's backpack with toys and activities. See the list above.

Pit Stops

Take a fifteen- or twenty-minute rest stop every two to three hours of driving. Your goals for these stops can be: a potty break, lunch, running around in a grassy area, or going shopping at a store for more activities or trinkets to put in the backpack.

The Grassy Area

Just letting your child run free for a while is a wonderful thing. You too can run, play, tickle, or give a piggyback ride. If you plan ahead, here are a few toys that are ideal during breaks:

- Rocket balloons—if you have a big grassy area at your disposal, pump up these long colorful balloons with the enclosed pump, and let them go screeching into the sky. Your children will love chasing them and trying to find them after they fall back to the ground.
- T-ball and bat, the toddler version—pack this toy if you have space, and bring it out for some exercise at your rest area.
- Soccer ball or plastic golf set—also fun to play with in a grassy area.
- Beach ball—great for playing catch and easy to store.

What if...

It's wintertime?

Nowadays McDonalds offers some fairly healthy food choices. I think they should be commended for this transformation in cuisine. If you go to the McDonald's Web site, you can put in the start and end points of your trip to get a list of every McDonald's Playland or Playplace along your route. Let's face it; on a winter road trip you really don't have many options for letting your kids burn off energy. Just wash their hands after you leave, and you'll feel better about it.

Commonly Overlooked Necessities for Car Trips

- Sanitizing hand wipes or gel
- Regular wipes
- A roll of paper towels
- Extra clothes for children
- Plastic bags for soiled clothes and trash
- Bottles of water

- Emergency snacks like nutrition bars
- The "lovies"—favorite blankets, binkies, or stuffed animals
- Two bath towels, kept handy in the car, to cover up a child about to vomit
- Check this out: a company called Potette makes a portable potty that uses plastic grocery bags as liners (go to Kalencom .com). Excellent for roadside stops.

Games to Play in the Car

- Car or auto bingo—a reusable cardboard game with doors your child can pull shut when she spots a traffic light, a church, a cement truck, etc. (www.alliedbingo.com)
- While looking out the window:
  - Find the letters to the alphabet.
  - Find the letters to your name.
  - I Spy—only when you are driving slowly on back roads!
- Think of five words that begin with. . .
- Sing a song everyone knows but change the words. Then give everyone a turn to change the words. For example, "The big baboon by the light of the moon, was combing his polka-dot hair." "On top of spaghetti, all covered with mashed potatoes. . . "
- Learn some classic children's songs to sing in the car. See the Ongoing Adventures section on page 305 for CD suggestions.
- Have the non-driving adult take out some hand puppets and put on a puppet show.
- The non-driving adult can read a book out loud, if she doesn't get carsick.

Buy a Video Player

These days you can buy a good travel DVD player for under $200. You can find models that hang over the back of the seat and have multiple headphone jacks. If you can swing it, it will pay for itself in hours of stress reduction. Yes, travel is a time for breaking rules, but don't compromise your standards when it comes to video content. Show your children videos that are enriching as well as entertaining. There's no place for violence in media for two- to five-year-olds. As a rule, only let your child watch characters whose behavior you wouldn't mind seeing him copy. See page 305 for a list of terrific videos for little kids.

Reality Check

There's always a moment in every family trip when I seriously wonder, "Is this all worth it?" Had we just stayed home in our cozy routine, I fantasize, there would be no luggage, traffic, cruddy children, or lousy food to deal with. And then I fantasize some more about all the sleep I could be getting at home. When I look back on our family trip to New York City when our triplets were eight weeks old, I think we must have been crazy. Stir-crazy was more like it. We parents deserve a change of scenery, too, even if it takes a strenuous effort to get it. That means expecting and planning for the worst-case scenario. (For example, your child is likely to do one or all of the following while traveling: get sick, spill a drink on the floor, pee in the car seat.) If you plan your adventure with two strategies in mind—entertainment and disaster planning—you can pull off a surprisingly successful trip and create some great memories, too. When you get your little ones safely back home, take credit for the extraordinary feat you have accomplished!

CHAPTER 10

Health and Hygiene

Little kids can do some really disgusting things. They don't necessarily see their own actions as revolting, but we certainly do. I remember a situation with my children that was so stomach turning I can't erase it from memory. We were eating lunch at a pizza restaurant, and our three-year-olds took the lids off their cups in order to drip the liquid from their straws onto the carpet (one of my all-time pet peeves; who invented straws, anyway?). Before we knew what was happening, they pounced on the floor to lick up the drops from the carpet. They got a real kick out of it. I spent the rest of the day stunned, as I tried to figure out how my otherwise normal children could sink so low. Usually I can look back and laugh at all the amazingly gross things my children do—but this occasion still makes me queasy.

Picks Nose

Is your child just "fixing a problem up there" or does he put his finger up his nose to self-soothe? There's a difference. For toddlers, always help them when something in their nose bothers them. You can give your child the choice of who will clean out his nose—you or he.

Let's get a tissue and clean up your nose/mucus. (I always use the
word "mucus" so that my children have a better word at
their disposal than "snot" or "boogers.")

*Is there something in there that's bothering you? I can help you get
it out.*

Can you please get a tissue? Mucus goes in a tissue.

Also teach your child how to blow his nose, by helping to block
one nostril and then the other, if he will let you. Technically you
both must wash your hands after you are done.

___

What if. . .

After your kind offers of help, your child still refuses to clean her
nose or let you clean it?

Sometimes nose cleaning falls in the category of things parents
just have to do. Get your spouse to help hold your child while you
get that stuff out!

If your child has a habit of putting her finger up her nose, then it
becomes an issue of manners or social acceptability, both of which
should be explained to your child more than once.

*There are some things that are not pleasant to see. People don't like
to see your finger in your nose.*

*It's not a good idea to put your finger in your nose—there are
germs in there. And it's not good manners.*

For a persistent problem with a child older than four, you can try
to give him a small soothing object to hold in his pocket, like a large
smooth stone. Establish a special hand signal or a tap on the shoul-

der that means, "Take your finger out of your nose and pick up your stone." Other soothing objects include a large bead on a loop of string; a small stretchy frog or reptile; a large pom-pom (a colorful fringed cotton ball); or a squishy ball. The key is that it's small enough to fit in a pocket, and it's something your child likes to rub or hold. (For smaller children, make sure the object is large enough not to be a choking hazard.)

All kids pick their noses sometime. And yes, we do become more intolerant of it as they get older, because by then they should be more capable of understanding and learning the cultural norms. Fortunately, nose picking is rarely a problem after the age of five. When this bad habit really gets under your skin, so to speak, adopt a neutral, objective, non-scolding voice.

Please get a tissue.
Would you like to see what you look like? Let's go to the mirror.
In our family we have good manners. If you really have to do this,
 you can go somewhere to be alone.

What not to say: do not scold you child in public by demanding, "Take your finger out of your nose! That's disgusting." It's likely to stress him out and increase his need to do it again.

Sucks Thumb

Thumb sucking is a natural extension of the self-soothing behaviors of babyhood. Most children stop their habit between the ages of two and five. After five, the habit usually goes away on its own when your child's peers start noticing it. It's not worth pressuring your child to stop, since you don't need yet another battle in your life, and it will most likely diminish on its own. Dentists don't like thumb sucking—especially vigorous sucking—because it can cause problems in the developing mouth. They even prefer that your child suck on a blanket rather than his thumb, since it's not attached to the body and can be taken away. Luckily most thumb-sucking habits die out before permanent teeth come in. If a habit persists beyond that point, you can offer your child a few ways to help that are listed below. Your intervention should never evolve into discipline or punishment, because this will make your child feel more anxious and further ingrain the habit.

You're still sucking your thumb, and I don't know if you are embarrassed by it, but I have something that can help you stop.

The American Dental Association recommends that you:

- Praise your child for the periods of time when she doesn't suck her thumb, instead of scolding her when she does.
- Involve your dentist in explaining to your child the negative consequences of her habit. Sometimes the voice of an authority resonates with our children more than our own warnings.
- Always involve your youngster in selecting the approach you will take for stopping—a prescription ointment, a bandage or Band-Aid worn on the thumb, a sock to wear over the hand during sleep.
- Since nighttime thumb sucking is the toughest to stop, start with daytime interventions first.
- If your child is a particularly vigorous or intense thumb sucker, make sure to have a dentist examine her to assess the impact it has had on her mouth thus far. This is a good time to have a dentist talk to her about breaking the habit.

See if you notice any patterns when your child sucks his thumb. Does he do it when he is tense, anxious, or needs comfort? Does it happen around transition times? Is there any way to provide support or comfort at these times that would distract your child from sucking his thumb, like a hug, cuddly toy, back rub, cuddle, or book you can read together? Is your older child sucking his thumb out of boredom? Can you engage him in an activity instead?

Spits

Toddlers love to play with their spit. They get a real kick out of watching you squirm when they dangle it out of their mouths. If you get grossed out, all the more entertaining for them! They spit when they're angry; they spit when they're in a silly mood. They like to paint with it. So now you have to come and ruin the party because, of course, it's your job to teach them that spitting is not OK. Rather than expecting, warning, or threatening them to stop cold turkey, tell them about the places where they can spit, for example:

- Outside on the dirt where people don't walk (not on sidewalk or concrete)
- In the toilet
- In the sink
- In the bathtub

When spit ends up in the wrong place, give your child a wipe and have him clean up at least some of it. This logical consequence, like when your child must pick up the food he intentionally drops on the floor, should always follow a spitting episode. She can even clean it up when it lands on other people.

If you see your child starting to spit, ask her:

Where are you allowed to spit? Where is it OK to spit? (Pass her a wipe.)

Occasionally you may want to say:

Saliva (or spit) belongs inside your mouth to help you when you chew food.

Or

Remember when we talked about spitting? People really don't like to get spit on them because it's sticky and messy. And it has germs in it that might make them sick.

Still Uses Pacifier or Bottle

Although it can be quite the bane for a parent, it's physically harmless for a two-year-old to use a pacifier. After age three, like thumb sucking, pacifiers sometimes can affect a developing mouth by causing teeth protrusion, an overbite, or other problems. It was once thought that pacifier use inhibited a child's speech. Today there is not much evidence to support long-term negative effects. Most children will discontinue use of the pacifier on their own, after being exposed to peers at preschool. If you would like to encourage your child to stop, try using only positive reinforcement, and no negative feedback.

- Try a sticker chart, and give a reward for a certain number of minutes, hours, or days spent without a pacifier.

- Get your child involved in an activity, and then smoothly take away her pacifier and tell her you'll put it close by.
- Make it a rule that whenever your child talks, she has to take the pacifier out of her mouth. Shrug and say, *I can't understand you when your mouth is full.* Assist in removing it if necessary.
- Talk to your preschool teachers and make sure they have a plan for gradually removing the pacifier.
- Continuing to use a pacifier at naptime and bedtime is fine.
- When your child starts detaching from her pacifier because she is feeling "bigger," involve her in the process of disposing of it. For example, she can help throw it away, give it as a gift to another baby, or perform any other ritual that gets it out of sight!
- Going cold turkey is not recommended because it is so stressful for everyone, and because the negative effects of pacifier use are usually minimal. But when all else has failed, you might have to do it. Explain what you are doing, and then do it. Don't let the next few days of misery change your mind. Provide lots of comfort and comforting activities in its place.

Is Your Two-Year-Old Still Using a Bottle?

One of my daughters used a bottle until she was two and a half! Why? She was underweight, and it was the only way she would drink milk. We decided she needed that milk more than she needed to act her age. If your toddler is still drinking from a bottle, but doesn't have to, you should start phasing it out, because it's high time to start learning the skills needed to use regular cups.

- First, never let your child go to sleep with a bottle of milk or juice. This practice is known to cause tooth decay, and drilling into a small child's teeth is something you'll want to avoid.

- Don't let your child walk around with a bottle, or use it as if it were a pacifier. There are many reasons for this: it causes tooth decay; it becomes a crutch that could prevent him from engaging in other activities; it's not hygienic; and it prevents the opportunity to develop the motor skills needed to use an open cup. Make it a rule that he must sit down in a chair or at the table when drinking.

- Get him interested in sippy cups and open cups by exposing him to other children who are using them. *You're growing up/getting bigger, and you need a cup for older boys!* Restrict bottle use to prebedtime and prenaptime.

- Involve your child in throwing the bottle away or giving it to another baby in the neighborhood, for example. Once it's gone, it's gone for good. Drinks can be served in sippy cups or open cups from now on.

Security Blanket Use

There is no reason a two- to five-year-old can't have a favorite blanket or stuffed animal to carry around if she wants it. But if it starts to interfere with her activities, or makes her less likely to engage, then you should intervene. Both you and your child's teachers can establish a policy of putting the object away in a special place—a cubby or a shelf, for example—during playtime. She can always return to it later. You can try to cut back on blanket usage by restricting it to "only at home," "only at night," "only in the car," or some combination of these. This is a much more peaceful way to phase out the habit than going cold turkey. You must give a good solid reason for cutting back:

You can have your blanket whenever you ride in the car. But
when we get out, we need to leave it in the car so your hands
and feet will be free to walk/so we don't lose it in the store.
You are growing bigger and don't need to carry this in your hands
all the time. From now on, we are going to keep your blanket
in your bed so you can cuddle with it at night/bedtime.

Most likely she will discontinue her habit when she gets older and
notices her peers do not carry blankets or "lovies" anymore.

Hair Brushing Battles

If you have daughters, welcome to the wrestling match of hair brushing. After the experience of having four girls, I've learned one important truth—there is no need for a youngster to have long hair! Long
hair might look nice to you and fit your image of what a little girl
should look like, but it's not worth it if hair care becomes a horrible
experience each day. As your child approaches ages five and six, she
should be able to take more responsibility for brushing her own hair,
and that will make a world of difference. If your daughter is adamant
about having long hair, make sure she understands your family policy about hair. For example:

- No one can have long hair unless she allows a parent to help
  her brush it (or does it herself) once a day.
- If a child continually struggles to avoid getting her hair
  brushed, a parent can make an appointment for a haircut.
  (Note: Your threats to cut her hair will only work once or
  twice. Then she will stop believing you, and you will have to
  act. Before you get on the phone with the salon, give her a few
  extra chances to comply.)

- If your child's hair is in a mad tangle, and you have the time, offer to wash her hair right then and there. You'll wash all the tangles out with conditioner.
- Use "detangling" conditioner every time you wash her hair. Your use of this product is directly proportional to the peace and quiet you will have when brushing out her hair after a bath.
- For really thick hair, brush it out while the conditioner is still in.
- When brushing out dry hair, use a detangling spray or a spray bottle of water.
- Have someone your child knows (and likes) with long hair (a cousin, teacher, or babysitter) talk to your daughter about how she takes care of her hair. Your daughter will be surprised at the work involved and may decide she doesn't want it after all!
- For very long hair, keep it in a loose ponytail during sleep to minimize tangling.

What if . . .

Your child just doesn't look right in short hair?

How could a little girl not look cute in short hair? This is your battle to pick, or not. You can opt for beautiful but hard-to-take-care-of hair in exchange for less peace and calm in your lives. Remember, shorter hair can always grow out when she gets older and is ready to take on more of the work herself.

What if . . .

You are running really late for school, your child's hair is a mess, and she is not cooperating with your attempts to brush it?

Put her in the car, give her the brush, and tell her it will be her job to work on her hair while you drive to school. If she doesn't do it, or does only part of it, that's the hair she brings to school. Don't argue about it. Offer a barrette or ponytail holder, perhaps, but don't scold. Review your family rules about hair sometime after you get home. (Many teachers are willing to help finish up a morning task with your child upon arrival—like brushing hair or finishing breakfast. You may simply need to ask for their help.)

What if. . .

Your child refuses to let the stylist cut her hair?

Offer her a lollipop (or another rare treat) if she sits for the hair stylist. Also, choose a stylist who will let you sit in the chair with your daughter on your lap. Explain to your child that the haircutter will be making her hair a little shorter, and this will make it a lot easier to brush.

If your child still refuses to cooperate, try buying a pair of blunt-ended haircutting scissors and a spray water bottle and doing it yourself. (You may have to go to a beauty supply store for the scissors.) If you have no idea where to start, stick with trimming the ends to shorten the overall length. It's not going to be perfect, but shorter hair will make grooming a lot easier. Set her up outside, if possible, on a bar stool or high chair. (It will be a lot less messy.) She can wear a painting smock or other cover-up, and play with something in her hands while you work. Two-year-olds will not have much patience, so you must work fast. As children get older, they amazingly comply with longer periods of staying still.

Reality Check

Admit it, you feel like a slacker when you send your child to school with a rat's nest in her hair. The whole world can see you don't even have it together enough to take care of your own daughter's hair. Oh, and here's a classmate (who arrived on time) with long gleaming braids adorned with bows. You imagine this child sitting obediently in her mother's lap as her tangles release under skillful maternal hands. But that's not your daughter. No way. What are you doing wrong?

If you have already engaged in a full-out battle with your child about hair brushing, you should step back and take a break. You must take the misery out of the task. Either give the job to your spouse for a while, let your child go to school with messy hair, or arrange for a haircut. As for the messy hair days, just let them go. Learn to care a lot less about your youngster making a pristine appearance. If you have tried all you can to be helpful but have received only push back, let him or her go. You have done all you can right now.

Teeth Brushing Battles

Nearly all parents have faced teeth-brushing resistance from their kids. And it usually comes after a long, tiring day filled with negotiations in various other battles. Two-year-olds are too young to really understand the importance of brushing their teeth, let alone why they must spit out the toothpaste! Yet we must start this healthy habit early, before they are capable of really serious resistance. Before you throw up your hands and give up, and before you get to the point where you forcibly brush your child's teeth, try to get him interested in lots of different ways.

- When it's time for brushing teeth, do your own first, and make it look like you are having fun. Make a point of spitting out the toothpaste, etc. Tell your child what you are doing. If you have to, brush your teeth with your child every night.

Now I am going to clean all the dirt and food off my teeth. . .
Now my teeth feel so clean and look sparkly white. . .

- Go shopping and let your child pick out his own toothbrush and toothpaste for kids. Some toothbrushes even have flashing lights that pulse for the length of time you brush. Others play music for the recommended one to two minutes of brushing. Some children love the battery-operated brushes with spinning bristles, while others hate them.
- Show him his own teeth in the mirror. Explain that if he doesn't brush his teeth, the little bits of food (or "sugar bugs," as our dentist likes to say) can make holes in his teeth. Brushing helps wash them away.
- Read your child books about brushing teeth. Some have songs you can sing to make the process more appealing; others have interactive toothbrushes your child can use to brush animals' teeth. (See page 304 in the Ongoing Adventures section for book suggestions.)

Brushing teeth falls into the category of things your child has to do. Period. If you have tried everything and are facing a flat refusal every night, you and your spouse can try physical intervention. Hold your child in a bear hug, or with his arms crossed over his chest, and quickly brush his teeth while his mouth is open (as it likely will be). With luck, you will have to do this only once. Use non-fluoride toothpaste until your child learns to spit properly. For really tough cases, you can use an infant product: a plastic cover for your finger with bristles on it. If you are brushing a reluctant child's teeth, stay calm and pretend you are a detached, only-doing-my-job dental professional. Remember the folks who draw blood from children? Feel lucky you don't have to do that! Your battle will be short, and the next time you can say:

Would you like to open your mouth for me, or should I hold you while I do it?

Important note: kids should have their teeth brushed twice a day. Dentists advise parents to brush their children's teeth for them one time per day until age eight, when they can do an effective job on their own. That doesn't mean your child should not be encouraged to brush on his own—it just means you have to go over his work when he's done. For example: an older child can brush her own teeth in the morning, and a parent will do it at night. Or with younger children, you can count the brushes each time: *Five for you and five for Mommy.*

What if. . .

You've had a really tough morning (or night) and you skip brushing your child's teeth?

Every parent skips a brushing now and then, when life gets really hectic. Just remember to brush at the next opportunity.

What if. . .

Your child constantly swallows the toothpaste?

Use a non-fluoride toothpaste and practice, practice, practice. Show him how you spit out toothpaste and water from your own mouth. Have him practice spitting out water into the sink. Don't expect your child to control his urge to swallow until he is closer to age three. Keep practicing and it will pay off.

Oh no, we don't swallow our toothpaste. We spit it out.
Toothpaste is like soap that cleans your teeth, so we have to spit it
out. You can try to spit next time.

Won't Take Medicine

With all the candy-sweet chewables on the market these days, taking medicine has never been more appealing to kids, but parents still face struggles when it's time for their children to take medicine. Younger children are more likely to reject medicine than older children. For reluctant toddlers, you can try to sneak liquid medicine into their drink if you time it right—that is, do it when they are thirsty, and use a small serving of juice so it gets finished.

If you have no success being sneaky, find another way to administer the medicine.

Try telling your child the doctor says she should take the medicine so that she will feel better/stay healthy. Also, many pharmacies now have a variety of flavors they can add to medicine; ask your child to pick out her favorite.

What if . . .

Your child spits out the medicine or chokes?

Then you must go back to sneaking it in her food or drink. Be careful that you have the accurate dose, because if the food is only partially eaten, you no longer have a clear idea of how much she took. Be sure to record what happened. Write down the time, the dosage you hid in the food, and how much of the food was consumed. You will need this data to keep track of how much your child has taken, and to avoid an overdose. Some other favorite delivery devices are ice cream, applesauce, and Jell-O. You can also offer a bribe by promising a small candy or chocolate "chaser" after your child has taken his medicine.

If you are really struggling, ask your pediatrician for more techniques for delivering medicine to your child. They know all the tricks in this department.

Won't Take a Bath

Some kids take a bath once a week, others take one every day—whether they like it or not. Parents can set the rules about bath frequency. Unless he's filthy, a child doesn't need a bath every day, but establishing a regular routine (for example, Sundays and Wednesdays) will make your child more cooperative. Before you resort to forcing a child into the bath, try to lure her there by selling it as an opportunity to play. Act like taking a bath is a really exciting thing to do.

- *Let's go make lots of bubbles in the bath.*
- Bring a container of bubbles to blow in the tub.
- Let her pick out a toy she can try out in the tub (plastic only). Forget the boring rubber duckies. Try something novel, like a funnel, watering can, plastic bowl, plastic cups, a straw for blowing, swimming goggles for older children, balls, and Frisbees.
- Buy soap-based "crayons" or "paint" for bath-time use. Crayola makes fizzy colored pellets to drop in the water that are nontoxic and non-staining.
- Special windup bath toys (frogs, fish, motor boats) are great enticements, especially if they're brought out only at bath time.
- Finger paint with shaving cream. Children can do this in a dry tub first. Then wash off and run the bath water.

In spite of your tremendous sales pitch, your child balks at the idea of a bath?

Happily go off to start the bath.

Well, I'm going to start the bath and I'm going to wind up the frog and watch it swim!

In a few minutes, your child may come to investigate.

Nothing is working and your child will not buy into the bath plan?

Now it is time to get physical. Make sure you have the washcloth handy and all the bubbles you need. First say:

Mommy and Daddy have decided it's time for you to take a bath. Here are your choices: You can climb in by yourself, or I can put you in.

If there's no response:

OK, I'm going to count to three, and then I'm going to put you in. One, two. . .

At this point, do a quick job washing with the washcloth and soapy water. If your child is clawing to get out, take off your clothes and get in with him, if you can. Do this at least once with your child if she is fearful of the water. Try to make it a fun or calming experience, in order to relax her.

Washing and Rinsing Hair

Here's where the volume turns up. Kids hate getting water and soap in their eyes (even though you use tear-free products). The lifesaver of all bath experiences is a handheld sprayer for the shower. You can buy one for under $30 at the hardware store. It's one little thing that can make your life dramatically easier during the toddler-plus years. But if you don't have a sprayer, you can use a cup for rinsing. Either way, encourage your child to look up at the ceiling so that water won't roll in her eyes. Have an older sibling demonstrate, if you can. Children may not get the hang of looking up until around age three. In the past I have put stickers on the ceiling or urged them to find the clouds out the window. Other hair-rinsing strategies:

- Use a special hair-rinsing container with one soft side that you can rest against your child's forehead as you pour.
- Some children agree to wear a rubber bath visor that fits around the crown of their head with hair sticking out the top. The water rolls right off the edge of the visor. (Some children, however, despise these.)
- Since water will get in their eyes, and there's no way to avoid it, show your children that it's no big deal. Instead of jumping for a towel each time, simply wipe the water away with a quick swipe of the fingers, as if you were in a pool. *Just brush away the water.*
- Give your child a dry washcloth to hold over his eyes. This is great for younger children who won't look up. It will only work until it gets saturated, so rinse fast.

Be warned: If you don't use tear-free products, you're in for stinging and yelling, and you'll need to rinse out your child's eyes with fresh water. Not fun.

Note: You can get grooming tasks done more efficiently when you do them all together at bath time or bedtime, when you have your child's attention and, hopefully, cooperation. Getting them all out of the way at once beats stretching out the tasks—nail clipping, ear cleaning, teeth brushing—over the whole day.

Hates Going to the Doctor or Dentist

Prepare your child for their next trip by demystifying the experience. If your child has a tendency to worry, wait until the day before to try out some of these suggestions:

- Read some books about going to the dentist or doctor. There are some terrific ones listed on page 304 in the Ongoing Adventures section.
- Buy a toy doctor's kit. You, the parent, give your child a checkup first, and explain the purpose of what you are doing. (*I'm checking your throat now to see if it's red. I am listening to your lungs. Can you take a deep breath?*) At the end tell him how healthy and strong he's growing. Then reverse roles.
- Buy a battery-operated spinning toothbrush and play dentist at home. Have your child lean back in a chair or couch, just like the dentist's chair. Brush, count her teeth with your finger, floss, and even practice spitting in a cup if you'd like.
- Guess the reward or prize they will receive at the end of an appointment—maybe stickers or colored Band-Aids.
- Offer a trip to the toy store, or other reward, if you know that a shot is involved. What better time to treat your child than

after a scary shot? As the nurse is preparing the shot, distract your child by asking her: *What will you pick out at the store today? What name will you give the baby? Oh, you want a lollipop? OK, what flavor will you pick?*

Things you might like to say about the purpose of your child's appointment:

You're four years old now. Dr. Jane is going to tell us how big you have grown.
She's going to make sure you are growing healthy and strong.
Dr. Davis, the dentist, is going to polish up your teeth and make them so sparkly.
The dentist is going to count up all your teeth and see how big they are growing.

Won't Get Fingernails Clipped

Two- and three-year-olds can be tough customers when it comes to nail clipping. There are times when your child can understand a rational argument—such as, when you don't clip your fingernails, they can scratch you—and comply with your wishes. Other times, it's just an outright battle of wills. In any case, try a little reasoning first to see if it works.

Explain that when nails grow long:

You can accidentally scratch yourself or your friends.
All the sand and dirt from the sandbox can get stuck under there.
See that black line right there? That's dirt.
A fingernail can accidentally break off and pull your skin.

Long toenails can poke holes in your socks. They can make your feet feel uncomfortable and scratchy in your shoes.

- Sometimes little children are intrigued by the nail clipper and want to play with it. Make a deal that you cut three of his nails, and he can cut one of yours (with your help, of course). Or tell him he can hold the clippers (in the closed position and fully supervised) once you have finished cutting his nails.
- Another idea is to give your child a really short video to watch while he sits on your lap. Cover his lap with a towel and clip away. Don't put in a long video, or you will not be able to peel him away after you're done. (See page 305 in the Ongoing Adventures section for video recommendations.)
- Some parents find they can clip nails when their toddler is asleep. This method can work for very deep sleepers.
- If nothing else succeeds, try another day when your child is in a different frame of mind, or is distracted by something else, so that it will no longer seem like a battle of wills.

Note: Some children fight against toenail clipping because they're very ticklish. To avoid touching the foot, wrap a towel around it with just the toes poking out.

Reality Check

The best way for your child to learn good hygiene is to set up a regular routine for things that happen repeatedly—like caring for teeth and hair, and bathing—and following through without being punishing. You are bound to get resistance somewhere in the hygiene spectrum because young children have not internalized the importance of cleanliness. That's when you really have to be calm, creative, and just a tad manipulative. (*Would you like me to clean your nose with the white tissue or the pink fluffy one? Let me take you to a place where you can spit. Here's a special purse you can put your binky in.*) But sometimes, you will have to let something go until the next day. When routine maintenance turns into a battle, just disengage, and assume that other parents and teachers understand perfectly well why your daughter has dirty fingernails today. (And if they don't? Well, they will just have to puzzle it out.)

CHAPTER 11

Particularly Annoying
Refusals

When youngsters give us a flat refusal, they test our ability to be flexible, creative, and calm. Your request may seem entirely reasonable to you, but not to your little rascal. Many times, a little creative persuasion can secure your child's cooperation. But other times your tyke may be too tired or hungry to absorb any information. Some no's you can honor, and some you just can't. When there are no choices or compromises left, you can exercise your right as a parent to do whatever needs to be done.

"No!" is a Favorite Word

When two-year-olds discover the power of saying "No!" they can't help but explore its potential. They want their voice to be heard, loud and strong. When your child is involved in a No! opera, the best thing to do is avoid correcting or contradicting him, to the best of your ability. It's not important that what your child says or believes is accurate or correct at this young age. If you are at a loss for what to do when faced with a wall of no's, simply give a little nod and say, "Mm, hmm," as in "I hear you." That will buy you some time to think about your next move, if any. You should always respect your child's wishes—because we parents shouldn't control every behavior and choice unless there is something dangerous or time critical involved. He doesn't want to get his diaper changed right this second? Fine. If nothing is oozing down his leg, you can wait. Give him a certain amount of time to keep playing before you bring him to the bathroom. *Do you want two minutes or three minutes to play before I clean you up?* Indicate with hands or fingers: *Do you want this much time, or this much time?* Better yet, ask him to come and get you when he is ready. (Not all children will be this cooperative, but you'll never know until you try.) Instead of feeling bossed around, he will feel like he is in control. And control, that magical sensation, makes a child very happy and self-assured. Not every situation is flexible, but when time permits, why not give your child a choice instead of an order?

What to avoid:

It's time to finish breakfast so we can go to school.
"I'm not going to school."
Yes, you are.
"I'm nooooot!"
You have to go today—it's not a choice.
"I am NOT going. I am staying home today. (Cries.)"

If you decide you really need to move your child from "No" to "Maybe," you can try some of the following, in order of urgency and time investment:

- Use silliness or humor.

This works best on younger kids. Pretend to put her clothes on you and announce that you will wear them to work. Start to put her shoes on her hands. Really, there's no end to the silliness you can invent on the spot. The idea is to make her laugh enough to change gears.

• Talk to the air.

This is another light approach. Talk to the air, or to another person nearby. This is not meant to be mocking or making fun of your child.

> *Oh dear, Matthew is not putting his shoes on. I guess that means*
> *we can't go to the library now. I guess we will miss reading all*
> *the dragon books. . .*
> *I wonder why Bevin keeps saying no. I guess I will go upstairs and*
> *read the fire truck book by myself. . .*
> *You silly goose, you want to go to school in your pajamas?*

• Redirect.

Try to focus his attention on something along the way he might enjoy doing.

> *Let's go ride on the elevator now. Do you want to push the but-*
> *ton?*
> *Let's go outside and see if we can find some birds. Do you think*
> *they are eating worms?*

(There's no end to the exciting things you can dream up when your child is participating in the adventure.)

• Keep moving forward.

In many cases, if you subtly move your child along through the paces, she might chant "No no no," but will actually follow along. For example, while you are nodding Uh-hum to your child, acknowledging her no's, you might be able to slip her raincoat on without protest. The key word here is "might," as in, you might be able to get away with it.

- Give a choice that doesn't have a "yes" or "no" answer. Enough creative manipulation, now you must get down to business.

    You can walk to the tub by yourself, or I can carry you. Which one do you want?
    Would you like to wear the sandals or the sneakers today?

- Count down.

As a last resort, tell your child you will count to a number and then you will pick him up and do whatever it is you must do.

Won't Get into Car Seat

After you have exhausted all of your standard enticements about where you are going, and what you will do at your destination, you might try a few of these:

- Offer a snack.

Keep pretzels in your glove compartment. After your child gets clicked in to her seat, she can have some. It's a harmless bribe that children never seem to get tired of. Don't forget to rotate the snacks.

- Stay put.

The reasoning goes like this: You can't drive the car until everyone's buckled in, so you will just have to wait in the car together for as long as it takes. For this tactic to be successful, you should act calm and willing to sit in the front seat and meditate (in your own way) until your children finish selecting their seats. This can be hard to do if you are a naturally anxious or tightly wound person, and can't tolerate being fifteen minutes late to wherever you are going. You might even say out loud but to yourself: *I guess we'll have to stay here in the car and miss playing at the park.* Keep looking at your magazine and act indifferent. Children can't tolerate inaction for very long, and will eventually get into their seats.

- Stand outside.

Roll down the windows a bit, lock the doors, and stand outside with your back toward the car. Wait here for a few minutes while your child squirms inside the car. This is a good time to take a breath and laugh or roll your eyes at the pickle you are in. Remind yourself that it will pass. Then get back in the car and comfort your child for a few seconds, if needed.

Please get into your seat so we can go.

- Use appropriate physical intervention.

If you are not in a position to wait it out or find diversions for your child, you may have to pick her up, put her in the car seat, hold her in, and fasten the buckle. (See page 286, "Using Physical Force on Your Child," for details.)

Won't Get Dressed

- Try humor. Pretend to put the clothes on you. Or pretend to put the pants on the wrong part of her body. Your child may laugh at you and then show you she can do it the right way.
- Offer a compromise. *You put on your shirt, and I'll put on your pants. You put on one shoe, and I'll put on the other.*
- Set a timer. Give your child about fifteen minutes to get dressed. After it rings, you should pack up her clothes in a bag and, if you're on your way to child care, bring her out in her pajamas. Do not get huffy or frazzled by her stubborn behavior. Remember, little kids are supposed to act like this! And you should act like it's part of your ordinary routine, too. You will get more cooperation if you have a little family meeting the night before and explain what you are going to do with the timer in the morning. You can frame it as a little adventure, a game, or a low-key race against the clock. As for going out in her pajamas, try to accept it as "one of those crazy things little kids do." In other words, don't sweat it. If you bring a bag of clothes along with you, your child can decide when she's ready to change later.
- If dressing in the morning is a huge problem for your child, it could be that he is overwhelmed by all the choices. Revamp his clothing by putting only four mix-and-match outfits in his drawers and storing the others in a sealable bin under his bed. (This is for you to access, not your child, so store it when he's

not looking.) If there's too much pressure in the morning, ask or help him to pick out clothes at night and lay them out on the floor. Kids are usually ready to do this, with your help, around age three.

⎛ **What if. . .** ⎞

What if your child picks out clothes at night but refuses to wear them the next day?

Try not to reopen the whole issue; present just one or two choices as alternatives. If you're not in crisis mode, ask what the problem is with last night's selection. You might get an informative answer, or it could be that your child simply changed his mind. If the process is getting dragged out, consider having a small logical consequence as a result of morning mind changing.

Well, we had to change your choice of shirts from last night, and now there is no more time for reading a book/playing catch before we go. Maybe tomorrow you'll decide to stick with your choice so we have more fun time in the morning.

If you're in crisis mode, and your child is refusing to make a choice, say calmly:

It's time to get dressed now. I need you to decide which clothes to wear while I count to ten. If you don't pick out some clothes, I will do it for you. One, two, three. . .

If your child is still digging in her heels and won't let you dress her, remember you can always pick her up and carry her to the car

in whatever she is wearing. Bring her clothes and shoes in a separate bag.

What if. . .

Your child dresses herself in a hideous combination of battling stripes
and clashing colors? You can't let her out of the house looking like
that! Or can you?

A potential battle is at your fingertips—one you do not need to
have. Let your child wear whatever she fancies. Think about it: when
in your life can you get away with dressing yourself without any con-
cern for what other people will think? Only during the first years of
childhood, before we start internalizing the cultural and social messages about proper dress. Just be glad your child dressed herself! That
is a tremendous show of autonomy, and you don't want to crush the
positive feelings she has about herself for doing it on her own. If you
feel like distancing yourself from your youngster's fashion faux pas,
you can smile and say:

> *Guess what Karen did today? She picked out her own clothes and
> got dressed all by herself.*

Or

> *Karen really likes to pick out her own clothes.*

If clashing patterns really offends your sense of decorum, try to
exert control over the clothing that goes into the drawers in the first
place (by giving her only three or four mix-and-match outfits that are
visually compatible), rather than urging your child to change clothes
once she has dressed.

Your child seems to be genuinely sensitive to the clothing on her skin, complaining about scratchiness or tags rubbing on her neck?

This is a legitimate complaint that needs to be accommodated. Feel free to cut tags out of clothing, as long as the remaining bits don't create more irritation. Provide loose-fitting cotton shirts, and let your child wear the same three or four over and over again, if he wants. Don't force variety of dress; it's more important to make sure your child is comfortable. And if that means getting her favorite shirt out of the dryer, then so be it. You can also take your child shopping to find clothes that feel good. Overall, soft brushed cotton is the best choice. However, it's not always the fabric content but the feel of the fabric that matters most.

Won't Eat Breakfast

There is no point in battling with your child to get her to eat in the morning. Maybe she's just not hungry yet, or maybe she can't decide what to eat. There are only a few things you can do that won't amount to pressuring or bossing her.

- Give her a choice of two breakfast foods. *Do you want cereal or waffles?*
- If you think dawdling or distraction is keeping your child from eating, try to set a timer. Tell your child that when the timer goes off, you will clean up the breakfast dishes.
- This is the one I resort to most: put a waffle, cheese stick, or granola bar in a bag and bring it in the car if you're on your way to school. You can't pack up uneaten yogurt or cereal, so

you have to grab alternatives that need little or no preparation. If your child still does not want to eat in the car, give the snack to her teacher or caregiver to hold for later.

- If your child decides not to eat, try not to be swayed by her subsequent laments of being hungry. Don't quickly resort to a snack. (Of course, give snacks at the regular times.) You can try to serve lunch a little earlier that day, but it's important for you not to give in to the whining immediately. Wait a little while (within reason) so your child can understand what it feels like when she skips a meal. You can say:

Wow, it's no fun to be hungry, but breakfast is all cleaned up. Lunch (or snack) will be ready in a little while.

Won't Clean Bedroom

Been there. . .

You can't walk across your four-year-old's bedroom floor anymore because it's strewn with puzzle pieces, unfinished artwork, dirty clothes, books, and a renegade group of rocks. You have asked her to clean up after she finishes playing. You have even given her a box to put things in. Still, nothing gets done. When you ask her again, she pouts and goes to a corner of the room to play with something. You start to wonder if this is a sign of an attention problem.

You know your child is capable of picking up objects and putting them into boxes; in fact, she mastered that skill as a baby. Isn't this what cleaning a bedroom is all about? So, why isn't she able to do it now? Somehow, cleaning a room is so much more than the sum of its scattered parts. Two- to five-year-old children need help cleaning up a room. It is overwhelming to them, and they don't know where to begin or how to separate the components. They need a grown-up to join them. Your expectations about how much they can do should be pretty low with two-year-olds, but as they get older, their fraction of the workload can increase.

- First, reduce the amount of stuff in the bedroom. The younger the child, the less overall stuff should remain. Keep the high-frequency use items, and put the rest into storage bins and get it out of sight. Force yourself to store or give away the possessions that get very little use, even if they were gifts.

A child may feel it is an invasion of her privacy to see her parents rifling through her stuff. You can involve her by deciding together what stays and what goes. However, you, the parent, probably will have to make some unilateral decisions just to get the job done.

- Make an announcement about the cleanup project. Say you are planning a weekly cleaning project on Saturday mornings. Remind your child (or children) the night before.

Tomorrow morning we are going to clean up your bedroom together before you go out to play.

You can explain the importance of cleaning a bedroom:

We all have to learn how to clean up our rooms so we will have room for friends to come and play.

*We have to take care of our toys so that they don't break and we
can use them again.
We have to put away our toys so that we don't lose them.*

There are some great books about cleaning up; children are fascinated by stories about other kids' messiness. (See page 304 in Ongoing Adventures for book recommendations.)

- Ask your child where she would like to store certain items.
  Provide bins, boxes, or baskets labeled with tape. Or, if desired, you can tape photos or pictures of the toys on the outside of the bin.

Give your child a discrete, limited task to do. For example, she
can put the dolls in a specific box, while you put the books back on
the shelf. Parents have to be actors all the time, so act like you're enjoying it. Make the activity upbeat, or turn it into a game, if you have
the energy to be a little silly.

A two-year-old might fill up only one or two boxes. An older
child can do perhaps three or more before getting irretrievably distracted. But again, as they get older, they will not only buy into the
idea that it's part of taking care of oneself and one's own space—
they might actually do it on their own sometimes. That's not to
say they will be consistent about it! Oh, no. Parents have to uphold
the weekly plan.

- For all those "collections," buy a small stack of plastic drawers.
  Put one collection in each drawer, and the number of drawers
  will be your limit. This will work for beads, rocks, coins (too
  small for two-year-olds), spinning tops, and more.

- Young children need adult direction and participation at the end of playdates. Near the end of the visit, announce to the children that it will be time to clean up in five minutes or other amount of time. Don't worry if the job is not thorough; any amount of effort from the children is better than none. Here's the challenge: get them to participate in the cleanup before they are at the end of their rope, or you will have whiny, tired little people who will not cooperate.

Before a playdate, give your child the chance to remove important or special toys he does not want to make available to his friends.

What do you not want your friend(s) to play with today?

"Sharing" is a very abstract word, so use it only if your child is old enough to really understand it. (See page 42 for more on sharing.)

What if...

Your child makes a good show of sulking and moaning, as if the act of cleaning a room is sucking the energy right out of her?

Acknowledge that it's hard to work on a cleanup project when you are tired. Take this premise and go with it:

You look so tired. I find it really hard to clean up when I'm tired. We are going to stop the project right there, so you can rest in your bed and take a nap.

Put the whole endeavor on hold, take a potty break, bring in the comfort items, turn out the lights, and see how far you can get toward the proposed naptime.

Won't Make the Bed

If you are really on the ball, you can model making your child's bed every morning. Then get him involved, whether it's straightening a corner for a two-year-old or having your five-year-old pull up the sheet or blanket. If you do this every day, chances are your child will fall into the routine if given parts of the job to do. If you are not all that fastidious, at least get your child to help make the bed during bedroom cleanup time.

What if. . .

You are so tired of cleaning the bedroom over and over that you have half a mind never to touch it again?

Theoretically, a child's bedroom is his domain, and he should be able to do what he wants with it. Besides, won't the natural consequences of not being able to walk, play, or find things teach him the importance of neatening his room? Yes to all of the above. If you go this route, though, you have to be a purist and really, really not care about social expectations. And you really have to refrain from bailing out your child when he can't find something. Our recommendation would be not to take this approach until your child is older than five, when he has more capacity to understand the consequences.

Been there. . .

After your three-and-a-half-year-old son mastered dressing and undressing, you bought him a nice laundry basket for his room. He quickly learned to put his clothes in the basket after taking them off. And you've already taught your five-year-old that the clothes she wants to wear again should be put into one of her drawers. (You don't even ask her to fold them!) In fact, you've even had a practice session with your kids, and everyone really seemed to understand the drill. But what do you see day after day as you walk into the kids' bedroom? A carpet of clothes. Are small children incapable of doing this minor chore? Is nagging the only way to get the job done? Should you bribe them? Is it a losing battle?

I don't think two- and three-year-olds care one iota about a clean bedroom. As for four- and five-year-olds, well, they are just starting to understand that it's important because Mom and Dad say it is. If you want compliance, you will probably have to join your child in a clothes-picking-up session every day or so, much like the bedroom-cleaning strategy above. As your child approaches age five, you can give him reminders and a little pep talk to get him motivated, but you still may have to work in parallel. What you really want is your child to pick up his clothes because he enjoys having a clean room. But this value probably will not develop until he is much older. That's not to say there aren't inducements to get your child to pick up his clothes.

- Positive reinforcement: it goes without saying that the best way to win your child's cooperation is with encouragement and a little praise. If words aren't enough—and they probably won't be for this job—you can try to hang a calendar in your child's room and put a sticker on the days she picks up her clothes. Make sure you have the packet of stickers taped onto the back of the calendar, because your efforts will lapse if you don't have the stickers at your fingertips.

- Another type of positive reinforcement is to make a chores chart, and have your child check a box or make a mark on it after he picks up his clothes, makes an effort to pick up the playroom, puts his dishes in the sink, etc. It's like converting the chores into a game. Don't include too many chores, and list only those he already knows how to do.

- Give your child a piggy bank. Each time she picks her clothes off the floor, and puts them where they belong, you can drop a penny in her bank. Your child should not be able to open it until it's full, at which point you can decide how the money can be used. Make a counting game out of it, for example, and then take a trip to your bank to turn it into larger coins or dollar bills. This is a kind of low-grade allowance. If, however, you frown upon allowances, this is not the right option for you.

- Tie the clothing pickup to another event. For example, your child can go outside (or get out the finger paints) after he has picked up his clothes. (Definitely don't hold food, drink, hugs, or any other necessity hostage until the chore is done.)

- For younger children, limit the clothes picking up to placing pajamas under a pillow or hanging them on a hook. Then progress from there.

- The logical consequences for not picking up clothes are, of course, running out of clean clothes and/or not being able to locate the clothes you want. Unfortunately, this kind of lesson won't be effective until age seven or eight.

- Try saying "Thank you!" for a job well done. Sometimes we parents get so focused on crossing off everything on our to-do lists that we forget our good manners. Saying thanks not only teaches good manners but also lets our kids know we appreciate their efforts.

Can't Give Up the Artwork?

Those lovely, messy little offerings seem to collect in all the wrong places around the house. Who can contain them? Where do you put them? Why do we feel so guilty about throwing them away?

First of all, you can't save everything. (Well, technically you can, if you have a big attic, or want to rent an outside storage facility.) For practical reasons, though, we have to get used to the idea of letting go of some drawings or paintings. That means throwing them away. (Or recycling them, depending on whether or not there are little objects glued on.)

Take a daily, weekly, monthly, or even yearly approach. Each day, let your child hang up her artwork, using either magnetic clips on the fridge, or clips on a string mounted to a wall or mantle. You might have another display idea, such as a horizontal wall-mounted wire with clips (available at stores like Ikea and Pottery Barn Kids). Let a few pieces collect under the same clip. Instead of letting the clutter accumulate on your refrigerator, pick one small wall in your house (usually in a kitchen or playroom), paint it with magnetic paint, and you have an instant magnetic board to hang drawings! I saw this at a birthday party once, and it looked great.

Once a week, get rid of half the artwork. Put the date on the saved items (this is important) and place them in a storage bin or a flat portfolio folder. You can try to enlist your child's help in making the selections, but chances are he will not want to part with anything. In that case, you make the decisions. What are your criteria? Think of what you might appreciate seeing ten years from now, and what your child might appreciate seeing later in life. You will feel better about tossing artwork if you have a little discussion about the work first.

Examples:

Can you tell me about this drawing? Is there a story that goes
   with it?
Is it a design or a picture? What do these lines represent?
How did you get this color to spread out? Why did you put this
   here?
What were you thinking about when you painted this?
Where did this color come from? Is it paint or crayon?

You can try to involve an older child in the weeding process by asking her to help select the number of drawings to keep.

These three are similar in color/design; which one do you want
to keep?

If you are working on your own, and are really on the ball, you can revisit the art bin once per month, and weed out about half of the work once again. If you are like me, however, you'll probably revisit the bin only once a year. Try to save about twelve pieces of artwork per year per child; that's a reasonable annual goal.

What if. . .

Your child wants to keep everything and is distressed when a piece of artwork is missing?

The unilateral approach to tossing artwork (after it has been displayed or at least acknowledged) is based on the assumption that your child won't remember every drawing, and therefore won't miss the ones that get weeded out. There are exceptions to this rationale. Some children are very attached to their creations, and remember almost every one. In this case, the child's sense of ownership should not be violated. There are creative ways of grouping artwork for long-term display or storage.

- One mom I know collects a group of drawings made within a certain time frame, punches holes in the edges, and binds the pages together with yarn to make a kind of album.
- If you are handy, you can display drawings under the transparent top of a coffee table, or frame them (with real frames or paper ones) and have your child give them to relatives.
- If you have a good computer setup at home, consider scanning the artwork (or take a picture of your child holding the artwork) and store it on a disk or drive. Don't forget to include the date and any other commentary.
- My favorite solution comes from my husband: store all the artwork in a big plastic bin and drop it off at your child's house when he's twenty-five!

Trouble with Transitions

On the mornings you get out the door in a civilized, happy way, you swear it's a good harbinger for the rest of the day. Most kids, however, can't suddenly move from one frame of mind to another just because you want them to. They need to be prepared, and reminded ahead of time what's going to change.

When you have a specific time you need to be at work or at the airport, you need to set pretty strict cutoff points for getting ready. If you are just going to the playground, you might decide to be flexible and give your child more time to finish whatever it is he is doing. It's your judgment call. There are some pretty basic ways to signal to your child that a transition is coming.

- Give a ten-minute warning. Some children also need a five- and a one-minute follow-up reminder. For two- or three-year-olds, you may want to indicate the time with your fingers—*You have this much time to play, and then it will be time to clean up.*
- If your child will not let go of a project he is working on, offer to put a "Reserve" sign on it so no one will touch it, and he can return to it when he gets home; or offer to put it on a high shelf, a reassurance that it will be kept safe from siblings.
- Ask your child to pick out a special toy or stuffed animal to take along with him. You can think of it as a "transition toy."
- Keep a special box of toys inside the car, for use only when on the move. One great idea is a little cassette player or headset and earphones for playing parent-approved music. Some good car toys include car bingo, sunglasses, kaleidoscopes, pinwheels, and removable sun-catcher stickers (or window clings) for decorating the windows. To encourage your child to get out the door, remind him of what he can play with in the car. (You may have to rotate the items in the special box when your children become too familiar with them.)
- If your child is whining and resisting, and you must leave, acknowledge his feelings first:

You really want to finish your railroad track. I understand. But we have to go now.
Would you like me to pick you up, or would you like to walk by yourself?

If you receive no answer:

You don't want to decide, so I will count to five, and then pick you up.

Disengage and stop giving alternatives. Don't lecture or explain anymore. Do your best to stay calm and unaffected when you carry him to the car. Hum as you remind yourself that you are just doing your job . . . and your child is doing his!

Dawdling

Perfected by the age of five, dawdling raises the question of whether children intentionally want to dismiss us, or they are just blissfully unaware that the whole world is waiting for them. Your child's most likely excuse will be that she is busy doing something and doesn't want to stop. And it will be the truth. Children's powers of concentration improve as they get older. Being able to focus intently on a task is a wonderful thing. It's just too bad the focus seems to intensify when we are trying to get out the door, or when it's time to clean up the playroom. Dawdling is here to stay; it's part of a young child's job description. So we parents have to tolerate a certain amount of it, even though it can make us feel like we are talking to a wall. Always start out gently but firmly when you try to switch your child's point of focus. You can use the same pointers listed above under "Trouble with Transitions."

Reality Check

Why do we parents need to be so darn creative just to get from point A to point B? Can't we just say "No" or "Get in the car, please" and that's that? A terse refusal or direct order might work on occasion, but it is more likely to start a verbal tennis match between you and your child. In authoritarian families, a single "No" is very effective because it is usually accompanied by the threat of physical punishment. Clearly, we do not aspire to this style of parenting. So we are obligated to assess each refusal on a case-by-case basis and figure out if we can honor it; and if we can't, to at least explain why. After that, we must do what needs to be done.

CHAPTER 12

Miscellaneous Bugaboos

Sometimes the best responses to our kids' puzzling behaviors are the most counterintuitive. We reverse a "no" decision and give our little one what she wants just to stop the noisy complaining. Or we might come down hard on our child for lying or stealing because important moral lessons are at stake. Remember that two- to five-year-olds need time, and many chances, to learn right from wrong. In this age range, heavy issues are best handled with understanding and explanation, rather than punishment. Little kids are happily oblivious to their own behaviors most of the time. There are, of course, small things they do that drive you mad, like running away from you at the park or changing their mind all the time. Because they love to do things over and over, it's easy for youngsters to get stuck in a behavioral loop, at which time they might need an adult to help them out. This is achieved somewhere on the spectrum of calmly explaining why a behavior has to stop (and redirecting the child) to setting a specific limit and following through with it.

All by Myself: Stubborn Independence

Those wonderful, huffy, self-righteous two-year-olds! You have to love it when a tot wants so badly to put on his sock by himself that he ends up writhing on the floor in frustration but still won't accept your help. They are so determined to be bigger and act bigger that they will pursue their goals against all odds.

As tedious as it may seem, it's a good idea to support these displays of independence (even when she wants to open and close the door three times). Not only is this the way children learn new skills, but acquiring these new skills will launch them into a new developmental phase. For example, once your child learns to zip his coat, he can start to help others zip their coats. And mastering something on his own will give him the confidence to take on more challenges.

When your youngster is attempting a new task, avoid being the overbearing or over-correcting parent. Give him the space to get it wrong and be frustrated. You can stand nearby and offer help, but don't give it without permission.

Would you like some help?
How about if I put on one shoe, and you put on the other one?
It's tricky at first, isn't it?
I'll help you put your toe in the sock, and then you can pull it up.

If your child abandons his valiant attempt and walks away in frustration, don't try to change his mind. He'll return to it another day.

In general, if he loses control out of frustration, and you have to intervene, show him that you respect his independence by casting yourself as the "helpful parent."

I can help you calm down by holding you on my lap for a little while.

I didn't see who had the toy first, but I can help you by giving you each the same amount of time to play with it.

You had an accident; that's OK. Mommy and Daddy are here to help you learn.

I know you really want to hit today, but we don't hit our friends because that hurts. I can help you find something else to hit, like a pillow.

Whining, Harping, Hounding, Insistence/Persistence

Shouldn't we all be passionate about the things we want in life and fight for them? Our kids know all about this; they're out in front with their demands, all the time. Whining is an effective way for your child to get attention and get what he wants—that is, if you give in. The king of all parental peeves, whining tests our ability to stay our course in the face of an exquisite kind of torture.

Reality Check

If you feel the urge to pull out your hair when your child is whining, you are not alone. Whining is like having a car alarm go off inside your house as you frantically look for the keys. The incessant siren has a way of blocking out all rational thought and eating away at your self-control. When you give in to whining, you step onto a slippery slope. Children learn so fast what it takes to get you to change your mind: all they have to do is drive you bananas. Don't fall into this trap. If whining is getting out of hand at your house, and skillful ignoring doesn't work, you must adopt a no-tolerance policy. Give your child a countdown to stop his whining, and if he doesn't stop, give him a time-away without negotiating or compromising. No exceptions. Does this mean we parents can't ever change an initial "No" to a "Yes"? No one's perfect, and when you are pulled in many directions, it's sometimes hard to think straight about the boundaries you are setting. But too much compromising looks like a cave-in, and teaches your child that her whining is effective. If you do change your mind in the middle of setting limits, there are two things to remember. First, don't do it often! Second, always explain to your child that you have changed your mind and why. Otherwise he will think it was his whining that did it.

Some ways to respond to whining:

- Main rule: don't give in to whining. Expect your child to change his tone before you respond or fill the request.

Can you say that in a conversation voice, please?
I don't speak to people who whine. (If your child keeps whining, go about your business but do not respond.)

- When he switches to a reasonable tone, make a point of telling him you liked hearing it.

Ah, that sounded so much nicer.
I'd be happy to get you a spoon, because you asked so politely.
I like the way you said that.

- Give examples of a "conversation voice" and a "whining voice." Ask your child if she can identify each one. Then ask her if she can demonstrate each voice.

- Record her whining on a tape recorder. At another time when she is calm, and you are discussing the topic of whining, play back the recording so she can hear what she sounds like.

- Sometimes your child may correct his tone of voice, but you still can't fill his request right away because you are tied up with something else. In this case, describe a specific time frame when you will do it. If the whining continues and morphs into hounding, tell your child that you will have to remove him from the room. Count to five out loud before you do it.

Yes, you can have some milk. When I am done cleaning up the dishes, I will give you a cup of milk.
Yes, after you put on your pajamas, I will read you that book.

What if . . .

Your child is hounding and pounding while you are driving, so you are unable to give him a time-away?

- Try to use humor to diffuse the hounding. When a child is demanding something you already explained you don't have—"I want water now!"—try this: *I know you want water right now. But wait a minute. Do I have a sink in this car?* (Pretend to look around.) Or when a child demands different shoes to wear or something specific to eat: *Do I have a shoe store in the glove compartment? Do you think there's a grocery store in the trunk? Do I have an ice cream store in my purse?*

- To cut off the back-and-forth, be more direct and firm in your response, but do not yell. For example, if your child is begging and hounding for more crackers, after you have already given

her plenty, you can say: *I said no more.* Then try to tune out
the protesting.

- If your child's ranting escalates to deafening noise, try a sidewalk time-out, as described on page 19.

What if . . .

Your child is doing so much groaning and whining that she can't hear
you talking to her?

This is my favorite question. "What's the point of all this talk, talk,
talking if my child can't hear me anyway?" Here's a fact to remember:
You can't negotiate with a child who is at the end of his rope.

I can't help you until you calm down.

Disengage, read a book, look at a magazine. After a while you
might say:

Would a drink of water help you?

If the whining and moaning does not abate, give a warning or
count, then pick her up and carry her to the time-away room.

Obsessive-Compulsive-Like Behaviors

Before I could leave her bedroom, my two-year-old daughter had to
have her blanket smoothed flat across her chest (no bumps) and the
top edge folded down about two inches. If I didn't get it right, she
would shriek. Also before I left, she made me orient her rubber duck
at a certain angle on her table. ("No! The other way! A little more!")
Around the age of two and a half, her obsessions were getting even

zanier. I started to get worried. Then her preschool teacher told me the story of the time that she, the teacher, ruined a toddler's entire day because she peeled a banana for her instead of letting the child do it herself. There was no recovery from that one.

In short, most toddlers go through an obsessive phase, marked by fetishes, repetitions, and hoarding behaviors. They might not grow out of it for a year or two, but it should ease up a bit by age four or five. If you have a good sense of humor, use it! Write down these zany behaviors, or take pictures of the infamous purple rubber shovel your child carries around everywhere, because it will be hilarious to revisit them five or ten years from now. (And you will not remember it later, no joke.)

How should we respond? If the behaviors do not interfere with the functioning of the family, accommodate your child as much as you can bear it. He is just trying to wrest some control over his life and environment, and it probably makes him feel secure when certain things are in the right place. The blue block must always be in the tall can? OK. You like the door open only this much? Uh-huh. If the obsessions become a disruption or great burden, try to explain to your child why his need is interfering, and suggest that you strike a deal.

I moved this doll around five times, and now I am getting tired. Now you will have to put it where you want.

I will arrange it one more time, and then I am all done.

You really want to carry all of these toys in your hand, but that's slowing you down. Why don't you use this bag from now on?

I know you really want the blue blanket tonight, but someone spilled milk on it, and it's stinky. I have to wash it. How about you go to the closet and pick a different blanket for tonight? Then tomorrow you can have the blue blanket back.

(If your child's attachment to an object, like a blanket or pacifier, is interfering with social interactions, see page 202.)

If your child is still exhibiting odd ritualistic behaviors by age six, definitely mention it to your pediatrician.

Changes Mind All the Time

Children's palates and interests change constantly, and so do their minds. Of course we try to accommodate our little chameleons as much as possible, but only up to a point. If you see a pattern developing, where your child is changing her mind a lot just to delay sitting down for dinner or getting in the bath, for example, then recognize this as her way of exploring how much she can control or manipulate the situation. You have to admire her for trying, even though you'll need to set limits. The other thing to remember is that too many choices tend to overwhelm young children, causing them to have strong reactions, from mind changing to paralysis to real distress. Help your child by limiting the number of choices. For example:

Clothing

Hard as it may seem in today's world of irresistible kids' clothing, your child will do much better if she has four or five mix-and-match outfits in her drawers. Store the others away in a bin and rotate them through the drawers when necessary.

Food

Mealtime will be more peaceful if you give a child one of two choices. This is true at the ice cream store as well. At dinnertime, the second choice should be a standard, easy-to-make food that you know she likes, such as a PB&J or cheese sandwich. (For more about eating and mealtime behaviors, see Chapter 4.)

Material Objects

After my children got flu shots last year, I told them, "You can pick any toy under $10." I didn't get out of the store until an hour later due to all their mind changing. Stores are tough for kids. The next time, I selected a specific "prize" ahead of time. So, after haircuts, the children could choose any color balloon they wanted. The idea is to narrow down the options.

Seating Arrangements

To put an end to musical chairs, you can enact a first-come-first-served policy, where the first child who arrives at the car or dinner table can choose any seat.

> *I'm sorry; Donna was ready first, so she got to pick out her seat. You can try again tomorrow.*

Alternatively, you can indicate ownership of a seat as long as the seat is labeled in a way that everyone can see it. A placemat at the dinner table or name tag on a car seat can work.

If name tags don't work, and the survival-of-the-quickest strategy creates conflict, make a schedule for who sits where on which days. For example, Nancy sits behind the driver on Monday, Wednesday, and Friday; and John sits there on Tuesday, Thursday, and Saturday. Like any policy worth upholding, you will have to write it down and display it on the wall or bulletin board. (Also see the Family Policy Book on page 36.)

How much mind changing can you bear? Every parent has his own limit but after, say, two or three changes, you can rein in your child:

You only get one more change; that's all.
I've given you several different spoons. The last choice is the one
   you need to use.

Or

I've offered you several different spoons. If you want to change it,
   it's your turn to do it by yourself.
(Only say this if you know—or expect—that your child can do it on his own. But, if you know your child can do it, don't help in the first place; encourage him to do it.)

Or

No more changing spoons. You may have the green spoon or the white spoon. ("I want the purple spoon!") *That's not a choice right now.*

Been there. . .

At a picnic, someone brings out Popsicles for all the kids. Your child is handed a green one, before noticing the red and pink ones, and starts whining that he wants one of those. Should you ask the host if she has more? Should you offer to get your child a raspberry one the next time you go grocery shopping?

There is no harm in asking the host for a trade on the Popsicle if there are other Popsicles left, and if it doesn't start a cascade of other kids changing their minds. Inevitably, however, you will face a situation when all of the items have been handed out, there's no room for choices anymore, and your child balks.

Here are some ways to handle the situation:

In our family we have a saying. It goes: You get what you get and you don't get upset. That means when a friend gives us a treat, we keep the one we get, and we say thank you. It's best to explain this concept in advance, and give examples, rather than trying to teach it in the moment.

You can offer to buy his favorite color Popsicle the next time you go shopping. You might even take out a little notebook and jot it down.

Can you remind me what color you want so I'll know the next time I'm going to the grocery store?

Without laying it on too thick, you can point out what is unique about the treat he chose originally.

Is that bright green like your socks? I bet that tastes yummy.

If your child simply does not recover from his disappointment, it might be time to put the pop in the freezer and take him for a walk until he calms down. You can also say: *If you don't want this one, I can see if a friend wants to eat it.*

Notice when your child tends to change her mind a lot and try to head it off the next time. This takes some advance thinking. For example, if your child has a "bowl thing," then before you pour the cereal, ask your child if he wants a blue or red bowl. The pink or purple socks? Sandals or sneakers?

Loses Things

Like fighting, losing things is part of the background noise at my house. Whenever you let goody bags, holiday gifts, or hand-me-downs into your house, something is bound to get lost. Does this have to happen? The "I Can't Find" epidemic is simply a function of having too much stuff, and no place for it to go. Here are some ways to dig yourself out:

- Allow only five to ten toys in the play area. (It's up to you whether your child helps you choose them.) Keep some of the leftover toys stored away in bins. You don't have to keep everything. Find ways to donate to charity, recycle, or store in limbo. (To enlist your child's help, see page 228.)
- Whether it's bins, boxes, or shelves, give each category of toy a place to live. You can get as detailed as you want, such as a box for chalk and a box for paints, or you can group all art supplies together in one big bin. If the art box gets unruly, it's time to break it into subcategories.
- Have a sorting day once a month. Enlist your children to help you reunite puzzle pieces and fill up the designated bins or boxes with the appropriate toys. Depending on the ages of your children, you will probably do most of the work and coaching. But getting them to put in some effort on a regular basis is the key.

So, what about the constant refrain: "Mommy, where's my. . . ?" Before you go off on an expedition, encourage your child to look for the object on his own by giving him clues—lots of clues for a two-year-old.

I can't help you right now, but I have some ideas—
First of all, animal toys go in the red bin. Did you check there?
Did you look under your bed? Inside your blankets? In your sis-
ter's room? In the bathroom?

Try to teach older children how to retrace their footsteps, using a "solve the mystery" theme.

Where did you put them when you came in the house?
What did you do next?
Where did you get undressed?

And so on.

- After your child has given a good effort, you can go around the house once with him, but don't tear apart the place. No luck? Just shrug and tell him he'll have to find another pair of shoes (or another toy) for now.

They may turn up on another day.
When we clean up your bedroom, we might find them.
Do you remember where we put our shoes when we take them off?

Reality Check

In even the most organized houses, kids lose things. A toddler will carry a toy around and then just drop it when he's done. Possessions become more precious as children get older, and the more precious the object, the better a child will take care of it. It is up to parents to help them find a special place for their special things.

Steals

Like biting, stealing is something most kids do at least once in the toddler-plus years. "Steal" is a harsh word; avoid using it with little kids.

Treat the first few incidents as an opportunity to teach.

In our family we don't take things that don't belong to us. We ask first.

Even grown-ups sometimes want things that we can't have. But we never, ever take something that doesn't belong to us, even when we really, really want it. We ask to see if we can borrow it.

Been there. . .

Your daughter comes home from school holding two unfamiliar barrettes. You ask her about them, and she insists that they are hers. "They really, really are mine, Dad. Really!" You explain that they don't look like the ones you bought and you've never had them in your house before. They do not belong to your family. Your daughter says, "Angela gave them to me. Angela said these were hers but she said I could have them." So, which story is true? Did your child take them or were they a gift? Should you take them away? Should you interrogate her more?

First of all, don't be harsh. Remember, this is a chance to teach values. Also remember not to browbeat your child, because you do not know if the story is fictionalized or not.

Remember when we talked about how we don't take things that don't belong to us? Well, I am going to take (the object) *and keep it in a safe place until we can figure out who it really belongs to. The person it belongs to might be sad because she can't find it. Tomorrow we will bring it to school and see if your teachers can help us, or maybe Angela's mom can help us figure this out.*

(Don't set up a showdown between your child and the teacher/ parent/other adult. Frame it as "getting help from" another person.)

You can also let your child keep the object until the next morning, when you bring it back to school, considering that you don't know the real story. However, if your child gets into a pattern of taking things home, you should remove the item upon discovery. Resolve the issue the next day at school, or with a phone call to the other parent.

What if . . .

You discover a toy your child has carried home from a playdate?
  Stay as neutral as possible.

  It looks like you forgot to ask Joey if you could borrow his car. Let's keep it in a safe place, and we'll give it back the next time we see him. (Or you can telephone the friend to let him know.)

What if . . .

Your child starts stealing regularly?
  Each time, take away the object and have your child give it back as soon as possible, with your help, of course. Make caregivers and teachers aware of the situation and talk to them about how they will respond.

What if . . .

You notice a friend stealing something from your child?
  You can say to the friend:

Megan, it seems like you really want to have that ball. Let's ask Jonas if you can borrow it.

What if Jonas says no?

Jonas doesn't feel ready to share this ball today. I'm sorry. Maybe you can play with it together the next time.

If it's not a precious toy, you can say to the friend:

We are happy to let you borrow the ball, but next time, can you please ask first?

Runs Away in Public

Some kids seem to have the running-away gene and others don't. A runner is the kind of child who has a gleam in her eye as she boldly skitters down the block, not once looking back to see if her parent is following. Imagine the courage, the audacity! Imagine a small child who has no sense of danger. Unfortunately, there is not much you can do in this situation but be on your toes and control your child's whereabouts.

- Make sure that your child is not making a game of it. This is just the time when you want to scold your child, but it may not be effective. If your child keeps getting an extreme reaction from you, she may come to enjoy it.
- If you have a child who likes to run away, keep her in a stroller, or hold her hand during dangerous transitions, or when you are in a setting with no borders or boundaries, like at a fair, concert, or even strolling on the sidewalk. Let her run free

only in enclosed areas. As she gets older, gradually experiment with more freedom.

I know that you always like to run away from me. But you are getting bigger now and you can learn to stay inside the fence. Let's give it a try while I sit right here (near the exit).

Or

You are really growing up, and I think you are ready to walk with me on the sidewalk.

Reality Check

Thankfully, "bolting" is a phase that your child will outgrow. As she gets older and internalizes your teaching about what's safe and what's dangerous, she'll gain a better awareness of her surroundings. But her awareness will never be as complete as an adult's, so that's why it's your job, indeed your reflex, to be vigilant. If the problem continues past the age of five, and you feel your child has difficulty using judgment, you should seek professional input.

Uses Baby Talk

When a child discovers that he is growing up and changing, it can be a scary realization. Sometimes he wants to remember how it feels to be a baby, and to be taken care of like a baby. This often happens during times of change, like the arrival of a new sibling or switching to a different preschool classroom. There is nothing wrong with a little regression. There's no need to scold, because it will only make your child feel more insecure. You might ask or say:

Lucas, you love to use that tiny voice, but I can't understand your words.
Can you say that in a growing-up voice this time? Because I can't understand.
Hmm. I really miss the four-year-old son I used to talk to.

Indulge your child a little. Show him how you took care of him when he was a baby. Hold him, rock him, and sing lullabies. He will benefit from knowing that he is still worthy of all your affection even though he's gotten bigger. However, if the baby-game goes on too long and is driving you crazy, describe to your child all the things that babies can't do, and all the fun things a bigger boy can do. Then pretend to enforce these limitations, such as, "Oh, no sandbox today, because tiny babies can't use the sandbox." Don't get too heavy-handed with this approach, because you don't want to generate distress. Baby talk is benign and will go away by itself.

Lies and Lying

Never call it lying; not at this age. Young children can't always tell fantasy from reality. They are even capable of creating a fiction that is so vivid to them that it becomes their reality. Your job is to patiently give them a way to classify what they are saying:

Tell me if that's a real story or a pretend story.
Is that something that happened, or something you wanted to happen?
It sounds like you wish you had gone to the circus.

If you know your child is lying just to get himself out of trouble, don't be punishing about it, since a four-year-old is just starting to understand the moral implications of his behavior. Around age five or later, you can introduce the concept of honesty and trust.

> *Friends and grown-ups need to believe that you are giving real information. That's what it means to be honest. It means that you are telling a real (or true) story.*
>
> *Do you know what trust means? Trust is when a friend knows that what you say is a true story. He knows he can always hear a real story from you. You can tell him a made-up story sometimes, too, but you say, "I'm just pretending."*

What if. . .

You catch your child in an indisputable lie? What if you saw the event or you have the evidence against him?

For younger children:

> *I'm not comfortable when I know you're telling me a made-up story.*
>
> *This time I know the real story. I'm going to tell you what I saw. . .*

A child might still insist he is innocent. Here are some ways to respond:

> *You really wanted to believe your brother told you to break the marker.*
>
> *I know that's the way you want it to be, but this is what I saw. . .*
>
> *Sometimes children wish things happened a different way, so they tell a pretend story about it.*

For older children:

I'm uncomfortable when I know you are telling me a made-up story.

Of course most of the time parents have not witnessed the alleged story or event.

Been there. . .

One afternoon you walk into the dining room and notice that someone has made a huge drawing on the wall with several magic markers. You look at your two children sitting at the table blithely drawing and playing. No one says anything, and, in fact, they don't even seem to be aware of you. Do they think you won't notice? Arrgh! You are about to blow your top. Instead you take a deep breath to keep your composure and say, "Excuse me, can someone please tell me who drew on the dining room wall?" Both children look up and say flatly, "I didn't." You ask them again. They look you right in the eye and shake their heads.

Gently huddle the children by the wall so you can all talk.

It sounds like whoever did this is feeling uncomfortable. In our family it's more important to tell the truth (or a real story) than to hide what really happened. I am not upset. But I will be very disappointed if my children won't tell the real story.

Another option is to tell a personal story:

I had a friend one time who accidentally stepped on my plastic egg. My friend didn't want to tell me because she thought I would be mad at her. But I wasn't mad at her. I just wanted to know how it really happened so that maybe I could fix it, or keep it safe the next time. . .

If someone confesses, say:

Thank you, Bevin, for telling me the real story. I'm glad I know what really happened. I am not upset with you, but I would like you to help me clean it up. After you are done cleaning: *I know you understand that markers only go on paper, not on walls, right?*

If no one confesses, say:

I can see whoever did this has decided not to tell me right now. So, I will need help from both of you to clean up the wall. . .

Reality Check

Clearly there are lies, and then there are *lies*. Because children are supposed to exhibit a vivid imaginary life, marked by colorful exaggerations, you can leave the playful, harmless lies alone. Which ones are the serious lies? Only a parent can make that judgment. If a child insists she has five horses at home, then fine, ask her what their names are. If your child says he already brushed his teeth, but you notice his toothbrush is still dry, then it's time to have a little talk about the real story, as described above. On the flip side, if your child is lying compulsively or is constantly blaming other kids and can't own up to her actions, it might be time to consult a trusted teacher or experienced parent.

Perfectionism/Self-Criticism

Your almost five-year-old son and his friend are calmly drawing together in the dining room, discussing the stories that happen to be on their minds, and choosing what to draw next. The friend announces that he can draw a knight on a horse, and demonstrates. Your son watches intently and then tries to draw one for himself. Suddenly he stops drawing and scribbles aggressively all over his work. "I can't do it!" he exclaims. You encourage him to try again, and he picks up a clean paper. But this time when he gets stuck, he balls up the paper and tosses it on the floor, then sits in a huff. His drawing looked fine to you. Should you have given him more encouragement and praise? Should you quickly distract him with another activity? Should you point out all the other things he's good at?

As his parent, your heart breaks at the thought of your child being so dissatisfied with himself. You want to say, "Take it easy; you're only a kid. There will be plenty of time to be hard on yourself when you're grown up!"

It's common to see perfectionism rear its head around the age of five, when kids are getting acutely attuned to the abilities of their peers. They discover, to their shock, that a peer can do something much better or faster than they can. But it's way too early to have conversations about talent—you'll have plenty of opportunity to broach that one in the preteen years. For now, it's best to be supportive and patient as you wait for this phase to pass. Here are some ways to be supportive to a self-critical child:

Don't try to reprogram what they are thinking, especially when a child is in a big huff. It's better to acknowledge a child's frustration in a low-key way.

It's tricky, isn't it?
Hmm, I bet it takes a lot of practice to get that ball in the hoop.
I know it can be frustrating to learn something new.

Ask if she wants some help, or if she would like you to show her a couple of tricks. We often have the urge to take over and "correct" something we think our child is doing wrong. Always ask first.

You're not satisfied. Is there a way I can help?
Can I show you a couple of tricks?

If she is receptive to your support, you can offer to bring out pictures of the object she is drawing, for example, and help her think about how she would start. *Look at that oval face. . .*

When your child is in tears, saying, "I can't do it!" you might say some of the following:

You're right; you can't do it right now, because you are too upset.
  This is a good time to take a break, and come back to it later.
It's hard to do this when your mind is not clear, or when you have
  so many things to think about. Let's take a break to clear your
  mind.
Looks like you are overwhelmed and there are too many things to
  think about. Let's take a breather, and get a snack.

Later on, when the heat of the moment has subsided, tell your child stories about something you had trouble doing at first, and how you practiced and worked hard even though you sometimes felt like giving up. Or you can point out a new skill that he could not do at first but eventually figured out. (For example: riding a bike with training wheels, swimming, or drawing his favorite subject.)

What if. . .

Your child is focused on a peer who can hit the ball (or do hula hoop) better than he can, and it makes him feel bad?

When your youngster is making comparisons to another peer who can do something better, always frame your response in terms of how much or how hard the other child is working on the particular skill, and not how "good" the other child is at something. For example, if your five-year-old is moping about how certain children in her class are reading already, and worries that she cannot do it, try to encourage her without turning it into a forceful pep talk. Some things you might say:

> *Becky can read because when she was younger, she probably spent a lot of time looking at books and trying to sound out words. Just like you are doing now. You are learning to read, little by little, every day. Remember the other day when you read (name of book)? You are doing exactly what you should be doing to learn to read.*

This response might seem a little wordy, yet some children will want this kind of support. Others may reject your encouragement and will prefer that you listen to them and empathize instead.

What if. . .

Your deepest instincts tell you that your child really does not have the talent for ballet or soccer, but he still wants to pursue it?

If your child is enjoying his experience, there is no reason to stop. Listen to what he says about the activity. If he continues, he deserves your support. If, however, he's miserable, don't make him continue just because you paid for the session. A two- to five-year-old is too young to understand the principle of making a commitment, and it's more important to take him out of an environment that is consistently making him feel bad about himself.

If self-criticism is a big part of your youngster's life, you should consider doing the following:

Give her plenty of opportunities to do the things that make her feel good about herself. Maybe your daughter is not having such a great time in soccer but always seems to enjoy putting on plays or shows at home. You might support this activity by setting up a "stage" or making tickets for the show. Perhaps you should investigate dance classes for her. It's not an immediate antidote to the breakdown on the soccer field, and she'll never buy it if you say, "Yeah, I can see how tricky it is to dribble that ball; let's put on a play instead." You have to be a lot more covert about changing the menu. There are so many exciting new skills that a five-year-old learns— swimming, hula hoops, writing short notes, drawing something new, mastering a new board game—that it makes sense to focus on the ones that engender positive feelings in your youngster.

Ask yourself the difficult question of whether or not you or your spouse spends too much time "correcting" your son's or daughter's actions. Even little comments over time—"Those pants don't match" or "You made the 'N' backwards"—can cause a sensitive child to become overly self-conscious and self-critical. Biting your tongue is often the best course to take when it comes to little imperfections.

Reality Check

It's a wacky ride, sometimes, parenting little kids. What is your least favorite bugaboo? Could it be when your child wipes his nose on the arm of the sofa? How about when your daughter screams, "Get away from me!" as she rolls on the floor with snow pants bunched around her ankles? The best way to cope with most of these disconcerting behaviors is with a little private humor. The madness we parents tolerate! The absurd situations we find ourselves in! If you can, document some of your child's quirkiness through scrapbooks or videos, because it probably won't last. By next year, the particular behavior will seem quaint, and far away.

On the other hand, more serious behaviors like stealing or lying require your consistent, calm response. As always, children need guidance from their parents to figure out clues to their own bewildering emotions, and how to navigate expectations of the grown-up world.

Epilogue

Whoever said we don't own our children was right; we are merely entrusted with their care. We build safe borders around these wild bundles of energy; gingerly tweak, redirect, remind, and, of course, love them. Then we wait and watch. As they grow, they surprise us in delightful ways. Perhaps the most breathtaking quality about our children is how fiercely they love us, even when they are being unbearable.

To be the parent of a small child is to find yourself in situations you don't want to be in, to repeat the drill you have done a hundred times before, and to put aside so many of your needs in the service of someone else.

It's no wonder we glimpse the edge of the cliff sometimes. Young children demand a lot. They expect to be understood when they are not acting rational. They want things to go their own way no matter what. It is reassuring to remember that nothing we give our children gets wasted. They may not learn the tenth time we patiently instruct them to sit down at the dinner table, but over time, they will. We soldier on, and know (or hope) that the rewards of growth and self-discovery will sneak up and excite us. Indeed, delayed gratification is the norm for parents. Maybe because we don't receive an immediate payoff for our hard work, when it finally comes, it is so much sweeter.

We parents demand a lot of ourselves, too. Being a parent is a role we play, and some of us are better prepared for it than others. The rest of us learn as we go. Any conscientious parent will sometimes wonder, "Am I doing the right thing? Should I give in, or should I hold the line?" It helps to be flexible enough to explore ways of improving a situation. But it's also critical to establish reasonable—but not too restrictive—boundaries that make sense for your child and your family, and firmly but calmly uphold them. And your positions will sometimes make your child unhappy for a little while. It is not our responsibility to protect our children from disappointment, but it is our job to help them deal with it. Over time—yet another surprise—our children will learn to handle small setbacks with resilience and creativity.

We have an impressive job description that requires mixing and measuring all the necessary elements a child needs to grow: love, respect, boundaries, freedom, and guidance . . . with just enough personal time to keep ourselves happy. It's a tough job, but one we will be able to grow with too.

Ongoing Adventures:
Final Thoughts

How Much Should You Negotiate?

If only there were a concrete rule for knowing when to put your foot down, and when to haggle with a child. Experiencing autonomy is critical for a youngster's development, but at the same time, a functioning household is critical to everyone's sense of security. So it's your-child's-freedom-versus-a-functioning-household that lies at the heart of when, and how much, we should negotiate.

Think of all your children's requests and actions arranged in a pyramid. At the very top are the absolutely non-negotiable things, and at the very bottom are the issues you could negotiate almost endlessly because they are not terribly significant. In the middle are the things you are willing to negotiate for a while, but then the situation either becomes so disruptive or chaotic that you have to put a stop to the back-and-forth.

The thing is, every family has to fill in those three levels based on their own values. For example, in our house we let our kids jump from couches onto pillows on the floor, but we do not let them bring food into carpeted areas, like the living room. Most certainly there are other homes where jumping on furniture is not OK, but kids can eat in the living room. (As children move into new settings, we can teach them that different families have different policies, and that's fine.)

How can you decide how strict or how carefree you should be? It usually helps to have a rationale for each non-negotiable rule. For example, my husband and I reason that our furniture is not that precious, so we don't worry about wear and tear. If our kids can jump and not get hurt, then it's OK. At the same time, we have a good reason why we don't like food in other rooms of the house. With five children eating throughout the house, we would be spending quite a lot of time scrubbing ground-in food out of the carpet. We hate to do that! And it would take time away from more important things. So, when we see a child wander into the living room with a snack, we ask him to please sit in the dining room or kitchen to eat. Sometimes, when our kids test us, we pick them up and move them. Because we are consistent about upholding the rule, they all seem to respect it.

The Non-Negotiable Top of the Pyramid

Are there a handful of universal non-negotiables—ones that most families would agree with? The things that come to mind are brushing teeth; taking medicine when sick; trying to use good manners; helping to clean up around the house to the extent of one's ability; and refraining from physically hurting one another. We would add one more category: any new routine your child is learning, like going to school or sleeping in a new bed, should follow an ironclad routine until your child is through the adjustment period. Everything else on your non-negotiable list is contingent on what is important for your child, and for the family—in other words, your values. It is extremely helpful to write down your non-negotiable rules in your Family Policy Book (see page 36). Any notebook will do, as long as it's handy and doesn't get lost in household clutter. Your policy book should be somewhat dynamic, because you always have the option of adding an important policy as a new need arises, and, conversely, you will remove items as the children get older.

The next two levels of the pyramid are for internal use only. For parents to share, but not for the kids.

Negotiable to a Point

This middle level of the pyramid represents those borderline areas where you can compromise with your child once or twice, but that's it; then you must move on to the next thing before your plans—or your sanity—go awry. Here are a few examples:

- Your child wants extra time to finish a project (or keep playing) before a transition, such as going out the door, coming to dinner, or getting in the tub. When the requests for more time become an obvious delaying tactic to avoid the necessary things she must do, you have to announce an ending point.

OK, Mommy has given you a lot of extra time. Now I am going to set the timer for two minutes and then we are going to leave.

Or

OK, your extra time is done now. I am going to count to ten, and then we are going to the bathtub.

If she still won't cooperate after counting, pick her up and go.

- More books or cuddles at night? You might accommodate some of these requests, if time allows, but you can't let it go on and on or you will be on a slippery slope to later and later bedtimes. Occasionally you will have to leave your child's room as she yells in protest—that's just part of the process of keeping your family on track, and teaching your child healthy sleep habits.
- Requests for a new toy, a fluorescent-colored cereal, a tattoo, for the chance to come along on a special errand, or anything that is not problematic in small amounts, but you certainly wouldn't agree to it on a daily basis. Take a deep breath and shake off some of your own inflexibility:

Make it a rare, special-occasion treat rather than a completely forbidden item. Moderation is the key. You can tell your child something like this:

> *I don't usually like this cereal because there's so much sugar in it, and that's bad for your teeth. But I'll buy it this time; just so we can try it.* And when your child requests it the very next time you go shopping, you can reinforce your policy and redirect.
>
> *Nope. We don't buy this cereal every time—only once in a while. You can pick a different cereal that you can eat every day.*

Or have a special day of the month when your child can have his favorite (otherwise unacceptable) cereal, or gum to chew, or other request that makes you cringe. Let your child enjoy the indulgence without any strings attached. Remember, you are the parent, so you get to draw the line at requests that you feel are out of the question.

For example, no amount of begging or arguments for moderation can convince me to let my kids watch particular videos. If a kid eats too much sugar, you can always brush his teeth. The impact of a violent video, on the other hand, is harder to erase.

Infinitely Negotiable

This is the bottom of the pyramid; the widest part containing all the uncountable things that you can pretty happily and harmlessly negotiate with your child because to do so will not throw your household, your family routines, your marriage, or your values off-kilter. Children need to get what they want sometimes—in fact, many times. They need to make their own decisions and feel like they are mostly in control of their world. If you don't perceive your child as going through the day happily making most of his own choices, perhaps this is a sign of too much parental control. By no means does this level of the pyramid represent demands you must fill *for* your child, but rather choices you can help your child execute for herself. Safely, of course.

Naturally, there will be times when you are just worn down by, say, winding up the yo-yo for the umpteenth time, and you must stop—because you have a right to rest your hand.

> *This is the last time I can do this. My hand is really tired, and I need a break.*

What If You, the Parent, Can't Decide What to Do?

Worse, what if you actually find yourself caving in and changing your "No" to "Yes" and thoroughly confusing everyone? It's useful to express your thinking process a little:

*I've been thinking about it, and that's a reasonable request. I've
    decided to change my mind.*
*I am not sure whether or not this is a good idea. I need to think
    about this for a while.*
*That is a reasonable request, but I need ten minutes to talk to
    Mommy about it first.*

Because I Said So

Well, it's true. You are the mom or the dad, and you get to make the
rules. But what child is ever satisfied with the answer above? You will
get more compliance over the long-term if you give a rationale for
your refusals or postponements. The "why, why, why" of repetitive
questioning can drive a parent right off his tightrope. When a child
repeats himself over and over, as if he did not hear—or did not want
to hear—then you might have to be firm, without yelling, to get the
message through. Here are some possible responses:

*I said no, and I already explained why. Please don't ask me over
    and over.*
I'm the mom and I do know what's best for you.
*There are things that you can take care of yourself. But Mom and
    Dad know when you are ready to do it.*
*I am in charge; that's my job as a parent. I know what's best for
    you—I know more than you because I'm older and I've been
    around longer than you.*
*Yes, we are the bosses of you until you learn how to do things your-
    self. I'm here to help you learn all these things.*
*Mommies and daddies know more than our children, and our job
    is to help you learn and grow.*

I can tell you don't like my answer, but I need you to listen.
Because I said so. (Hey, if it's the only thing that works, use it.)

After you have done your best to deliver the news, you must try to ignore subsequent pleadings and calmly walk into another room. *When you're ready to listen and stop repeating, we can make a plan/solve this problem.*

Breaking the Rules

Here's the fun part. Once your child or children are settled into their routines—the big ones being morning drop-off and going to bed at a certain time—it's actually a good idea to break the rules . . . on occasion. Having a special night out with friends that gets everyone to bed at 10:00 p.m. is an exciting departure from the norm, and it teaches children flexibility, too. On the next day, you can go back to your regular routine. I draw the line at special sleepovers in the parents' bed, if a child is already comfortable in a bed of his own. If it actually worked as a rare special treat, it would be fine. But it's likely that a child will insist on sleeping with his parents every night thereafter, and parents are faced with retraining him to fall asleep in his own bed. An undesirable price to pay, considering you will have to compassionately retrain your child to sleep in his bed after vacations and illnesses. What about sleeping bags in a parent's room? It can work, but there are two challenges with this idea. First, whatever portable bed you are using for your child has to be comfortable, or she will sneak into your bed for relief. If you really want your child to have the option of sleeping on your floor, as opposed to in your bed, then you must be in a position to gently remove her from your bed and return her to the sleeping bag in the middle of the night. (See page 66 for a discussion of the family bed.)

Is a Bribe or Reward Ever OK?

Bribing a child to do something is a very controversial issue among parents. Because a bribe removes your opportunity to teach him why something is important for him to do, it is a very shallow learning experience. Basically, your child learns that he will get a reward for picking up his clothes or staying in his bed all night. He will not learn the benefits of keeping a neat room or the rationale for not waking Mom and Dad up in the middle of the night (i.e., it makes them tired and cranky). Hold on, you say, young children are not always rational beings, and we can explain and explain to the point of exhaustion why something is important and still get no cooperation at all. You try to teach, teach, teach, and yet they may be too young to understand the important concept you are trying to convey. You're not going to give up teaching, but if you add a bribe now and then, who can blame you? To sum up our ideas about bribes, here's a list of parameters:

- Use them rarely, and only after you have made some attempt to explain, and reason, and encourage your child's cooperation.
- Instead of using candy treats, buy your child a calendar and tape some packets of stickers to the back for storage. (This way you won't be running around the house looking for stickers when you need them.) Hang the calendar somewhere convenient and have her put a sticker on the day she did that great, useful, or growing-up thing.
- There are some things that truly warrant a bribe or reward— really unpleasant things that your child must do, and a prize will sweeten the experience. Some examples are getting shots from the doctor, removing a splinter, or having a first visit to the dentist.

Believe it or not, the bribe inducement does not last forever, and your child's desire for the particular reward usually fades as he feels more confident with his new skill.

You get dressed every morning. Wow, you are really growing up. Let's celebrate. You can choose a special dinner/dessert tonight. You learned how to sit at the dinner table until you are done. We already had a party last night to celebrate. (Use if your child asks for another reward after you have stopped supplying them.)

Sometimes children can actually get stuck in a behavioral rut, and they need a little motivation to move out of it. This phenomenon may look a bit like regression. Typically a child who had adapted to a routine will backslide for no obvious reason other than to attract attention from the adults around her. A conscientious parent will respond first by trying to talk to her child about her feelings, then offering more support and time together. A parent can also make sure the routines are very consistent. But still the child acts out. The unorthodox measure of trying a bribe might actually work in this situation.

Been there. . .

Here's an example. After many months of happy morning drop-offs, my four-year-old daughter, Lucy, started crying, pleading, and pulling on us to stay with her at school each morning. It got to be very stressful for us. We tried talking to her and role-playing, and we were sure to be consistent and cheerful during drop-offs. But still, it was agonizing to see her so miserable every morning. We couldn't figure it out. Nothing out of the ordinary was happening to provoke the weepiness.

When I discussed Lucy's behavior with her teachers and with Barbara, we all realized that we were trying everything we could to address Lucy's issue—but what exactly was her issue? (OK, there was one suggestion that we couldn't really achieve—getting to school before 9:00 a.m. If she arrived before the "movement" part of class, perhaps it would be easier for her to integrate. But with five children to get ready in the morning, we consistently failed in that department.) Then Barbara made a suggestion that I immediately rejected. I should offer to give Lucy a little chocolate kiss at pick-up time to celebrate if she didn't cry that morning. My husband and I don't like bribes, and he turned up his nose at the idea. After mulling it over, I decided to try it as an experiment. I wanted to see if she would take the bait, and if I would then become a slave to chocolate kisses, as I predicted. Well, I tried it, and it worked. Lucy just turned off her morning collapses, and instead focused on what a growing girl she was becoming. She was proud of her new skill of not crying anymore at drop-off time.

So, should I have stuck with my principle of "no bribes" and have Lucy continue to act out each morning? By trying this one unorthodox bribe, I managed to make us both more comfortable. She stopped asking for chocolates after a week or so. We've had a good run with her morning drop-offs. If I sense her anxiety in the morning, I talk to her a bit about what she might do at school that day, and ask if she thinks she will be able to be happy and comfortable at drop-off. And on the days when she does become tearful, the teachers' support seems to calm her down much faster.

Losing Your Temper, Keeping Your Cool

What they say about being a parent is true: nothing can prepare you for the level of patience and self-control you must find in yourself to survive. Each of us has a different threshold for anger, it seems. We can see it in our own families. Why, for example, does whining make me want to climb the walls, while my husband can coolly tune it out? Why does one person become short-tempered when he hasn't had enough sleep, while his spouse can maintain an even keel on only five hours of rest?

One thing that we all can do is adjust our own attitude a bit. It's not fun to sweep the floor, but maybe if we whistle a song while we do it, it will feel better. Parenting coach Barbara Capaldo says that the difference between consequences and punishment is attitude. When you are setting a limit with your little one, it's good to think of your job as trying to help. As in, "I'm just trying to help my daughter learn to stop pushing," instead of feeling like you have to teach her a lesson.

For all the emphasis our culture puts on expressing feelings and being honest, to be a good parent, we almost have to do the opposite. We have to stay in control in spite of our true feelings. We can't say what we really feel when our child clobbers his brother for the third time, or when our toddler gets off the potty only to stand in front of us and let his pee run down his leg. (What we want to say is, "I am so sick and tired of trying and trying to potty train you and never getting anywhere!") We can't cover our ears and run screaming into the street, and we can't pick up our children and shake sense into them either. Do we fantasize about doing this sometimes? Yes! We cringe at the idea, but we are human, after all. Fantasies are fine, even healthy. As long as they stay in our mind. There are safe places to vent our real feelings, but it's usually not in front of small kids.

No one can play the parent role seamlessly. It is very much like acting, where our tone of voice, body language, and all the things we are supposed to say and do are constantly in play. Our true selves eventually come out, and we lose our temper sometimes. To be really honest, we must admit that we don't like this job of parenting every second of our lives. It's exhausting and frustrating, and it never stops. Trying to be the perfect parent is an ideal we will never reach, but, ironically, we are morally obligated to keep trying to do better. The rewards are always mixed in with the struggles. The same parent who is brought to tears by his defiant child will also feel like the luckiest person alive as he watches his child grow into a civilized, mature, and joyful person.

Parents need to diffuse their anger and frustration many, many times a day. When you feel your blood starting to boil, there are some things you can say to yourself to stay on the other side of the fence. Disengage, laugh to yourself, talk to yourself—figure out what works for you in the minute-by-minute frenzy of your day. Taking a longer view, when you build regular stress outlets or personal breaks into your week, your tolerance for your children will increase.

Here are things you can do to control your anger. What will work depends on your personality.

Disengage

This doesn't mean what it sounds like: crawling into a shell and refusing to respond to your child. When your best efforts fail, you must distance yourself mentally from your child's stressful behavior. Unpushing your own buttons, so to speak. You can do it through reasoning, humor, or both. Here's an example:

When you witness your child's ghastly behavior, head off your anger by describing what you have in front of you, almost like an anthropologist describing a member of a new tribe. Or think of your child as a little psychiatric patient whose mind does not work like yours—indeed, it has not finished growing yet. Run through a mental monologue along the lines of:

OK, I have a three-year-old here rolling on the floor, moaning like a wounded animal because she can't have chocolate chips. Hmm. I have tried to explain that chocolate chips are for baking, and she can have a different snack, like apples or crackers. OK, I'll offer her a cookie. No go. She keeps spinning on the floor, whining like a siren. Hmm. She thinks if she's loud enough to drive me insane I might just give in. It does sound tempting.

Wow. I wish I could act like this at work. I'm in a bizarre comedy skit right now watching my own stubborn daughter howl like a banshee while I look on dumbfounded. Only a three-year-old can get away with this. Poor thing. She can't even realize I'm offering her a cookie! Her mind has not developed yet to the point where she can control her emotions. She's like a giant explosion with no off switch. The most I can do to help right now is to contain this little tempest, by carrying her to the time-away room. I'll wait with her until the storm blows over. And I know it will. It always does.

Step Aside and Take Deep Breaths

If you feel like you are being hounded and pounded to the breaking point, take a few deep breaths. Turning away or stepping aside to take your breaths is even better. Those special breaths are a reminder to detach yourself. Tell yourself you don't have to talk right now. You can breathe, and think things through. There is always time for breathing. You can even say to your children: *I am not sure what I can do to help. I have to think about this.* Don't feel compelled to respond to every request or demand right away.

Give Yourself a Time-Away

Kids are not the only ones who need a time-away! You can't escape to a tropical island, but you can remove yourself from the scene of chaos and find another place to sit or lie down. You can do this when the noise is really disturbing you, or when you find your own anger rearing its head. Assuming your children can hear you over the din, tell them you need to give yourself a time-away and briefly explain why. It's great for your children to see you manage your anger in a constructive way.

Whisper or Stop Talking

When you need to break a cycle of yelling or loud voices getting out of control, drastically diverge from your child's volume level. Deliberately respond in a whisper or a very quiet voice. Stubbornly keep your voice low. Your children might get louder, then complain, then eventually quiet down so they can hear you. Resist getting sucked into a vortex of escalating voices, if you can. The other tactic is to stop talking altogether. Use nods or minimal hand signals to pantomime what you need to convey. It feels wonderful to give your voice a rest.

Identify When You Are Saturated

Saturated is when you can't think straight anymore; you don't care what your children are doing; you have no more energy to help; and you can't wait until bedtime. Perhaps you have been mediating tantrums or squabbles all day. Or maybe your eyes are glazed over from reading *Green Eggs and Ham* too many times, and you feel like a zombie at the playground. You are not a bad parent for having these feelings. You have simply reached your saturation point and need some time away from your children. Recruit your support system—spouse, family, and babysitters—and plan some time for yourself. Get a feel for how often you need this break—and you *will* need it repeatedly. Twice a week? Four times a week? A break for yourself once a day is very, very sensible. Set up these breaks for yourself, based on the support and resources you have. Just as your child needs consistent special time with you, you need to give your mind and body time to recover from the demands of your children. When you get to the point where you wake up and groan, "It just starts all over again today!" it is time to do the right thing for you and your family. Refresh yourself on a regular basis.

Find Your Stress Outlets

Parenting is hard work. It fatigues the mind and body. Take care of yourself by finding an outlet to diffuse some of your stress. (Don't say you're not stressed; every parent is stressed!) If you make it part of your weekly routine, you'll be surprised at how much more stamina you will have on an average day.

Suggestions for What to Do on a Repeating Basis

- Go for a long walk with your music and earphones (ideal frequency—once a day).
- Go out to dinner with a friend and immerse yourself in someone else's life for a while (once a week).
- Read a really good book or join a monthly book club.
- If you can't get out of the house, ask a family member or hire a high school student, for example, to watch your children for one or two hours while you relax with a book or watch a movie (ideal frequency—once a day).
- Take yourself to a movie—alone (once a week).
- Do gardening without interruption (three times a week).
- Join a knitting or crocheting circle.

- Play pickup basketball.
- Take an art, cooking, or music class.
- Attend meditation or yoga classes.
- Go out to dinner, see a movie, or take a walk with your spouse (at least twice a month).
- Some parents agree to babysit another family's kids for an evening, or afternoon, so those parents can get some alone time, and then the babysitting is reciprocated. When multiple families are involved, it's often called a babysitting club or pool. You might also find domestic help or child care through your community's family resource networks or religious organizations.

Get Regular Exercise, Whatever It Takes

It is hard to exaggerate the benefits of regular exercise. If people really knew about how fitness can change your life, pharmaceutical companies would probably make a lot less money. Regular exercise not only increases your overall energy level, it also raises serotonin levels in your brain, which reduces depression. (Getting enough sleep also raises serotonin levels.) Exercise helps you sleep better and gives you a satisfying sense of accomplishment—something that stay-at-home parents often long for. Here's the kicker, though. You only get these benefits if you do it on a regular basis. When you begin an exercise program, don't set overly ambitious goals for yourself. Make a commitment to exercise three times a week for one month, if possible. By the end of the month, you will be over the hump and will start feeling "addicted" in a good way. Keep with it. You can't get a better life-affirming high. Of course, you should get the OK from your doctor before starting a fitness routine.

If you can afford it, going to an exercise class is much better than planning your own workout because you deserve to let someone else take care of you. Just show up on time, and the instructor will lead you through your paces. Don't be discouraged because you can only do half of what the other naturally slim, I-never-get-cellulite people are doing. This is your workout and you'll get the hang of it over time. There are some great classes nowadays: yoga of every variety, Pilates, low-impact aerobics, even urban-rebounding (where you jump on little trampolines). The idea is to get hooked on something physical. It will be the healthiest addiction you will ever have. If going to a class is not practical, start out by moderate walking three times a week, and eventually build up to brisk walking. To get more cardio benefits, move on to biking, running, swimming, or other activities that increase your heart rate a bit more.

Go Back to Work

Whether a parent works or stays home to raise children depends on his or her financial picture and a sense of what's best for the children. There are some people who feel more comfortable in their role as a parent than they ever did at work. Even though parenting can be an exasperating and fatiguing job, they would rather be at home raising children than doing anything else. But what about the parent who really misses his or her professional identity and the work she used to do? Grown-ups have needs, too, and the drive or desire to work outside the home is a legitimate one. It's taken me years to realize what older, wiser parents already know: if a parent really wants to work, and good child care is available, she should go back to work. You can't just pick up where you left off, but you can find a new arrangement. If you deny the part of you that really wants to express its talent, you will be miserable, and sadly, you will eventually make your family miserable, too.

What to Do When You Lose It

I will never forget the day I threw a plate against the wall. I try not to think about it, but I can't deny that it happened. I was immensely pregnant on a hot summer day, and we had no air conditioning. My three-year-old would not eat her lunch, and stubbornly refused to go to her friend's birthday party. She would not cooperate with anything I asked her to do. The crash of the lunch plate in the next room caught my daughter's attention all right. She got the message that I was upset. I had a bizarre feeling of calm afterward—it actually felt good to get physical! Later, as my daughter sniffled up in her room, regret settled on me like a fog. When I entered, she looked up at me hopefully and said, "Mommy, I ate some of my macaroni. Isn't that good?" I felt horrible. What was I teaching her? This is not how a parent is supposed to act.

I apologized to her and explained that I should not have expressed my anger like that. I made a mistake. There were other ways I could have gotten angry, like stomping my foot or walking away. (Actually, I wished I had just burst into tears instead.) How would we all recover from this? I wondered. Would my children start destroying things out of anger because I taught them how? In the end, everyone turned out OK. Amazingly, I was forgiven.

In short, all you can do is apologize, and try never to do it again.

Using Physical Force on Your Child

It's the third rail of parenting discussions, and people are ashamed to admit it: when all else has failed, we parents sometimes use physical restraint on our children. This can come in the form of carrying a flailing child to a time-away, or the unfortunate forcing of a child into his car seat. We think we are doing something wrong, and that our neighbors are going to call child services, but in fact we are well within our rights to physically dominate our child for safety purposes, or to achieve a critical goal. (What if you must leave for the airport, but your child is refusing to get buckled in?) Using restraint is only justified as a last resort—and when it is done as gently as possible. All parents use restraint sometimes, so we might as well learn how to do it safely and get comfortable with it as part of our repertoire of interventions.

A Time for Spanking?

Is there any benefit to spanking a child? Most of the time physical punishment makes the situation worse, because it teaches children that hitting is an acceptable way to express anger and solve problems. It also humiliates and scares them. Do you remember how you felt after a spanking when you were little? You probably felt like a bad person. What about using spanking only in life-or-death situations? If your child has the dangerous habit of running across the road without waiting for you, and you have exhausted all other means of getting her to hold your hand, you may think the message will get through if you spank her. But, over time spanking will lose its effectiveness and quite likely do emotional harm. (On the other hand, very limited shouting can be effective when used in situations where a child is endangering himself or others. Make your voice short, quick, and loud—that is, out of the ordinary. Once you get your child's attention, return your voice to a noticeably lower level.)

As a general matter, spanking is neither useful nor practical in the vast majority of frustrating tangles we have with our children.

(Clearly, we don't hit a child for resisting getting into the car.) Instead, we parents have to find ways to keep a cool head, whatever it
takes. If you are heating up and yelling the whole time, your anger
will translate into too much force, and you will regret it later. Therefore it's helpful to learn how to disengage, laugh, or take breaks. (See
"Losing Your Temper, Keeping Your Cool" on page 278.) For those
times when we must use our muscle, here are some safe ways to do it.

Getting into the Car Seat or Stroller

If all the strategies on page 222 fail and you must get going, use
force, but gently. Take a minute to catch your breath, and check your
perspective, along the lines of: "Every child resists sometimes. And
yes, it is utterly insane. But I know how to get him in safely and that's
what I will do." Make one statement to your child, such as, "Mommy
is going to bend you into the car seat now." Don't keep talking
through this procedure because your words will fall on deaf ears,
which will make you even angrier! Use embracing holds, rather than
white-knuckled grips. Secure your child's torso against the back of
the seat by leaning into her with your arm, shoulder, or open hand.
From this position slip her arms under the straps. If your child arches
her back, lean your forearm against her pelvis, but just enough that
she sits back. Do your best to duck flailing limbs. Once the car gets
moving, calm usually settles in. Never grab a limb, the neck, or hair
as it could cause pain and possible injury. (The same procedure
works for a stroller, but you must lock the wheels first.)

Getting off the Subway or Bus

How many times have you seen a parent lifting a child into the air by
his wrist? Because the practice is ubiquitous, you might be inclined

to believe it's OK. However, it's not safe and can dislocate the elbow, as pediatricians well know. The same goes for playfully swinging a child around by the wrists or hands.

When you have to get off the bus or subway quickly and your little tike is resisting, bend down and pick him up by his midsection. That's the only safe way to do it. Yes, that means loading your bags onto your shoulders in order to free your hands. It's a burden, but it only lasts a few seconds and then you are back on the sidewalk. When sweeping a child through subway doors, you should lift him around the midsection with his arms secured to his body to avoid getting limbs pinched in the closing doors.

If disembarking is a recurring problem, try practicing at home what you will do if he refuses to get off the bus or subway. Ask your child to show you the "safe way" he will walk off with you the next time.

Stopping a Rampage or Destructive Fit of Anger

We are not talking about your run-of-the-mill temper tantrum here. When a child is out of control and destructive to the point where she can hurt herself or others, create a "containment circle" by sitting cross-legged on the floor with your child squirming in your lap. Then hold out your arms some distance to make a circle around her. Deflect her limbs if she lashes out at you. Keep your head up so you don't get thunked in the jaw by your child's head. As soon as her body relaxes, you can let go. While being contained by you, your child might cry out that you are hurting her, even when you are only lightly holding her. Most likely it is the force of her resisting that is causing the sensation of being hurt. This is a way to get a parent to sympathize and feel guilty, and not to follow through. Remember, you are not doing this in order to punish her. You are doing this because you care about her and are trying to help her control her destructive impulses, and you will hold the course until she calms down. We call it a containment circle in our book, but experts in early childhood development describe the method in many different ways. The Children's Hospital of Oakland provides more guidelines for the management of rage-type tantrums at www.childrenshospital oakland.org. You can also check the Web site for your state's department of early education.

For an older, stronger child, the containment circle maneuver may not be practical. Instead, usher your child into a time-away room. If she flops on the floor en route, tighten your abdominals, bend your knees a little, and pick her up as best you can to carry her away. If she is on her feet, but violent, stand behind her, reach both your arms around and under her arms, and hold her wrists as you walk together. Don't hold so tight that you hurt her. Keep telling yourself, "I am simply doing my job. She is just a child, and I am helping her calm down."

During the containment phase, don't talk much to your child; she is too distraught to hear anything you say. If you get a chance, you can make supportive or soothing offers, like:

I can get you a tissue to wipe your nose.
Sounds like a drink of juice might help your throat.

When your child's body relaxes, offer her a drink of water. Allow your child a few minutes to settle and then have her help you clean up some of the damage, if any. Don't lecture or scold her about her outburst; it's too much to process. She may not even remember what triggered it. Just try to resume what was happening before, or start a quiet activity.

What if. . .

Your child breaks loose from your arms and runs away?

Never chase him around the room, because this creates a game of increasing frustration for you and much excitement for your child. Just make sure he can't leave the room by standing near the door. If he manages to run away and continues his destructive behavior, you can either let him finish his destruction if it involves, say, taking books off a shelf or some other fairly benign act. However, you must stop him from doing something extremely destructive or dangerous by picking him up and bringing him back to your lap as mentioned above, or to a time-away room. Make sure that his anger doesn't trigger your own outrage. Proceed in a business-as-usual frame of mind. Remember, if your child sees you losing control, he will likely test you more. Testing is the way he makes sure you are still in charge and will keep him safe.

Stopping Your Child from Hurting You

If a child is coming at you with flying fists, catch her arms and turn her around so that her back is toward you and her arms are flailing away from you. If she is lying down and kicking you, catch her legs and turn her onto one side, holding the legs to the side to prevent them from swinging back at you. If your child bites you, try not to let her know how much it hurts. Paradoxically, a child prefers negative feedback like a sudden cry of "Ow! That hurt me!" to being ignored. If she forcefully tries to bite you in the midst of a tantrum, you may have to turn her body around so her back is supported by your chest, and her head is supported between your hands, so that she cannot bite again.

Once you are out of the line of fire, walk into a different room. Only after she has calmed enough to listen can you go back and try to solve the problem together.

If the attack on you continues, use the containment circle mentioned above. If violent outbursts become the norm, talk to your pediatrician.

What's Considered Quality Time?

You know it when you feel it. So does your child. She needs your closeness and attention every day—even if your life is so hectic that you can only manage fifteen minutes of special time (see page 145). Ideally, we would like to have more meaningful interactions than one short session a day, but depending on our work requirements, it can be tough. Like the average American, we have our work life and family life to manage, and sometimes we have to take our child to the hardware store while we talk to the doctor on the phone and push the shopping cart. We juggle, and we juggle some more. Our responsibility as parents, however, is to protect our relationship with our child, to make sure she gets enough of us, and that her fundamental needs are not overshadowed by the pace of our lives.

Since almost any good experience with your child can be labeled "quality time," it's helpful to remind ourselves what choices we make that take meaningful time away from our children. The purpose of this short list is not to criticize our choices—since every parent has a lot on his plate—but rather to keep us on track.

Ways to Keep the Quality in Your Time

Forget Multitasking.   It's hard to let go of your to-do list, and even harder to turn off the one that runs constantly in your head. If you are spending alone time with your child, turn off your cell phone for a while. Put down your reading material and phone and play along at the playground. Don't do your office work when you are supposed to be spending time or playing with your little one. You can call to check in with your spouse or order take-out food, but that's it. Turn off or ignore your phone if you're baking cookies with your daughter. If you start to do a puzzle with your son, don't wander off to tidy the house. Sometimes just sitting next to him as he plays is a good way to spend time together.

Reduce Logistics. If you are saddened by the lack of time you have with your child, don't take him on a huge trip to the zoo because you think it will be a bonding experience. All that time spent driving and packing is lost time. If your little one is missing you, he will get a lot more out of sitting in your lap as you read to him, talk, and ask questions about the stories. Reading is a simple, no-overhead activity that not only allows you to be in physical contact with each other but also nurtures developing language skills. It's impossible to exaggerate the benefits of snuggling up together with a book. (After you put in some close reading time, then you might go to the zoo.)

Get on the Same Level. It's hard for a child to feel like you are paying attention to her if she can't look you in the eyes. Either she can go up, or you can get down. If you are constantly distracted by other things going on in your environment, the time you spend with your child will be very unsatisfying. (Quality or special time should be one-on-one, with no other children around.)

Follow Your Child's Lead. Instead of setting the agenda, let your youngster decide what he would like to do today, in the next hour, or during the next fifteen minutes—whatever amount of time you have.

Give him choices if he is not sure. Maybe he just wants you to build a tower with him, in which case you should be present with him and observe how he goes about the job or recruits you to help him.

Don't Interrupt, but Do Ask Questions and Tell Stories about Yourself.   Whatever your child wants to ramble on about, let her do it! Instead of telling her what the right approach is, or the accurate way of doing or saying something, ask her questions about what she's doing or how she's thinking about something. Acknowledge her fantasy stories and pretend playmates. Pretend right along with her. Whatever you do, don't interrupt, talk over her, or change the topic. You hate it when people do that to you, right? It makes you feel like your ideas are worthless, and no one is taking you seriously.

Show Affection.   Always add a few hugs, squeezes, and kisses when you spend time together. Don't smother your child, but don't forget to have skin-to-skin contact, either. It's also great to say: *I like spending time with you. It's fun to take a walk with you! I really enjoy painting together.*

Turn Mundane Errands into Little Adventures.   Trips to the grocery store or doctor's office are filled with opportunities to watch people doing their jobs and equipment serving a certain purpose—not to mention opportunities to count numbers, identify colors and animals, and watch for taxis, elevators, construction sites, clouds, and much more. This is the part of parenting that we once dreamed of—the chance to show a child all the amazing things the world has to offer. Regardless of our income, education, or skills, noticing the wonders around us—pointing out, explaining, teaching—is something all parents can do with their children. There is only one catch: to do this we have to slow ourselves down for a little while and live in the moment.

EASY BUT MEANINGFUL ACTIVITIES TO SHARE IN A PINCH

- Read to your child, allowing him to interrupt and ask questions.
- Page through a family photo album, or create a new photo book.
- Bake something in an unhurried way.
- Take turns doing each other's hair and "dressing up."
- Draw together (but don't draw everything for your child).
- Put play sand on a flat tray and practice drawing letters and designs in it.
- Take chalk out to the sidewalk and draw.
- Grab a bucket and go outside to collect something—pine cones, pebbles, leaves.
- Write (or draw) a letter or thank-you note to a loved one, and drop it in the mailbox.

What to Look for in Your Child's Caregivers

If you are fortunate enough to have options for child care—toddler school, preschool, home care, or a nanny—your standards can and should be very high when deciding the best arrangement for your child. Assuming you find a candidate who has experience and first-aid training, or a school that follows all safety and licensing regulations, you can focus on the interpersonal aspects of a teacher or nanny. The attributes of a good caregiver that are not written down in a rule book are much harder to evaluate, and they turn out to be mostly intuitive on the part of the parent. You need to spend a certain amount of time observing the person or people who will be taking care of your child. Putting all logistical issues aside, here are some important qualities to look for.

Universal Qualities to Look for in
Teachers, Caregivers, or Nannies

- No matter what the arrangement, caregivers or teachers should be warm and loving toward your child and other children. They should be your partners in the nurturing of your little one. Caregivers must be tuned in to the developmental needs of your child, and be able to communicate their observations to you. You must feel confident that they have the presence of mind to take a sincere interest in your child and the social skills to get to know him. What you want to avoid is anyone who projects boredom or indifference, has a withdrawn nature, or yells at children. Look at the candidate's body language and dress. Does he or she convey a feeling of being approachable, flexible, and ready for anything? Is he or she always standing up looking down on the children, or does he or she easily go down to a child's level and back?

- A caregiver should often lower herself to the level of your child and other children, and make eye contact as she speaks. You want a person who is conversational, but who does not give directions to your child all the time. He or she should facilitate play, but not control it.

- In a group setting, teachers should be able to make individual connections with children, rather than "herding" and "processing" them in groups all day. If you select a family care setting or opt for a nanny, you should do a background check on the candidate or call as many references as possible to find out how the caregiver has worked with other children, or if former clients express any reservations or concerns.

- There is such a thing as "chemistry" between your child and a caregiver, and it means that the two personalities are compatible. For example, nannies, like kids, can be animated and active or quiet, calm, and cuddly. If possible, set up a paid or unpaid trial run for a few days before making a long-term commitment to a nanny or caregiver. Keep in mind that experience and safety consciousness are right up there with being warm and loving.

• If you can afford it, send your uncertified nanny or regular babysitter to a children's first-aid training class at your local hospital. It's relatively inexpensive and requires only about four classes. It will do wonders for your peace of mind. If you have trouble locating classes, call your local fire departments for advice.

Selecting an Early Childhood Program

Some child care centers have programs for two-year-olds, often referred to as a "Toddler Class" or "Sprouts." Preschool, prekindergarten, and kindergarten come next. (Not all child care centers include kindergarten.) Rather than list all the licensing, safety, and teacher-student ratio requirements, I want to mention the more intangible qualities you should look for in an excellent child care center.

• Teachers should have a degree and training in early childhood education, and should without fail have a warm and loving personality with children, as mentioned above. Your child doesn't need to click with every teacher but should eventually bond with at least one of them. Teachers should respect children and listen and acknowledge them when they are talking. You should feel that the preschool environment is one where your child will be recognized and included, even if he is shy and withdrawn.

- Teachers should have a system for communicating with parents, and be responsive to parents' concerns and questions. You must feel that teachers will take you seriously and work with you in good faith on any issue concerning your child. Teachers should be able to suggest creative ways of dealing with a particular issue, and be willing to try another approach if something is not working. If your child is working on a particular issue, say taking turns with peers, a teacher should be able to work with your child progressively and over time, not erratically. On top of it all, teachers should be able to anticipate a child's needs and vary their responses depending on the particular need. For example, a child who has been biting a lot might get a 10:00 a.m. snack to dissipate her urge. As the child grows and develops, the teacher can fade out the special snack.
- In settings with many rotating teachers, you should always know which teacher is in charge each day. This is not only a comforting fact for parents but also a sign of good management and organization within a school. This structure ensures consistency in how teachers respond to children. In other words, it gets all the teachers on the same page.
- You must feel comfortable with the school's methods of discipline. Be sure to ask detailed questions about what happens when a child gets disruptive. Does she get a time-out? Avoid a school whose policy is to isolate a child or scold him in front of others. (For example, at one kindergarten, I saw a "doghouse" chart listing the children who did something out-of-bounds that day.) Teachers must be able to handle difficult behaviors in a compassionate manner, without yelling, scolding, or threatening. If your child is having a more serious developmental problem, teachers and directors should describe it to you, and possibly refer you to outside professionals for eval-

uation, but they should never diagnose, label, or act like you have a "problem child" and throw up their hands.

- Since teachers are your partners in the care of your child, they should be ready to help you at morning drop-offs. When you arrive, a teacher should immediately be present to gather up your child and comfort her if she is having a tearful separation. You should also be able to arrive with a small snack in a baggie if your child has refused to eat that morning. A teacher should also be ready to receive clothes in a bag if your child is having one of those days when he won't get out of his pajamas. Sometimes all you have to do is ask for help.

- The child care facility you choose should be ready, willing, and able to handle a child who has not yet been potty trained. The potty-training program should include regular trips to the bathroom throughout the day and gentle encouragement, but no pressure to perform. Being exposed to peers who use the potty is often all that is needed to get a child motivated, even though an individual child may not decide he is ready for months.

- Avoid programs that are too academic in nature. Young children learn best through play. They should have access to toys that stimulate their development, as well as lots of unstructured playtime with peers. A program that emphasizes numbers and letters, at the expense of exploratory free play, misses the boat. The three kinds of play to look for are unstructured (a child can choose what to do), instruction (listening to a teacher read a book, for example), and developmental activities that exercise a child's area of growth (such as fine motor and gross motor skills).

- Teachers should give parents feedback about their child whenever possible, not just during parent-teacher meetings. The single most important indicator that a teacher really knows my child is when he or she tells me what interesting thing my child said or did that day. Of course this quality is hard to assess when investigating a school, but you can ask other parents if they feel the teachers really know and care about their child, and how they have come to feel that way.

- Ultimately, you want a sign from your child that he or she is growing and learning in the preschool environment. After he gets adjusted in the morning, is he usually glad to be there? When you drop in or at pick-up time, does she look engaged and interested? Does your child tell you animated stories about what he did at school? Maybe not every day, but often? Teachers should share with you the developmental changes in your child, both the high and low ones. Throughout the school year, you should see your child grow in positive ways.

- A good child care center should allow you to drop in unannounced at any time to observe your child's class. (Of course, you run the risk of your child seeing you and wanting to go home, so you will have to choose the time carefully.) The center or school should also give you an open-ended invitation to lead an activity if you wish, such as reading books to the class, sharing a specialty, organizing an art project, etc. Children absolutely love special visits from parents.

Finally, the school should host regular events or functions for the parents, like potlucks or teas. This is an important part of building a sense of community. Not only can parents meet each other, but children can also see that parents are part of the school community too. (If a school lacks the resources to hold casual functions, it should be open to having parents organize them.)

Excellent Books for Young Children

Chapter 1: Meltdowns, Tantrums, and Screaming Fits

Alicia's Tutu by Robin Pulver (New York: Dial, 1997).

The Chocolate-Covered-Cookie Tantrum by Deborah Blumenthal (New York: Clarion Books, 1999).

Hannah's Temper by Celia Berridge (New York: Scholastic, 1993).

I'm Frustrated (Dealing with Feelings Series) by Elizabeth Crary (Seattle: Parenting Press, 1992). (Also: *I'm Mad; I'm Furious; I Want It; I Can't Wait;* and others by the same author.)

Chapter 2: Social Graces, or the Lack Thereof

Good manners

Excuse Me! A Little Book of Manners by Karen Katz (New York: Grosset & Dunlap, 2002).

It's a Spoon, Not a Shovel by Caralyn Buehner (New York: Dial, 1995).

Sheep Out to Eat by Nancy E. Shaw (Boston: Houghton Mifflin, 1995).

This Little Piggy's Book of Manners by Kathryn Madeline Allen (New York: Henry Holt, 2003).

Sharing

Connie Came to Play by Jill Paton Walsh (New York: Penguin, 1996).

Sharing: How Kindness Grows by Fran Shaw and Miki Sakamoto (Pleasantville, NY: Reader's Digest, 2006).

This is Our House by Michael Rosen (Cambridge, MA: Candlewick Press, 2005).

Separation and school transition

Betsy's First Day at Nursery School by Gunilla Wolde (New York: Random House, 1976).

Don't Go! by Jane Breskin Zalben (New York: Clarion Books, 2001).

I Am NOT Going to School Today! by Robie H. Harris (New York: Margaret K. McElderry, 2003).

The Kissing Hand by Audrey Penn (Terre Haute, IN: Tanglewood Press, 2006).

Umbrella by Taro Yashima (New York: Puffin Books, 1977).

When Mommy and Daddy Go to Work by Joanna Cole (New York: HarperCollins, 2001).

Will I Have a Friend? by Miriam Cohen (New York: Aladdin, 1989).

Yoko & Friends School Days: Mama, Don't Go! by Rosemary Wells (New York: Hyperion, 2001).

Babysitters
Don't Forget to Come Back! by Robie H. Harris (Cambridge, MA: Candlewick
  Press, 2004).

Bossiness
Clara and the Bossy by Ruth Ohi (Toronto: Annick Press, 2006).

Bullying and bossing
Brave Little Pete of Geranium Street by Rose and Samuel Lagercrantz (New York:
  Greenwillow Books, 1986).
King of the Playground by Phyllis Reynolds Naylor (New York: Aladdin Books,
  1994).
Martha Walks the Dog by Susan Meddaugh (Boston: Houghton Mifflin/Walter
  Lorraine Books, 2003).

Making friends
Do You Want to Be My Friend? by Eric Carle (New York: Philomel, 1988).
Franklin's New Friend by Paulette Bourgeois (New York: Scholastic, 1997).
Wemberley Worried by Kevin Henkes (New York: Greenwillow Books, 2000).

Interrupting
My Mouth Is a Volcano! by Julia Cook (Vienna, VA: CTC Publishing, 2006).

Chapter 3: In Search of Sleep
Bedtime for Frances by Russell Hoban (New York: HarperTrophy, 1995).
The Boy Who Wouldn't Go to Bed by Helen Cooper (New York: Dial, 1997).
Good Knight by Linda Rymill (New York: Henry Holt, 1998).
I Hate to Go to Bed! by Katie Davis (New York: Voyager Books, 2002).
I'm NOT Sleepy! by Robie H. Harris (New York: Little, Brown, 2005).
The Night the Scary Beasties Popped Out of My Head by David Kamish (New York:
  Random House, 1998). (For ages four and up.)
The Something by Natalie Babbitt (New York: Farrar, Straus and Giroux, 1987).

Chapter 4: Eating Your Heart Out
Dinner Time by Jan Pienkowski (Los Angeles: Piggy Toes Press, 2000).
Never Let Your Cat Make Lunch for You by Lee Harris (Berkeley, CA: Tricycle
  Press, 1999).
Pancakes for Breakfast by Tomie dePaola (New York: Voyager Books, 1978).

The Vegetables Go to Bed by Christopher L. King (New York: Crown, 1994).
Yoko by Rosemary Wells (New York: Hyperion, 1998).

Chapter 5: The Trials of Potty Training

My Big Boy Potty and *My Big Girl Potty* by Joanna Cole (New York: Harper-Collins, 2004/2006).
Once Upon a Potty—Girl and *Once Upon a Potty—Boy* by Alona Frankel (Richmond Hill, Ontario: Firefly Books, 2007).

Chapter 6: Fighting

Best Friends for Frances by Russell Hoban (New York: HarperTrophy, 1976).
Don't Call Me Names! by Joanna Cole (New York: Random House, 1990).
The Island of the Skog by Steven Kellogg (New York: Puffin Books, 1993).
It's Mine! by Leo Lionni (New York: Dragonfly Books, 1996).
Matthew and Tilly by Rebecca C. Jones (New York: Puffin Books, 1995).
No Hitting! by Karen Katz (New York: Grosset & Dunlap, 2004).

Biting

No Biting! by Karen Katz (New York: Grosset & Dunlap, 2002).
Teeth Are Not for Biting by Elizabeth Verdick (Minneapolis: Free Spirit Publishing, 2003). (I always edit this one to say teeth are not for biting *people*.)

Jealousy

Christina Katerina and the Time She Quit the Family by Patricia Lee Gauch (New York: Putnam Juvenile, 1999).
Frog Face: My Little Sister and Me by John Schindel (New York: Henry Holt, 1998).
I'm a Big Brother and *I'm a Big Sister* by Joanna Cole (New York: HarperCollins, 2004).
Julius: The Baby of the World by Kevin Henkes (New York: HarperTrophy, 1995).
Mail Harry to the Moon by Robie H. Harris (New York: Little, Brown, 2008).
Twinnies by Eve Bunting (New York: Voyager Books, 2001).

Chapter 7: Getting Really, Really Angry

Benny's Had Enough! by Barbro Lindgren (Stockholm: R&S Books, 2005).
Danny, the Angry Lion by Dorothea Lachner (Zurich: North-South/Night Sky Books, 2000).
If You're Angry and You Know It! by Cecily Kaiser (New York: Scholastic, 2004).
I'm SO Mad! by Robie H. Harris (New York: Little, Brown, 2005).

When Sophie Gets Angry, Really, Really Angry by Molly Bang (New York: Scholastic Paperbacks, 2004).

Chapter 8: Manipulators and Clever Cons

A Children's Book About Disobeying by Joy Berry (New York: Grolier, 1988). This author covers many topics in her "Help Me Be Good" series, including being destructive, fighting, throwing tantrums, lying, tattling, whining, and more.

Chapter 9: Travel Survival

Are We There Yet, Daddy? by Virginia Walters (New York: Puffin Books, 2002).
Bumper to Bumper: A Traffic Jam by Jakki Wood (London: Frances Lincoln, 1999).
The Car Trip by Helen Oxenbury (New York: Puffin Books, 1994).
The Eentsy, Weentsy Spider: Fingerplays and Action Rhymes by Joanna Cole and Stephanie Calmenson (New York: HarperTrophy, 1991).
Jamie Goes on an Airplane by Jill Krementz (New York: Random House Books for Young Readers, 1986).
Wee Sing: Children's Songs and Fingerplays by Pamela Conn Beall and Susan Hagen Nipp (Los Angeles: Price Stern Sloan, 2005).
We're Going on a Trip by Christine Loomis (New York: William Morrow, 1994).

Chapter 10: Health and Hygiene

Benny and the Binky by Barbro Lindgren (Stockholm: R&S Books, 2002).
The Berenstain Bears Go to the Doctor and *The Berenstain Bears Go to the Dentist* by Stan and Jan Berenstain (New York: HarperFestival, 1981).
Brush Your Teeth Please by Reader's Digest (Pleasantville, NY, 1993).
Dad's Car Wash by Harry A. Sutherland (New York: Aladdin, 1994).
Going to the Dentist by DK Publishing (New York: DK Preschool, 2007).
My Friend the Doctor by Joanna Cole (New York: HarperCollins, 2005).
Owen by Kevin Henkes (New York: Greenwillow Books, 1993). (About attachment to a security blanket.)
The Pumpkin Blanket by Deborah Turney Zagwyn (Berkeley, CA: Tricycle Press, 1997).
Sam's Bath by Barbro Lindgren (New York: HarperCollins, 1983).

Chapter 11: Particularly Annoying Refusals

The Berenstain Bears and the Messy Room by Stan and Jan Berenstain (New York: Random House Books for Young Readers, 2005).
Fritz and the Mess Fairy by Rosemary Wells (New York: Puffin Books, 1996).

The Funny Dream by Kaethe Zemach (New York: Greenwillow Books, 1988).

I'm All Dressed! by Robie H. Harris (New York: Little, Brown, 2005).

No! No! No! by Anne Rockwell (New York: Simon & Schuster, 1995).

Oh, Bother! Someone's Messy by Betty Birney (New York: Golden Books, 1992).

The Ornery Morning by Patricia Brennan Demuth (New York: Dutton Juvenile, 1991).

Chapter 12: Miscellaneous Bugaboos

Arnie and the Stolen Markers by Nancy Carlson (New York: Puffin Books, 1989).

The Berenstain Bears and the Truth by Stan and Jan Berenstain (New York: Random House Books for Young Readers, 1983).

No Whining! by Janice C. Villnerve (Anchorage, AK: Paradigm, 2004).

Ruthie and the (Not So) Teeny Tiny Lie by Laura Rankin (New York: Bloomsbury USA Children's Books, 2007).

Excellent Videos for Young Children

The Scholastic Video Collection—Short video adaptations of award-winning children's picture books by Weston Woods. There are so many wonderful stories packaged on these DVDs, you won't need to add any more videos to the house.

The Best of the Electric Company—Talk about educational video. Although it's billed for kids ages seven and up, even two-year-olds will be riveted by these simple, upbeat skits that really teach them about phonics and reading. You'll recognize some famous actors as well as a few songs from your 1970s childhood by the Sesame Workshop.

Feature films

There are very few films we know that are enriching for two- to five-year-olds. *Mary Poppins* and *Meet Me in St. Louis* are wonderful films, no matter how many times you and your kids see them. Honestly, Hollywood doesn't get much better than this for the toddler-plus group.

Singable Songs for Parents (and kids love them too)

Music Together series—You will find ten different collections of very accessible songs with American folk and international roots. The CDs are named by instrument, such as bells, drums, fiddle, flute, tambourine. Bells is our favorite.

Whaddaya Think of That? by Laurie Berkner. A single CD with very clear, articulate, original songs for kids that you can really get hooked on, especially "We Are the Dinosaurs."

Session Americana's *Table Top People* is a set of two CDs with some zany and some quiet but all eminently singable songs your kids will love, such as "Froggy Went A-Courtin'" and "Merzidotes."

SOURCES AND BIBLIOGRAPHY

Chapter 3: In Search of Sleep

Sleeping through the Night: How Infants, Toddlers, and Their Parents Can Get a Good Night's Sleep by Jodi A. Mindell (New York: Quill, 1997).

Healthy Sleep Habits, Happy Child by Marc Weissbluth (New York: Fawcett, 1999).

The amount of sleep youngsters need, by age, can be found in:

Solve Your Child's Sleep Problems (revised and expanded edition) by Richard Ferber (New York: Fireside, 2006).

"Behavioral Treatment of Bedtime Problems and Night Wakings in Infants and Young Children: An American Academy of Sleep Medicine Review" by Jodi A. Mindell and others, *SLEEP* 29 (November 2006).

Chapter 4: Eating Your Heart Out

"Your child will learn his body's natural cues for hunger and fullness if his eating is not coerced." *Let Them Eat Cake! The Case Against Controlling What Your Children Eat* by Ronald E. Kleinman, Michael S. Jellinek, and Julie Houston (New York: Villard, 1994).

Chapter 6: Fighting

"Children actually take responsibility for their actions and generate their own solutions more often when an adult is absent . . . Even children as young as three have been shown to come up with their own resolutions if given a chance." "Peer Conflicts in the Classroom: Drawing Implications from Research" by Edyth J. Wheeler, *Childhood Education* (January 1994); "The Dynamics of Preschool Children's Conflicts" by Brett Laursen and Willard W. Hartup, *Merrill-Palmer Quarterly* 35 (1989): 281–97; "Assisting Toddlers and Caregivers During Conflict Resolutions: Interactions that Promote Socialization" by Beverley A. Kovach, *Childhood Education* (September 1998).

"[M]ake a can with just the right number of Popsicle sticks in it. . . " "I Had It First: Teaching Young Children to Solve Problems Peacefully" by Donna Sasse Wittmer and Suzanne K. Adams, *Childhood Education* (September 2001).

Chapter 7: Getting Really, Really Angry

"What's Normal?" by Jerome Groopman, *New Yorker,* April 9, 2007.

The *New York Times* published several articles about diagnosing behavior disorders in kids. The first article in the "Troubled Children" series appeared on October 26, 2006.

"National Trends in the Outpatient Diagnosis and Treatment of Bipolar Disorder in Youth" by Carmen Moreno and others, *Archives of General Psychiatry* 64 (2007): 1032–39.

Ongoing Adventures: Final Thoughts

What to Look for in Your Child's Caregivers

A flyer from the Clearinghouse on Elementary and Early Childhood Education, University of Illinois, titled "Multiple Perspectives on the Quality of Early Childhood Programs" by Lilian G. Katz was a source for some of our tips on what to look for in an early child care center.

Other Helpful Parenting Books

Children: The Challenge by Rudolf Dreikurs (New York: Plume, 1991).

The Emotional Life of the Toddler by Alicia F. Lieberman (New York: Free Press, 1995).

The Highly Sensitive Child by Elaine N. Aron (New York: Broadway Books, 2002).

How to Raise a Responsible Child by Shirley Gould (New York: St. Martin's Press, 1982).

Siblings Without Rivalry by Adele Faber and Elaine Mazlish (New York: Avon, 1987).

Your Two-Year-Old: Terrible or Tender; Your Three-Year-Old: Friend or Enemy; Your Four-Year-Old: Wild and Wonderful; and *Your Five-Year-Old: Sunny and Serene* by Louise Bates Ames (New York: Dell, 1980).

ACKNOWLEDGMENTS

We would like to thank our medical advisor, who generously shared her knowledge and little-kid strategies with us:

Julie Dollinger, MD
Medical Director, Lexington Pediatrics, Lexington, MA
Director of Community Pediatrics, Children's Hospital, Boston

The authors would like to thank the following people for sharing their insights and suggestions: Maxie Chambliss, Connie Biewald, and Nina Araújo from Fayerweather Street School; Dana Ansel, Susan K. Lewis, and Teri Mendelsohn for their tips; Diane Hendrix and Libby Shapiro for their encouragement; Barbara's first and most important mentor, Molly Shapiro, of Brooklyn, who called her students "friends" back in the 1950s; and especially to Mat Dolan and former director Gwen Hooper and the staff and families of Arlington Children's Center. Finally, our deepest gratitude goes to our families, for supporting and teaching us.

INDEX

Bath visors, 214
Bathing, 212–214
Bathroom excuses, and bedtime fears,
    72–73
Battles, avoiding, 4–5, 27, 35, 38, 218
  at bedtime, 69
  over choice of dress, 226
  over cleaning room, 233
  over clipping nails, 216–217
  over eating, 88
  over hair brushing, 205–208
  over potty training, 97
  resulting in enema use, 109
  over teeth brushing, 208–211
  over thumb-sucking, 199
  when visiting others, 59
"Because I said so," 274–275
Bed transitions, 67, 73–77
Bed wetting. *See* Diapers, overnight
Bedroom, refusal to clean, 228–234. *See
    also* Cleaning up
Bedtime fears, 69–73
Begging, 245–246
Behavioral problems, 81–82, 176
Behavioral rut, 277
"Big girl/boy" use of, 3, 105
Binkies, 194. *See also* Lovies; Pacifiers
Biting, 130–131, 165–167, 291–292, 303
  serious cases of, 131
  See also Physical aggression
Blanket sucking, 200
Bolting. *See* Running away, in public
Bonding, 178, 180, 293
Books, for young children, 301–305
Bossiness, 48–52, 302
  of parents, 51–52
  reasons for, 52
  toward parents, 185–186
Bottles, use of, 203–204
Boundaries, 2, 38–39, 57, 268
Bragging, 52–53
Breakfast, refusal to eat, 227–228

Bribes, 276–278
  and bedroom, refusal to clean, 234
  and doctor and dentist visits, 215–216
  and medicine, ways to administer,
    211–212
  parameters for, 276
  and potty training, 99
  and vegetables, refusal to eat, 88
Bullying, 48, 52, 302
Bus, refusal to get off, 288–289

Calendars, use of, 234, 276
Call backs, and crib/bed transition, 74–77
Calming down, 7–8, 9–10, 11, 14, 16, 17,
    18–20, 24–25, 26, 149, 166, 246. *See
    also* Containment circle; Tantrums
Car seat, refusal to get into, 222–224, 288
Car travel. *See* Travel
Caregivers, 295–297
  first-aid training for, 297
Cars, tantrums inside, 17–20
Caving in, by parents, 21, 179, 244,
    273–274
Cell phones, 292–293
Changing your mind. *See* Mind-changing
Child development research, 2
Childcare, 284
Childcare centers, qualities to look for in,
    297–300
Children's Hospital of Oakland, 290
Child's lead, following, 293–294
Child's level, getting on, 293
Choice
  and breakfast, refusal to eat, 227
  and mealtime, 248–249
  and picky eaters, 85, 89
  and refusals, 222, 224–225
  and tantrums, in restaurants, 12
  and tantrums, while shopping, 9–10
  See also Mind-changing
Choking hazards, 199
Chores chart, 234